The White Dog Sacrifice

A Post-1800 Rite with an Ornamental Use for Wampum

The White Dog Sacrifice

A Post-1800 Rite with an Ornamental Use for Wampum

Marshall Joseph Becker
and
Jonathan C. Lainey

American Philosophical Society
Philadelphia • 2013

Transactions of the
American Philosophical Society
Held at Philadelphia
For Promoting Useful Knowledge
Volume 103, Part 3

ISBN: 978-1-60618-033-4
US ISSN: 0065-9746

Library of Congress Cataloging-in Publication Data
Becker, Marshall Joseph.
   The white dog sacrifice : a post-1800 rite with an ornamental use for
wampum / Marshall Joseph Becker and Jonathan C. Lainey.
      pages cm. — (Transactions of the American Philosophical Society held
at Philadelphia for promoting useful knowledge ; volume 103, part 3)
   Includes bibliographical references and index.
   ISBN 978-1-60618-033-4 (alk. paper)
   1. Iroquois Indians—Rites and ceremonies.   2. Iroquois Indians—
Domestic animals.   3. Iroquois Indians—Material culture.
4. Wampum—New York (State)   5. Animal sacrifice—New York (State)
6. Dogs—Symbolic aspects—New York (State)   I. Title.
   E99.I7B338 2013
   974.7004'9755—dc23
                                                        2013042214

Contents

Introduction

The region controlled by the confederated Five Nations Iroquois formed the epicenter of a "Core Area" within which wampum beads (*porcelain* in French; see Fig. 1) became central to intercultural interactions and diplomacy (Becker 2008b, 2012c). The Core Area originally included the lands of the Huron and Susquehannock confederacies (Fig. 2). Wampum, a shell bead commodity with a roughly standardized size and shape, was developed during the period 1590–1605 (Becker 2002). The technological ability to drill small shell beads was an achievement that depended upon the use of imported metal awls, called *muxes* by native users. Wampum as a commodity soon emerged as an important aspect of an expanding trade between Mohawk and Dutch merchants. Thus William Beauchamp's (1888: 195) brilliant observation that there is "no instance of any of the small council wampum [true wampum] before the beginning of the seventeenth century" was confirmed by several studies a century later (Lynn Ceci 1985, 1988; Becker 2002, 2008).

Wonderley (2004: xx–xxi) correctly notes that "wampum undoubtedly is the most symbolically charged substance known to Iroquois people today." Pan-Native interest in wampum shifted considerably after 1950, when "wampum" in various forms gradually began to join Plains tribes' feathered headdresses as part of the regalia used in pan-Indian activities. The origins and distribution of wampum, as well as its varied uses, are now better understood. We now know that wampum woven into flat bands only emerged about 1620–1630, when they became important elements of trade as well as diplomacy

(Becker 2002, 2012c). By the 1700s, the numbers of diplomatic belts noted in the many treaty records are so large that a simple listing has been recognized as a daunting task (New York [State] Assembly 1889: 234–365; also Shattuck 1991). Despite the vast numbers of bands and strings used in diplomacy after 1650, Beauchamp's insightful observation (1888a: 195) that the use of wampum for religious purposes "seems of a yet later date" now can be more explicitly confirmed as being after1800.

Prior to the 1790s, only secular uses for wampum, in economic matters and in politics-diplomacy, can be documented among the native populations of the Northeast. This corresponds with Tooker's finding (1994: 96, also 110) that among the many Iroquoian names for wampum that had been identified by Morgan, none appear associated with ceremonial items. The following documentation for the origins of the WDS, around 1800, includes a review of the several scholars who a century ago recognized the late origins of these rituals. Another of Beauchamp's impressive observations was that White Dog rituals had begun as the "great dream feast; the white dog sacrifice was

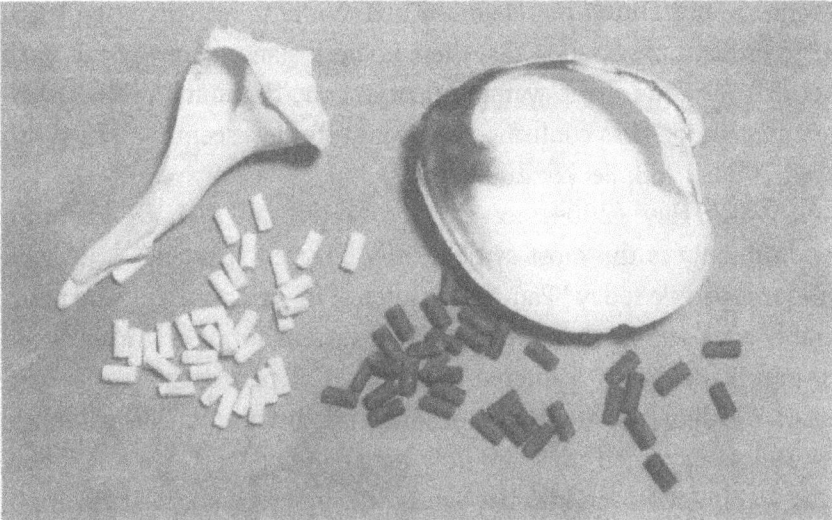

FIGURE 1: Marine shells used to make wampum beads, with reproduction beads (acrylic clay 'wampum')
(*courtesy of Rich Hamell*)

grafted upon this in recent times . . ." (Beauchamp 1895a: 211, see also 1888a: 198). In 1888, Beauchamp concluded that the White Dog Sacrifice (hereafter WDS) was a recent innovation among the Seneca, but he did not suggest a specific date for the origin of these rituals. Boyle (1898) also recognized that the WDS was a "recent" (post-1800) innovation. In addition, Boyle's first person account of a WDS remains the best record of this rite based on direct observation. Boyle's account, however, remained obscure and possibly unknown to even scholars such as William Fenton before its recent recognition in importance by Jonathan Lainey.

Despite Beauchamp's insights and Boyle's valuable account of the WDS, within a few decades after 1900 several scholars were suggesting a great antiquity for this ritual. The belief that the WDS antedates 1800 results from errors in "upstreaming," an approach made popular by William Fenton. In 1953, Fenton (1991: xi) borrowed this concept from Sir Flinders Petrie and suggested that we could peer into the Iroquoian past by examining the trajectory of more recent behaviors in a culture. Similar inferences had been made by Morgan (1851: 64–65) in the mid-nineteenth century when he inferred that the 50 "chiefs" of the League of the Iroquois reflected a system that went back "to the very dawn of the League" (see Starna 2008: 288, n36). Such beliefs continue to be made implicitly, or by tacit inference, by many scholars, perhaps part of the "invention of tradition" (Hobsbawm 1992). Fenton made his inferences explicit, and thereby provided a logical basis for testing them. Becker and Lainey accept the potential utility of upstreaming, but also recognize that one may erroneously "impute" great antiquity for relatively recent cultural innovations. Such has been the case with the WDS.

This research began not as a study of the WDS but rather to examine the various ways in which wampum might have been employed in a ritual context. In placing the WDS into historical and geographical perspective, we discovered that ritual uses for wampum, recently imputed to this commodity, were entirely absent from all the early records but did appear linked to the WDS after 1800. We soon found that all recent statements suggesting that the WDS long predated the nineteenth century were based on errors in evaluating these rituals as developments in ancient rites rather than recognizing them as post-1800 developments. Our original goal, to demonstrate the use of wampum as part of the rituals of the WDS, led us to discover that the WDS itself was a post-1800 innovation and that Beauchamp was correct in calling the WDS a "modern" phenomenon.

Returning to review the origins of wampum and its association with the WDS, we recognize that "true" wampum (also called "belt" wampum) became an important commodity in the Northeast in the decade between 1590 and 1600. Marine shell beads of various sizes had long been valuable trade items in North America, but the small wampum beads were a late innovation. That last decade of the sixteenth century correlates well with the dates demonstrated by Kuhn and Sempowski (2001) for the formation of the League of the Iroquois based on calumet use and exchange (also see Starna 2008). Strings of wampum may have been used in diplomacy as early as 1600, with woven bands, or "belts" (*colliers* in French), first appearing between around 1615 and 1620 (cf. Becker 2006). There is no question that during the early 1600s wampum became a prestigious material among several native groups. The value of wampum as a commodity is difficult to separate from other possible attributes. The marine shells from which wampum derives, and the fashioning of these beads by native makers, particularly prior to 1700, imbued this commodity with special meaning. We have no doubt that wampum was held to be vastly different from glass beads, especially when used in diplomacy. Bands with the design patterns similar to those seen on diplomatic belts but fashioned solely from glass beads, and bands in which metal and/or glass beads were included with wampum, were purely ornamental.

Throughout the region formed by the territories of the three great confederacies (Wendat/Huron, Five Nations Iroquois, and Susquehannock; see Fig. 2) the specific type of shell beads identified as wampum evolved uses beyond the traditional functions once held by marine shell beads. The earlier examples of marine shell beads used within the Core Area reveal that all the known examples were invariably larger in size than those beads specifically identified as wampum. Smaller examples

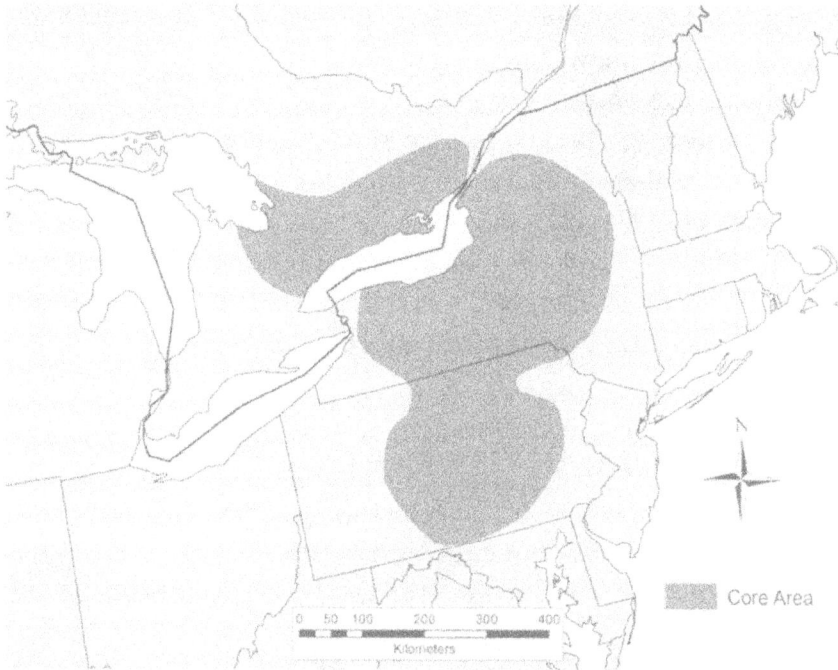

FIGURE 2: Map of the Core Area of wampum use, comprising the territories of the three great confederacies traditionally engaged in wampum diplomacy. The five nations of the traditional Iroquois confederacy occupy the center, in present New York state. The Huron (Wyandot) realm lay north of Lake Ontario, and the Susquehannock confederacy occupied central Pennsylvania (see Becker 2008b) *(Map created by Rhett Mohler)*.

of shell beads in the pre-1600 period were uniformly discoidal in shape rather than tubular. We may infer that the earlier uses of marine shell beads included ornamentation, but some contexts suggest possible ritual functions. Soon after wampum beads became standardized and commodified, around 1600 CE, they also became central to diplomatic protocols. Wampum diplomacy in the Core Area, as a mode of political interaction, may have begun as early as 1610 to 1615. By the 1650s, wampum "prestation," as we call a formal presentation of these strung or woven beads that was made in conjunction with a specific request, had largely superseded calumet ceremonialism at intercultural meetings in the Core Area. During this period, calumet rituals remained a powerful aspect of diplomacy in the western Great Lakes region and beyond. Within the wampum Core Area, however, the smoking of the calumet at councils, or what in the English documents are identified as "treaties" (cf. Becker and Lainey 2004), soon became of minor importance in these "ritualized" proceedings involving two or more cultural groups.[1]

Sir William Johnson (Fig. 12), a central figure in diplomatic relations with the Five Nations and others in the middle of the eighteenth century, summarized the need for wampum to verify all diplomatic messages:

> "It is obvious to all who are the least acquainted with Indian affairs, that they regard no message or invitation, be it of what consequence it will, unless attended or confirmed by strings or belts of wampum, which they look upon as our letter, or rather bonds."
>
> Johnson [1753] in O'Callaghan 1849, II: 624

O'Callaghan's publication emerged as Lewis Henry Morgan was organizing his data on the Iroquois. Morgan (1851: 114–115, n1) found this summary to be quite to the point.

Since strings and belts of wampum became essential to diplomacy in the Core Area, a central question in this study of the WDS relates to the alleged "sacred" nature of these items. A string of wampum accompanied even the most simple of requests, such as a request to attend a meeting (Fig. 11). Significant requests, such as to join as an ally in war or to uphold a treaty, involved the presentation of belts of wampum generally proportional to the importance of the request. This might seem as if the wampum belt that was presented was a proportional payoff, but acceptance almost invariably involved a return presentation of wampum of equal proportion. All of these details call into question the religious nature of diplomatic wampum. One could make the case that wampum presentations were like swearing on the Christian Bible, a formality with vague religious associations. However, were the two acts comparable, one would expect to swear on larger Bibles for more significant events such as capital crimes and on smaller examples for traffic offenses.

By 1800, wampum diplomacy was rapidly coming to an end, and wampum used as currency was being superseded by a relatively abundant United States coinage. The fate of the individual wampum belts then existing has become a matter of some interest. Today, approximately 250 surviving bands of wampum are known, almost all of which were made for diplomatic purposes (see also Becker 2008). The few ornamental bands that are known include those fashioned by the Penobscot (Becker 2004, 2005b, 2012b) and those recovered from Pequot burials of the 1600s (K. McBride, pers. Com. Aug. 2009). When considering the use of wampum bands within the Core Area, three central questions must be asked: who made it, why it was made, and to whom was it given or presented. Strings of wampum beads, either as a single strand of variable length or a cluster of two or more strings bound at one end (called "hands" or "branches") were fashioned for diplomatic and condolence presentation, serving as "low-end" items in formal wampum prestation (Becker 2008). Diplomatic wampum bands (commonly called "belts" in English and *colliers* in French) were the most commonly noted woven type of band used at "councils (Figs. 3 and 4)." A subset of diplomatic belts, constructed in the standard way, was made and used only within the Roman Catholic Church and its convert communities. These "ecclesiastical" bands, generally with distinct design elements such as a Latin cross, were made for presentation only among Catholic groups. They were presented by members of one religious "community" to members of another or sent to religious officials or even the Pope (see Becker 2001, 2006a) as "calls" to the faithful or as a show of faith (see also Sanfaçon, in review).

Ornamental or decorative bands of wampum (McBride 1993), also described as "personal" wampum, were made and used by people living in the "Periphery" of wampum use, and beyond (see Fig. 2). These bands, like those made and used by individuals in tribes living within the Core Area, sometimes were used for diplomatic purposes (cf. Becker 2005c). Ornamental wampum items generally remained among their makers, although they may have been given as personal gifts to people outside the community or presented in lieu of diplomatic wampum, should one be needed (Becker 2005b). Many other questions remain regarding nondiplomatic uses for this shell bead commodity, among which are possible uses in religious rather than diplomatic rituals. While individuals claiming native ancestry ("claimants") as well as modern native descendants commonly allege past uses of wampum in religious contexts (rituals), records documenting such uses remain extremely rare or completely specious (cf. Fenton 1998). Among the few religious rituals known that sometimes employed wampum are several post-1800 examples associated with the WDS (see Becker and Lainey 2008; also Becker 2007b).

A detailed review of the WDS provides some interesting insights into the history and uses for wampum. Research into the ritual uses for wampum in association with the WDS, perhaps the only well-documented ritual with which this commodity was associated, led to some surprising conclusions. Both the WDS as well as the use of wampum in association with this ritual appear to be late innovations among two of the Five Nations. Dogs were a favored food across North America. The ritual consumption of dog meat, associated with a period when food resources were scarce, appears to have morphed after 1800 CE into a ritual in which the meat of the sacrificed dog was not consumed. Only in this later context do we find the addition of wampum to the events. The goals of these rituals, and their functions within the changing paths of the histories of the Seneca and other groups, reveal changes in the cognitive role of wampum use in these societies.

Wampum and the Five Nations Iroquois

The Haudenosaunee (People of the Long House, or more recently the Six Nations, as some of the Five Nations Iroquois now prefer to be called) occupied the center of the Core Area of wampum use. As documented by records that span the 200 years of traditional wampum use, they remained the principal native users of diplomatic wampum throughout that period (see Ceci 1982; Becker 2002, 2006a). Of note is the fact that within the traditional Core Area of wampum use, very few examples of woven wampum of any type now survive or can be found (Becker 2007a, 2007b).

Most of the diplomatic belts that were presented to the Five Nations Iroquois, either collectively or to any combination of groups of these peoples, had been held at Onondaga. James Folts (1999: 152, from Beauchamp 1916: 215) notes that during that period of the mid-eighteenth century the "Six Nations Council at Onondaga had custody of a 'whole pile' of wampum belts" that were held in the cabin temporarily occupied by two Moravian brethren (Becker 2007b, 2013). These Moravian missionaries, Charles Frederick and David Zeisberger, took up residence at Onondaga from 1754 into 1755 in order to learn the language. Folts (1999: 153) also points out that most of the diplomatic belts known from the documents had been recycled or otherwise lost. These factors add to the considerable difficulty in using the numerous documents that record the use of belts in diplomacy to track the actual bands to the present. Folts's important comments on the recycling of wampum reflect the ways in which native users cannibalized strings and belts of wampum to produce different products for use in a variety of other contexts (Becker 2008).

Although the greatest concentration of diplomatic belts and strings in the eighteenth century may have been held at Onondaga, each of the many villages of the Haudenosaunee may have held significant numbers of diplomatic belts that pertained only to that specific group. In addition, items of personal adornment are rarely noted in the literature. We suspect that each collection of wampum held at a specific village included no more than a dozen diplomatic belts and probably fewer than 20 other wampum "pieces" such as strings of wampum used as condolence gifts (see Beauchamp 1895), various types of ornamentation, and any possible ritual items of that specific locale that incorporated wampum (cf. Becker 2007b, 2013). There are vast quantities of wampum noted in the various diplomatic records of each colony, especially in the eighteenth century (see Hauptman 1999) but only sporadic ethnographic references to non-diplomatic uses of wampum among the Five Nations groups and the Tuscarora. Non-diplomatic reports of wampum artifacts are so rare that we have no idea as to what kinds of items were most likely to be held locally, or if they were specific to the single culture from which they are mentioned or to an individual.

Among the many questions that we posed when this study began was "how significant was the post-1800 decline in the use of wampum in ritual contexts among the Five Nations Iroquois?" We discovered that the supposed "sacrifice" of one or two strings of wampum during the WDS, and the WDS itself, was a late innovation that began around 1799 CE. The first two decades of the nineteenth century saw the end of significant wampum use for political purposes. As wampum belts became obsolete in diplomacy, around 1820, even recall of their specific functions began to fade. Some Canadian First Nations, however, presented belts at meetings to recall past agreements. These include Nicolas Vincent Tsawenhohi's 1825 presentation before King George IV in London (Lainey 2004: 148). Another belt presentation, from 1829, involved the Wendat reaffirming hunting ground boundaries with their Algonquin neighbors (Lainey 2004: 182).

The Huron of Lorette had interpretations for the origins of the belts they held in 1846 (Lainey 2004: 108–110), but by the 1880s the original purposes for which all known wampum belts had been made were largely forgotten (New York Assembly 1889; Becker 2002, 2006). The evidence now suggests that as this decline in secular uses for wampum beads and bands accelerated, the use of the beads in rituals actually began. As Hale (1897: 237) observed, "it was the habit of the modern Indians, when wampum beads were needed for messages, presents, or sacrifices, to have recourse to the ancient and, so to speak, obsolete belts, which were thus gradually pillaged." Hale suggests that the use of wampum for delivering messages and as presents continued to the end of the nineteenth century, and that use for "sacrifices" took third billing in this list of functions. We have been unable to document the use of wampum in association with messages (attesting to their validity) beyond the 1890s, a period when wampum ornamentation in association with the WDS was also ending.

In the final decades of the nineteenth century and into the twentieth, the primary function of wampum among native-descent peoples

FIGURE 3: These eight wampum belts were preserved in the council house of the Hurons of Lorette (Wendat of Wendake) in 1846. Six of them were then briefly explained by the keeper of the belts.
Reference: Huyghue, Samuel Douglas Smith. "Some Account of Wampum". Dec. 1879, Hawthorne. Museum Victoria, Indigenous Cultures Department, Ethnohistoric Materials, Melbourne, Australia, 14 pages. Ms XM1495.

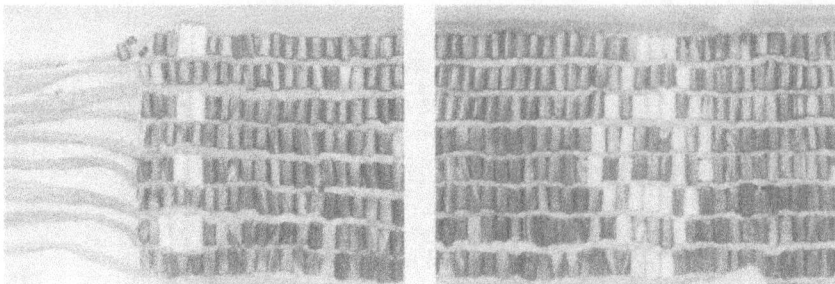

FIGURE 4: Wampum belt
Musée de la civilisation, Québec, Canada, item no. 1992-1288. Photo J. Lainey.

was a source of "cash" for the "keepers" (see Becker, in review A). The idea of hereditary keepers emerged among these egalitarian peoples, but the "keepers," whose titles varied, soon shifted from being representatives of the culture who were charged with "holding" these bands to becoming their de facto "owners." After 1850 their sales of wampum and other artifacts to people outside their native communities accelerated. Identification of the native vendors of these bands and strings now serves to help us to identify who had held wampum and to reconstruct genealogies of these people. The effort to construct culture histories for individual wampum bands has been a focus of research for many years (Lainey 2004). Lainey's data also reveal how the idea of appointed keepers emerged, and when and how they functioned within each of the Five Nations as well as among other wampum using peoples (Becker, in review A).

The exact numbers of separate villages occupied at any one time by the Five Nations Iroquois in New York, including the Tuscarora who joined the alliance around 1722, remains uncertain. Even the mythical founding of the confederacy (Wallace 1958) has been refashioned within as well as among the several participants. Cultural differences within each of these Iroquoian tribes were and continue to be considerable. Each of these cultures requires detailed study for us to understand any variations in wampum use and ritual activities, as well as changes through time. Snyderman, in his important studies of the Iroquois, recognized considerable variations "from village to village within the same

tribal group" (1961: 572). He saw this as reflecting an adaptive flexibility, a theme recognized by Wallace (1961: 39) as meriting attention.
Variations among various groups continue to this day, as demonstrated,
for example, by replacement of the use of various types of tobacco in
rituals by other aromatic plants as "purifiers." This is particularly evident at powwows and other "public" events where some of the more
politically correct Iroquoian groups now avoid tobacco use in any
form. At Wendake (the current name for the Huron-Wendat reserve in
Quebec), traditionalists still burn, but do not smoke, Nicotiana rustica,
one of the many tobaccos of the family Solanaceae. This high-nicotine
content species of tobacco now is used for ceremonies held within the
Wendake longhouse and also is used by various contemporary native
peoples throughout the Americas. Rustica is believed to be the species
of tobacco smoked throughout the Northeast in the past. The power
of the nicotine content may explain why it was smoked infrequently,
even when combined with other plant materials.

The many variations on any known ritual theme, however, do not
demonstrate that these customs had ancient origins, as Snyderman often
implies. Snyderman (1961: 607) mistakenly believed that wampum
predated European contact, stating that the "use of wampum in religion closely parallels its use in the old days . . . ." Since true wampum
post-dates 1590 CE, the many ways in which woven wampum was
employed—either in politics or religion—all emerged after 1600 CE.
On the basis of the evidence gathered here, we propose that the use for
wampum in conjunction with what became the WDS was a post-1800
phenomenon and should be seen as part of adaptive cultural change
rather than as the survival of a pre-1800 ritual.

Linked to the development of the WDS was the process of con-
fessing "sins to the Creator over strings of wampum" at the midwinter festival (Fenton 1936: 10; also Beauchamp 1888a: 195). Speck
(1995: 51) notes the use of wampum by the Cayuga in their confessions during the midwinter ceremonies. The use of rosary beads by
French priests appears to be an obvious antecedent for the native variant. We now suspect that as diplomatic uses for wampum were ending,
in the decades after 1800 CE (Becker 2012c), various ritual functions

emerged for this commodity. Yet we remain uncertain if the situations in which wampum was used in the WDS represented part of a ritual offering or were only intended to verify the message "conveyed" by the bearer dogs. Wampum may have simply provided a traditional and valuable part of the ornamentation on the sacrifice.

1

The White Dog Sacrifice

One of the more interesting uses of wampum beads among the Five Nations Iroquois was as part of the WDS at the beginning of the nineteenth century. Following an earlier exploration of the WDS (Becker and Lainey 2008) we recognized that these rites had originated within and became an important aspect of the Midwinter Feast among some of the Five Nations. To understand the role of wampum in these ceremonies, we undertook a review of the literature. We began with the efforts of Tooker (1965, 1970) to review Iroquoian midwinter rituals. Several contradictions and strained interpretations in her work led us to generate a number of interesting questions that we have resolved through this study. Of specific note were our earliest findings that the WDS, embedded within the midwinter ritual, was only reported from among the Onondaga and Seneca and that the WDS itself was a modern, or post-1799, phenomenon.

In seeking the origins of the WDS, we reviewed the Jesuit Relations and other documents recording early ethnographic information. The presence of the Jesuits among the Iroquoian tribes generally dates from after the 1650s, when their confederacy had largely dispersed or dislocated the Huron confederacy. The complete absence of Jesuit commentary on anything resembling the WDS as part of native midwinter rituals (cf. Deardorff and Snyderman 1956) is notable. The few references to dog sacrifice reveal elements that appear ancestral to the WDS, which took on its Christian aspects about the time that Handsome Lake (ca. 1735–1815) had his visions, ca 1799. The lack of evidence for the rituals of the WDS among the Iroquoian peoples with whom the Jesuits interacted prior to 1800 demonstrates that the WDS did not evolve until a later date. Had anything like the WDS existed in the 1600s and 1700s, the Jesuit Relations surely would have included mention of it. The suggestion that the WDS had been kept secret from the Jesuits is negated by the ample Jesuit descriptions of the rituals and ceremonies of the Iroquoians. The only rituals reported that involved the killing of any dog or other animal for a specific sacrifice almost always included eating the flesh. Feasting with dog meat often is noted.

The earliest account known derives from observations made among the Huron during the winter of 1623–1624. Gabriel Sagard's

(1865: 197 [154]) description of a dog "sacrifice" from among the Huron in 1623–1624 reveals the ritual consumption of a dog during a midwinter feast, a rite distinct from a sacrifice, in which the flesh is not eaten. The "white" color of the dog appears to have been a modern addition to his text.

An account from Ihonatiria in Huronia in 1635 suggests that the sacrifice of a white dog was made for the purpose of gaining "information," as in augury. Unlike later sacrificial white dogs, the meat of the 1635 dog was eaten, and there was no apparent association of the event with midwinter ceremonials.

> There are here some Soothsayers, whom they call also *Arendiouane* and who undertake to cause the rain to fall or to cease, and to predict future events. The Devil reveals to them some secrets, but with so much obscurity that one is unable to accuse them of falsehood; [page 123] witness one of the village of *Scanonaenrat* [174] who, a little while before the burning of the villages before mentioned, had seen in a dream three flames falling from the Sky on those villages. But the Devil had not declared to him the meaning of this enigma; for, having obtained from the village a white dog, to make a feast with it and to seek information by it, he remained as ignorant afterward as before.
>
> Brébeuf 1634–1636, in Thwaites 1896, VIII: 121, 123

Dogs were a source of meat throughout much if not all North America. Dog meat was a delicacy among all of the Iroquoian peoples, commonly consumed only on special occasions. Ritual components of this feasting, such as the selection of a white dog, had been incidental to these celebrations. This is distinct from events among the Seneca after 1800 at which dogs appear as sacrificial agents during feasts at which supplication was involved, but the meat of the dog was not eaten. The specific season associated with dog sacrifice also was not established until a later date. We believe that the consumption of dog meat ended when prayers of request entered the ritual, and the economy of the participants (their available wealth) allowed the meat to go uneaten. The concept of linking feasting with supplication may have extended beyond the Five Nations Core Area.

Brinton (1885: 54, n2) reports that the "Delaware [Lenape?] had three words for dog." The third of these, *moekaneu*, "has its origin, and also, significantly enough, [in] the verb 'to eat' in some dialects" [sic]. The interesting variations offered by Brinton suggest that more extensive linguistic data from the Five Nations and Huron might be of interest. Butler and Hadlock (1949: 35) provide a number of native terms used for dogs. A recent, error-filled review of the history of the native use of dogs (Schwartz 1997: 169–170) offers an Oneida term for dog (*é:lhal*) supplied by Floyd Lounsbury. Schwartz cites Tooker (1964) for the Huron term for dog (*gagnenon*). That all the Iroquoian people and their neighbors ate dog is evident, but the specific killing and eating of dogs as part of Iroquoian midwinter feasts apparently developed into the WDS at some period around 1800 CE.

The rare references to non-diplomatic uses for wampum in the Jesuit Relations all appear in contexts that reveal the basic meaning of "feasting." These documents also reveal the absence of a native concept of sin, an observation that is important to our discoveries regarding the WDS. Lloyd (1922: 263, from the JR vol. 13: 30) reports that in 1636, Paul Le Jeune witnessed the Huron burning a dog alive. The goal was to cure a sick woman. The flesh may have been eaten by that woman. Lloyd also says Le Jeune reported a dog being killed as a sacrifice and eaten by the Huron in 1638 but offers no reference. Lloyd (from JR 23: 158) also says that in 1642 the Huron burned several species of animal as sacrifices, and that included clubbing and roasting a dog (from JR 23: 172), presumably to eat it.

In 1639, Paul Le Jeune (in Thwaites 1898, XVII: 207–209) mentioned the great numbers of "public ceremonies, the various dances, the feasts of Outaerohi and of fire, and like superstitions,—which have, I say, taken place this last winter" in his village alone. He observed that similar ceremonies took place in other villages but declined to list these important ethnographic events, as there were too many to record. Perhaps he felt that these rites were too pagan to merit his effort. Le Jeune did record that many individuals carried in a pouch their *Ascwandic*, an amulet representing a personal or guardian spirit (cf. Thwaites 1898,

XVII: [134]). The propitiation of this animistic spirit is described in the words of his native informant:

> When I go to trade, I have only to open the pouch where he is; I request him to procure for me a porcelain [wampum] collar of so many beads, or a robe or mantle of so many beaver skins; I throw him, in homage and gratitude, [170] some porcelain beads, and a piece or morsel of beaver; finally, I make a feast; then I go away [to trade], and what I have aimed at never fails me.
>
> Le Jeune 1639, in Thwaites 1898, XVII: 209

The term "collar" (the French *collier*) rather than the English "belt" commonly appears in early accounts, but it is not known if this indicated a small belt, a band of one row (beads placed side by side), or one or more strands of wampum. Various authors suggest the use of white beads only, but the color of the wampum beads used is rarely specified.

A considerable gap appears in the Jesuit records between the Le Jeune accounts and the next commentaries relating to dogs. Seventeen years after Le Jeune's observations on "feasts," a report from among the Iroquoians of lower Canada, possibly a Huron group, describes a celebration on 22 February 1656 that was identified by the Jesuits by the name *Honnonouaroria*. Later records place these rites at the end of January (169). The description of the 22 February activities opens with the statement that "This festival might be called the festival of fools" (153) as the Jesuits witnessed men running naked in the cold and others throwing water or firebrands at random. The tossing of coals and ashes as either a prank or a threat (163, 169) reminds MJB of the often lethal use of fireworks at celebrations in modern Latin American villages, or the dangerous versions of modern "trick of treat" using fireworks that he recalls from his childhood. The Jesuit account describes individuals celebrating while dressed in costume or disguise (159). One participant stated that he wished to kill a Frenchman (Jesuit?), but he was appeased by the presentation of two dogs by others in his village (157). The French observers linked these winter ceremonies with preparation for war (Thwaites 1959, XLII: 153–169). Fenton (1944: 159–160) suggests that the Five Nations "Midwinter Festival is the lineal descendant or an ancestral cousin to the Huron Dream Feast, *Onnonhwaroria*, 'An addled Mind.'" This must be the same term used in 1656, perhaps leading Fenton to believe that the WDS predated 1790 and to suggest an evolution that is at odds with the evidence.

In 1655–1656, one of three warriors returning from a long campaign against the Cat (Erie) people (then being exterminated by the Five Nations) recounted a vision of significance in this study. The "visionary," from an Iroquoian group in southern Canada, saw a demon in the guise of a dwarf who said "I am he who holds up the Sky" [Taronhiaouagui?], by whose powers you have conquered seven nations, each named. The demon gave instructions to the warrior; the third being "let there be sacrificed to me ten dogs, ten porcelain beads from each cabin, a collar [belt] ten rows wide, four measures of sunflower seed, and as many of beans" (Thwaites 1896, XLII: 195–199). The "dreamer" also was to be given "two married women . . . to be at thy disposal for five days." The elders complied with all this "as commanded, so [132] prompt are they to obey whatever resembles a dream" (Thwaites 1959, XLII: 145; see also Snyderman 1961: 576).[2]

The Jesuit narration of the 1650s links the "sacrifice" of ten dogs (feasting) with the use of wampum as part of the sacrifice, but how and who would receive the wampum or eat the dogs is not evident. This activity is in no way tied to any of the seasonal feasts that had become established by 1800, and certainly not to the midwinter rites. Quite probably the round of five feasts that were known by 1800 was a development that was dependent on increased food supplies that were somewhat guaranteed by the pelt trade.

Another gap appears in the record of the Jesuit Relations before a supposed account reported by Lloyd (1922: 264), who reports this 1672 reference (JR 57: 146): "To Agriskoue they commonly sacrifice dogs, of which they make a feast for the sick." Another of the few reports of the use of wampum as an offering also appears in that *Jesuit Relation* for 1672 in which the Jesuit observer wrote

> Kiouchin, an oussaki, . . . possessed a Stone Idol,—which, however, had not the slightest resemblance to The human form. Still, it was his

God; he offered it tobacco to smoke, dedicated his feats in its honor; adorned It with porcelain, and embellished It with paint; he kissed and Caressed It and bore It along with pomp, assuming an air of intrepidity when he had It on his back.

Thwaites 1896, LVII: 277

Two of these accounts link wampum to the objects that served as personal "deities," and each depicts the extent of ritual behavior needed to propitiate a personal god. The use of wampum as one of the items with which Kiouchin "adorned" his stone idol indicates that the wampum was not in itself "sacred," although once the wampum became associated with his idol the entire collection attained ritual status.

Dog Sacrifices Placed on Poles

Of considerable interest is the first documented reference to hanging sacrificed dogs on poles. The date is 2 December 1676 and the sacrificing natives were the Algonquin people of the Lake, according to Lloyd (1922: 264). The account is from a report written during the last winter mission of Father Henry Nouvel, Superior of the Missions to the "Outawacs" (Outaouais; Ottawa in English). Written after traveling in the country of the "Sachis" (Sac or Sauk?) near Lake Erie, Nouvel reported entering a fine river, apparently free of ice, in search of a group with whom he planned to winter. The natives in question had recently left, but the remains of a successful hunt were evident, including bear, deer, turkey, and pike. Having written of the success of his intended hosts, Nouvel added

". . . but I was much grieved to see a large Dog suspended at the top of a painted pole, as a sacrifice to the sun, We Overturned everything, Broke the pole, and cast the Dog into the river, with the scalp of an extraordinarily large and hideous bear which had also been immolated."

Jesuit Relations 60: 217–218

Nouvel was upset at finding such strong evidence of traditional activities, or pagan activities, among "the poor savages" he had hoped to convert to Christianity. His brief description, however, provides a glimpse of a complex set of rituals that are nowhere else recorded or explained in detail. Nouvel's account also offers a rare mention of the size of the dog involved. What we do not know is if this "large" dog had been sacrificed when the natives arrived at this encampment in order to bargain with their deities for a good hunt. Had the flesh been consumed and only the skin hung? Had the dog been ill or elderly? The "scalp" of the large bear "which had also been immolated" suggests that the dog also had been burned before hanging. If so, the purpose must have been to cook and eat the meat, and the same would apply to the bear. In 1676 the bearskin had considerable value in the pelt trade and would have been stripped for trade. Despite many records concerning dogs killed for meat, we know of no instance in which dog skin is mentioned in trade or for any purpose.

No mention of dog sacrifice has been found in any record dating from between the 1676 account written by Nouvel and the 1712 record by Marest. Writing on 9 November 1712 from Cascaskias, an Illinois village situated on the River *Ouabache* [Wabash], the Jesuit Pierre-Gabriel Marest wrote a detailed account of the situation to his colleague, Father Barthélemi Germon. "At that very time a contagious disease desolated the Village . . ." and Marest was, in effect, competing in curing the victims.

> In the meantime, the Charlatans withdrew to a short distance from the fort in order to make a great sacrifice to their *Manitou*: they killed as many as forty dogs, which they carried on the tops of poles while singing, dancing, and assuming a thousand absurd positions. The mortality did not cease . . .
>
> Thwaites 1890, LXVI: 237–239

Forty dogs is an extraordinarily large number, but the population of dogs at Cascaskias must have been proportional to the human population, which was dying at a frightful rate. Sacrificing large numbers of dogs was an effort to respond to the calamity. The reduction in the numbers of living dogs in the village also reduced the probability that they would feed on the dead or disturb new graves. The reduced availability of human offal from the remaining population also created a problem for feeding large numbers of dogs. Lloyd (1922: 264–265) makes reference to this 1712 account, referring to activities on the Wabash River, as well as to the accounts of other dog sacrifices placed on poles made by various Iroquoians in 1779.

Beauchamp (1888a: 198) presciently recognized that the WDS is very recent in origin, possibly post 1800 CE, and that it derived from "the ancient Dream Feast." Beauchamp's (1892: 86) notes on this period of transition, and his reference to reports of dog sacrifices among the Iroquoians reported in 1779, are of particular importance. Beauchamp appears alone (1892: 86) in pointing out the many reports made by Major General John Sullivan's officers relating to dog sacrifices that had been made by Iroquoians at villages in the path of that significant military campaign. We offer a selection of these descriptions, using the edition of Sullivan's narrations that appeared shortly before Beauchamp made his observations in print (1892). After that 1779 campaign, field reports were submitted by each of Sullivan's officers, a standard military procedure. These journals are the source of the information on dog sacrifice summarized below. Lieutenant Colonel Henry Dearborn wrote

> At several towns that our army has destroy'd we found dogs hung up on poles about 12 to 15 feet high which we were told is done by way of sacrifice. When they are unfortunate in war they sacrifice two dogs in the manner above mentioned, to appease their Imaginary god. One of these dog's skins they suppose is converted into a Jacket & the other into a tobacco pouch for their god.
>
> Sullivan 1887: 76

Major Jeremiah Fogg's report from Genessee country records that on the thirteenth they marched to a castle [palisaded native village] called Gohseolahulee:

> "Here appeared the heathenish custom of offering sacrifices. Two dogs were found suspended on a pole, which signified that evil spirit was to

be pacified by their skins, which should serve to make him a tobacco
pouch and waistcoat."

Sullivan 1887: 99

Of particular interest regarding the use of wampum at the WDS
is Adam Hubley's account of 10 September 1779. His report contains
the only account indicating that in one case the troops had found the
following:

> A dog was hung up, with a string of wampum round his neck, on a
> tree, curiously decorated and trimmed. On inquiry I was informed that
> it was a custom among the savages before they went to wars to offer
> this as a sacrifice to Mars, the God of War, and praying that he might
> strengthen them. In return for these favours, they promise to present
> him with the skin for a tobacco pouch.

Sullivan 1887: 160

Sullivan was referring to the Roman god Mars and made an equivalence with the native god of war. The recorded versions of the WDS
demonstrate a relationship with pre-1799 midwinter feasts, during
which the flesh of dogs was consumed. Harold Blau's study (1964) of
the evolution and symbolism of the WDS ritual among the "Iroquois"
misconstrues its origins and distribution and fails to relate them to
Handsome Lake. Blau, as many others, incorrectly extrapolated the
rites of the WDS to all of the Haudenosaunee groups.

A far more problematical interpretation can be found in Delâge's
(2005) error-strewn compendium purporting to survey the use of dogs
by Canadian and other native peoples. Delâge offers a distorted view of
the WDS, which he associates with the "winter equinox." Presumably
he meant the winter solstice, which usually falls around 21 December, a month or more prior to the midwinter rituals of the Haudenosaunee groups. Delâge states (2005: n133) that sacrificed dogs and
others were hung from tall poles that were decorated with wampum.
Delâge observes that these dogs are much like the sacrificial lambs of
the Christians. In fact, Delâge misses the fact that lambs generally are
born late in the winter, closer to the period during which the WDS

was held. Lambs also tend to be eaten, whereas the WDS involves the cremation or burning of the victim rather than the cooking of the dogs for consumption.

The very limited distribution of the WDS among the Five Nations Iroquois (cf. Hewitt 1912) reveals it to be a recent or post-1800 diffusion rather than deeply rooted and with different paths of evolutionary development. The possibility that these differences only indicate distinct styles of reporting or variations in the quality or selection of information cannot be eliminated. We suggest that they reveal some of the many cultural differences among these tribes and are not simply recording errors.

Tooker (1965: 129) correctly stated that of all the New York Iroquoian rituals "the most important, the longest, and the most complex is the Midwinter, or New Year's festival" (also see Tooker 1970). However, she incorrectly inferred that the WDS was part of this elaborate "festival" prior to 1800 (Tooker 1965), without being able to cite a single account in support of that conclusion. Her own observations of "virtually the entire Tonawanda Midwinter ceremony in 1958 and 1964, and parts" of the rituals in later years (Tooker 1970: xi) were made long after the WDS had shifted away from the use of dogs. Her published account, an example of a synthetic narration that has been projected back in time to before 1800, is the only one of the many assembled narratives that have been published to include a reference to the burning of a basket (see Table II). This entire category of synthetic "descriptions" is considered later in this volume at length, together with observations on what this technique means to anthropology.

The midwinter "festival" during the nineteenth century lasted from one to two full weeks, depending on which of the activities is described and in which village the ritual was observed. The "stirring" of the ashes, or ashes rite involving the symbolic renewal of fire, may have been a commonality among the Iroquoians (see Speck 1995: 53 for the Cayuga). Within the series of events comprising the midwinter festival, documented only after 1799, the WDS attracted a great deal of interest among non-native observers. This may reflect the parallels with ideas of sin and sacrificial atonement basic to Christian and other religious systems. The date at which the WDS became a formal ritual, as distinct from the killing and eating of dogs, was a question that this study now addresses.

"Blood sacrifices," or the ritual killing of a living being, once were part of the activities of most if not all of the dominant European religions. We now understand when similar sacrifices, along with their links to the concept of "sin," became central to several of the Five Nations Iroquois and were carried north by their descendent groups into Canada. These processes of culture change provide insight into how the WDS relates to Christian influences. Sacrificial lambs are well known.[3]

Feasting on dogs may have led to the ritual sacrifice of one, and then a pair, of which one was eaten and one was burned as an offering (see also Beauchamp 1888a: 199; Tooker 1965). Many reports of the WDS have been found among the Onondaga and Seneca but none among the Mohawk, Cayuga, and Tuscarora and only a vague reference among the Oneida. Wide variations are evident among the known records of midwinter White Dog rituals in the two cultures where it clearly became established (cf. Hale 1885, Fenton 1936: 4, also 22). Our research demonstrates that the WDS had developed among the Seneca in the late 1790s, spread to the Onondaga, but never took hold among the easternmost members of the Confederacy or to the Tuscarora.

An account recorded by Samuel Kirkland while he was living among the Oneida in 1791 tells of the call for the sacrifice of a white dog (see the later section "Oneida"). This record may reflect an event antecedent to the development of the WDS, but it is not a description of a WDS as some scholars have implied.

2

Synthetic versus Firsthand Accounts

In this volume, we have gathered and presented all the known first-hand reports relating to the WDS. These data enable us to review probable origins of this ritual and to understand the development or evolution of the ritual. We also note some of the problems with an approach that we identify as "synthetic." By "synthetic" we mean the creation of a narrative account derived by taking elements from several different eyewitness descriptions and combining them into a single story, without regard to discrepancies in the individual narratives or temporal variations. If cultural variation among non-literate peoples is considerable, how then do we go about describing culture, or writing ethnography? The production of a cultural narrative, by combining elements, may seem to be the essence of writing ethnography. But the combination of details to produce a synthetic account also may generate a fictionalized version that, in turn, inhibits our understanding of cultural change, and thus cultural processes.

While a "synthetic" tale provides a useful general view or even a useful template for the midwinter ceremony, the several "modal portraits" presented by various scholars have added fictional variations to the ethnographic accounts. A synthetic account may fall within the cultural norms permitted or accepted by the members of the society being depicted. But such accounts also may hamper our ability to reconstruct origins and the separate processes of cultural change acting within the culture, here represented by each of the Five Nations Iroquois, and to understand the range of variation within each of them. Tracing the different trajectories of these changes during the post-Revolutionary War period as recognizing that not all of the Five Nations instituted the WDS into their winter rites is only possible when we have all the evidence in front of us.

Anthony F. C. Wallace has provided us with numerous valuable insights into the course of Seneca culture history. His suggestion (1970: 207–208, 356, n50) that around 1799 one of the many prophets among the Five Nations convinced the Seneca, and perhaps the Mohawk Joseph Brant, to "renew" the WDS, assumes that this ritual was an ancient custom that had, by the late 1790s, "fallen into disuse among all the Iroquois except the Seneca (among the Oneida it had not

been celebrated for thirty years)." Wallace considered Christian influences to be a possible cause for what he assumed to be a hiatus but
offers no evidence for any earlier version of the WDS. Wallace's belief
that the WDS had been "revived" derives from an interpretation of two
of Kirkland's accounts, dated by Wallace to February and May of 1800.
Our search for evidence to support Wallace's idea of a "renewal" of the
WDS produced no record of a WDS or any similar ritual that predates
1799 but offers several clues to antecedent activities that became incorporated into the WDS.

A review of Wallace's (1970: 50–58, 344, n1) "synthetic" view of
the WDS, largely derived from Morgan's own synthesis of the Seneca
ritual, enables us to recognize the problematical aspects of such generic
reconstructions. His approach also leads us to consider what consti-
tutes an appropriate "ethnographic" description. Wallace, as others
before him, recognized that details of the WDS varied from community
to community and from year to year. His synthetic "portrait" of this
rite, however, introduces various errors. Wallace's smoothly flowing
narrative derives from a historiography that suppresses discrepancies
and invites the presentation of numerous unsupported inferences. This
method, as will be shown, interferes with an ability to recognize the
origins of the cultural process involved in Handsome Lake's efforts to
revitalize Seneca culture, a process that Wallace himself (1956) held
to be universal.

In Wallace's synthesis of the WDS, he recognizes that at "some time
in August or in early September" the Seneca held a four-day "Green
Corn Festival." Into his description of this event he inserted his belief
that on the third day, one of three ceremonial activities was "the burning of a white dog as an offering to the Creator Tarachiawagon." The
name of this chief deity among the Seneca, "Holder of the Heavens" in
English, had also been conferred upon Conrad Weiser (1696–1760).
Fenton (1942: 20) had described a chant of "Personal thanksgiving"
sung "principally twice a year when the rite of chant is celebrated on
the third day of the Green Corn Festival and near the end of the Midwinter Festival." No tribe is specified by Fenton, but his narration suggests that one aspect of the rites of the WDS may have been repeated

at different seasons. We doubt that the entire WDS was repeated at the Green Corn Festival and find no association of the WDS with any rituals other than midwinter rites. This suggests that either Wallace conflated two distinct ritual events or the sacrifice of the dog had shifted.[4]

The belief that the "Midwinter Ceremony," marking the beginning of the Seneca new year, lasted nine days, commencing five days after the first new moon that followed the zenith of the Pleiades (cf. Ceci 1978), is a part of Wallace's synthetic narration (1970, see also Tooker 1970: 147). Wallace also placed the strangulation of the white dog on the fifth day of the ceremonies,

> "and its body, garlanded with ribbons, beads, and metallic ornaments, [was] hung on the wooden statue of Tarachiawagon, the Creator, before the long house. Now [then] it was burned in the long house as an offering to the Creator . . . ."
>
> Wallace 1970

Wallace's description of the WDS employs a basic approach to presenting cultural process, creating a narrative of the events through the amalgamation of details from several accounts. As in the case of Wallace's version of the WDS, where details are assembled from across time and cultures, this technique creates a basis for errors in subsequent evaluations, including a masking of the post-1799 origins of this sacrificial ritual. A similar approach to the WDS had been used by Shimony (1961) in her brief review of the ritual, which included no direct observations (cf. Starna 2008: 298). Her focus on conservatism among the Iroquois at the Six Nations Reserve also presumed that the rites "preserved" were ancient, or at least inferred that they originated long before 1800.

Elisabeth Tooker is much more explicit than Wallace in indicating that her account of the WDS (1970: 135–143) was synthesized largely from Morgan's. Tooker infers that the "Iroquois" WDS existed "in the latter part of the eighteenth century" (1965: 129) or prior to 1799. Tooker, like Wallace, first constructed a homogenized or synthetic model of the WDS containing a basic error. She accepts Kirkland's inferences regarding the antiquity of the WDS. Tooker's review of the Kirkland account of a WDS reveals an extremely interesting point regarding the actual content of these records. Tooker (1965: 131) found that the Oneida account as published by Beauchamp (1885: 236), an account long accepted as accurate, differs vastly from Kirkland's actual written text. Tooker claimed that Beauchamp did not simply use one of the many variant versions of Kirkland's journals. She diligently traced the actual origins of the Beauchamp account back to an appendix in William Campbell's *Annals of Tryon County* (1831). Nevertheless Tooker accepts Kirkland's inference that the WDS was an old, traditional Iroquoian ritual that had been *revived* around 1799 after a long hiatus. She also presumes that the WDS existed among all of the Iroquoian tribes.

An examination of specific cultural events as reported by actual observers of the WDS, in chronological order, offers a means by which we may recognize early transitional aspects in the evolution of this ritual. Variations as recorded in the individual accounts do not reflect anomalies but rather reveal a "development," or differences in this ritual that in many cases are quite distinct from what was documented a century later, around 1900. In the 1790s Handsome Lake and other Seneca were negotiating a difficult transition from living in a village-dwelling, but basically foraging society sustained by low-level supplementary horticulture to an incipient agricultural system. Since we suspect that the WDS began and developed among the Seneca, the listings that follow will begin with descriptions that we have from that culture.

3

Seneca Accounts

Just as the Mohawk, on the eastern margins of Five Nations' territory, are often recognized as quite distinct from the supposed "League," the Seneca were often marginal to activities in the Iroquoian heartland. The various alliances that emerged during the American Revolution clarified many of the differences among and within these tribes. The 1794 treaty at Canandaigua was primarily concerned with the relationship between the Seneca and the new United States (Campisi and Starna 1995). Not surprisingly, there are significant numbers of documents that include firsthand accounts of Seneca life between 1797 and 1828, an important period of rapid change in their cultural history. Those three decades span the period during which numbers of Quaker missionaries and others worked among the Seneca in a specific attempt to provide training that would influence the Seneca transition to a "civilized state."

Ten interesting accounts of "visits" to the Seneca were collected by Frank Severance (1903). In describing Asher Wright's later work among the Seneca, William Fenton (1956: 569, note) listed Severance's important corpus of accounts (see also Fenton 1957). Wright's observations, according to Fenton (1957: 307), indicate that the Seneca saw the burning of the dog also as a means of providing clothing for the Creator, harking back to the pre-1800 period when a sacrificed dog's skin was used to make articles for the deity. This is an important bit of information relating to that important period of transition among the Seneca.

Boyle (1900b: 270), an extremely careful observer, reported that the midwinter feast lasted 10 days. Boyle did not recognize that the variations in the WDS could be great, as we have found them to be, although he recognized the strong influence of Christian teachings. Boyle's full account and his important inferences are presented later. We have chosen to present here, as a prelude to our review of Seneca examples of the WDS, an early account of a Seneca "sacrifice" as told to Ezra Stiles by Samuel Kirkland. Kirkland's first two years of missionary work had been among the Seneca, but he soon relocated to an Oneida village where he spent many decades of his life. During the summer of 1783, having spent 17 years with the Oneida, Kirkland supposedly related some details of the Seneca midwinter celebration to Ezra Stiles. Stiles, a New England Congregationalist minister, also had served as the president of Yale College. These significant data in Stiles's diaries were pointed out by Christine S. Patrick (pers. Comm. 1 April 2012). Stiles provided us with this important record through his diary entry for 27 June 1783. We infer that Kirkland's account relating to the Seneca is based on observations made before his removal to the Oneida village in 1766, nearly two decades prior to the time of his narration of the details to Ezra Stiles. However, there is the possibility that Kirkland had witnessed a Seneca Midwinter Feast at a date after 1766. We have also considered the possibility that Stiles erred in using the word "Senecas" to relate this information.

> 27. Visited by the Revd Mr Kirtland [sic] Indian Mission^y to the Oneida Tribe of Indians, who were 410 Souls before the War . . .
>   Mr Kirtland was present at a national Sacrifice of a Faun or Deer (they sometime use a Dog), among the Senecas [ca. 1765?]. It is annually the latter end of Janry or in Febry . . .

There follows a long description of a three-day Midwinter Feast as told by Kirkland.

> "The sacrificed Animal is eaten by the Sachems. The best of Venison & great abundance [of food is] provided for all the pple at the Feast. This is the only evidence wherein I have learned with certainty that the Indians ever really sacrificed . . ."
>
>   Stiles 1901, III: 76

The term "sacrifice" in this context appears to refer to the ritual slaughter, and eating, of a sacrificial animal. Stiles was familiar with many of the native peoples of Connecticut, and with other native peoples, through his readings and conversations with missionaries such as Kirkland. As described by Kirkland to Stiles, the meat of the Seneca "sacrifice" was specifically eaten by the "Sachems." The aspect of that rite involving a "sacrifice" was far from the WDS during which the entire corpse of the offering is consigned to the flames and no part is eaten.

The Seneca Prophet Handsome
Lake: Origins of the WDS

The transition from dog feasting, or a dog "sacrifice" followed by consumption of the meat, to the ritual burning (cremation) of a sacrificed dog may have taken several decades. We believe that these decades correspond to the last years in the life of Handsome Lake (ca. 1735–1815). His message became known as the "Code of Handsome Lake" and may have been a major impetus in this process. The period from about 1799 and into the 1820s witnessed two important paths in Seneca culture history. During the first half of this period Handsome Lake communicated his message of renewal. The latter part spans the period when Quaker missionaries were most active among the Seneca (Aborigines' Committee 1844: passim).

Cornplanter, the half-brother of Handsome Lake, was then the Seneca leader seeking accommodation to change through learning the skills used by the Whites. While some historians view this as a period of profound cultural metamorphosis (Dennis 2010), we join those who recognize this as part of a long and gradual transition within the Seneca community. Regardless of how one views the gradual process of change, most agree that the account of the WDS dating from 1799 represents the inclusion of several Christian-influenced innovations into the traditional Seneca midwinter ritual. Deardorff (1951) and others have suggested that some of these changes were in process at the time of Handsome Lake's visions, or in the year 1799 to 1800. These cultural innovations are suggested by several events surrounding the life of Handsome Lake.

Handsome Lake as well as Cornplanter had participated in hostilities against the colonies that became the United States. He was party to the 1794 Treaty of Canandaigua between the United States and the Six Nations Iroquois, but subsequently his alcoholism became problematic. His alcohol intake increasingly marginalized him among his own people. By 1799, during or perhaps as a result of an illness, Handsome Lake had a series of three visions that became important agents in his new quest for change among his people (see Wallace 1952: 47–51;

Tooker 1970: 103). Dreams had always been important vectors for decision making and change among the Iroquoians. Handsome Lake became a visionary leader or what Wallace terms a "dreamer" (1956: 273) for a small group of the Seneca. His illness led to what Wallace identifies as a "mazeway reformulation" (1956: 270). Handsome Lake used his visions to promote European-style housing and farming practices while retaining many Seneca rituals. His desire to employ Christian concepts of sin and confession within Seneca belief systems were incorporated into the "Code of Handsome Lake" (*Gai'wiió*, or The Good Message; see Parker 1912, also Wallace 1970).

Halliday Jackson (1771–1835) was one of several Quaker missionaries who lived among the Seneca at the end of the eighteenth and into the early nineteenth centuries. These young Quakers were sent to instruct interested Seneca in farming technology, in the framing of buildings, and other agrarian skills. Jackson's journal (Wallace 1952; see also Tooker 1970: 123–127) provides what is the earliest record of the WDS. Jackson's longer account (1830b) is less often cited for the rituals described in it. Jackson did his missionary service during the years 1798 to 1800, and made at least one brief trip to that region in 1806. His two books on the Seneca were published in Philadelphia (Jackson 1830a, b). They describe a group of native Iroquoians who, in the years around 1800, were beginning to shift from a lifestyle based on low-level horticulture, as a supplement to extensive foraging, to a life as somewhat settled farmers. Those Seneca who had moved north into Canada, or west into the Ohio territories, generally retained more traditional lifeways.

Shortly after the twenty-third day of first month (March) in 1799 Jackson went to Cornplanter's village to visit "Henery my fellow traveler" (Henry Simmons, Jr.; see Swatzler 2000). Jackson's journal, written in the ornate verbal style of the King James Bible, speaks of his spring journey taking place at "a time of much rain" and flooding (Wallace 1952: 142). He arrived on "the Seventh day of the feast, for the day of Pentecost was fully come" when the natives assembled "to worship and to offer their yearly sacrifice." On his arrival Jackson found those who had gathered were making music and dancing, and had:

set up an image of wood in the form and Similitude of a Man [probably Tarachiawagon], and put thereon the Skins of wild beasts of the Forrest, and Feathers of the Fowls of the Air, and Handkerchiefs and fine ribbons of variegated colours.—And the people were adorned in fine apparel even with Silk and purple and fine linen, and Breast plates, and earrings and Nose Jewels and Bracelets, and round tires like the moon; and with head bands and Silver Pins and the Ornaments of the legs & girdle about their Loins curiously interwoven with various Colours. And moreover it came to pass on the Seventh Day of the Feast that they Slew a dog and hung him on the image which they had set up, and put a String of Beads about his neck, and adorned him with Ribbons and fine apparel, and looked thereon and worshipped, and it came to pass afterwards, that they kindled a fire and laid him thereon for a sacrifice and burnt offering for their Sins. And moreover did they burn incense upon their Altar, and the smoak [sic] thereof went upwards. . . .

Halliday Jackson 1799, cited in Wallace 1952: 142–143

Before discussing the ethnographic merits of the young Jackson's account, note can be made of an earlier impression of MJB, who stated that Jackson wrote in the manner of the King James Bible. This has been more recently confirmed to a greater degree than previously thought. In searching for an explanation of the meaning of "round tires like the moon" we found that this is a direct quote from the King James Bible, from *Isaiah* 3: 18. "No dancing girl is in full dress without her round tires like the moon." But what are these "round tires" worn by these Seneca? We believe there is a typographical error in the King James translation that is used only in England and in the American derivations. All other modern English-language Bibles use "crescent shaped necklaces" or similar variations. The term "tire" does not even appear as a noun in the *Oxford English Dictionary*. Thus Jackson is using biblical description to portray a scene, with at least one part referring to the sterling silver crescents that became common in the Indian trade after 1760.

Jackson's 1799 account is extremely important as it places the event in early spring, somewhat later than midwinter. The dog killed, for which no color is specified, was burned as a sacrifice and apparently not eaten, as in a feast. Whether the sacrifice of a dog had become an established activity by 1799 is not evident. We propose that this was innovative and very different from the sacrifices described in 1779. How recently this sacrifice had entered the spring rituals, and when it shifted to the midwinter cycle, is yet another question. When the dog's color became important is yet another of the questions that cannot be answered using the available evidence.

How wampum was used, or what if any role it played in these activities, also remains unresolved. Were the beads on the "String of Beads" noted by Jackson made of glass or of shell in the form of wampum? No reference is made to wampum by Jackson on this occasion nor during any other event that he recorded during this time period. Since wampum was still in use as small change in Pennsylvania (Becker 1980), we assume that Jackson was familiar with this commodity as a currency. By 1799 the use of wampum at councils and treaties involving the Five Nations Iroquois in New York was coming to an end. These native peoples had largely if not entirely shifted away from the use of diplomatic wampum, both bands and strings, in favor of receiving good copies of treaty minutes to be held as records of what had transpired (Becker 2002). The role of wampum in Iroquoian rituals during the period just before Handsome Lake, and after, remains to be explored. Religious rituals employing wampum did not exist at that time but emerged only at a later date. The evidence for this progression is in contrast to assertions of some modern descendants of these native groups.

During February 1800, Halliday Jackson spoke of people gathering in Cornplanter's village "to offer sacrifice" and staying for several days, but he makes no mention of a white dog (cf. Snyderman 1961: 588–589). Possibly he omitted reference to a WDS, or of a midwinter festival, because he had described it the previous year. In 1800 this ritual may have been associated with the rites of spring.

The specific time of year of Jackson's 1799 observations remains as uncertain today as it was to Wallace (1952). The celebration described by Jackson, later associated with the Midwinter Feast in January or February, may well have been part of events held in March or April. The decision regarding when to hold this midwinter activity was a matter of some discussion within these communities, and annual variations of up to a month could be expected (variations that also occur with the use of lunar calendars). Jackson's account appears to have recorded events that took place in March or later. Pentecost falls 50 days after the Resurrection (the British Whitsunday), deriving from the Jewish feast of *Shavuot* which is celebrated 50 days after Passover. A date seven weeks after Easter Sunday, which also is Pentecost Sunday, would be in late spring.

Wallace cites Jackson's journal as indicating that at other "ritual" gatherings among the Seneca associated with Handsome Lake in the years around 1800, "they slew a white Dog and did eat the meat" but completely incinerated the skin (Wallace 1952: 147). Communal cooking and eating of a white dog "as a preventative against the Sickness" was part of one of Handsome Lake's visions, and specifically recorded by Henry Simmons:

> The afternoon of the same day they prepar'd a white Dog to eat, and burnt his Skin to ashes, During which time it was burning a number of them Circled around the Fire, Singing, Shouting & dancing greatly; after which they all partook of their Delicious dish of Dog Meat Etc.
>
> (in Wallace 1952: 343, 348; see also Tooker 1970: 105)

Dog "sacrifice" and the eating of its flesh also is documented in several situations by the Jesuits. Dog meat, however prepared, seems to have been the Iroquoian "chicken soup," a generic comfort food in much of modern America. The specific goal of burning the skin of the sacrificed dog "to ashes" clearly is part of the curative ritual, but the treatment of the ashes and subsequent rites are nowhere documented. Handsome Lake's revelations of events from his journeys taken while in a trance state offer further insights into the WDS. In one of these visionary states he supposedly reported having met a dog and

> "Then he recognized the animal as his own dog and it appeared just as it had when he had decorated it for the sacrifice in the Hadidji'yontwŭs [New Year's ceremony]. Then said the four, 'This thing attests to the value of our thankoffering [sic] to the Creator.'"
>
> Parker 1912: 75

This narration, of course, was written by Arthur Parker nearly a
century after the death of Handsome Lake, in 1815. Wallace consid-
ers the importance of Handsome Lake's meeting with the dog "whom
he had sacrificed at the white dog ceremony last New Year; it was
still decorated as for the ritual, . . ." (Wallace 1970: 245; cf. Shimony
1961: 185–186). Handsome Lake's involvement in various rituals at
Cold Spring, including the WDS or some variation of it, continued for
a number of years, but the documents that we now use to understand
what then transpired are far from eyewitness accounts.

Halliday Jackson's journals provide eyewitness accounts of these
events mixed with reports of contemporary narrations. These are of
importance in decoding a transformation of the feasting or "celebra-
tory" eating of dogs at festivals into an apparently Christianized ritual
sacrifice. Soon after making these observations Jackson returned to
Philadelphia.[5] In the fall of 1806 he made one more trip to the Seneca,
a rushed 32-day journey from Philadelphia and back. During a brief
stop at the Seneca New Town at Cold Spring, Jackson and his party
"were invited into the Counsel room which is a long building prepared
for that purpose" (Snyderman 1957: 574, 582). The description of the
meeting involves neither wampum nor ritual smoking of the calumet,
suggesting that it was not a treaty. The meeting ended with handshak-
ing. Jackson's party had arrived months before the date that the midwinter rituals would have been conducted.

Jackson's 1806 trip ended without his recording any details regarding fall rituals that might reveal important changes then taking place
among the Seneca. One of these changes resulted from Handsome
Lake's effort to ban, in 1806, the WDS. As Fenton (1936: 12) puts it,
Handsome Lake "preached against burning the white dog." Whether
the trauma of losing his own dog, as suggested by Parker (1912: 75),
or some other factors were at play are discussed by Snyderman (1961:
589). By 1809 several fissions among the various Seneca factions came
to involve the WDS. "Henry O'Bail, one of Handsome Lake's chiefly
nephews, now also openly took sides against the prophet." O'Bail "publicly objected to the burning of the white dog" (Wallace 1970: 293),
but whether in support of the Christian influences among the Seneca

or as a protest against this innovative aspect inserted into the midwinter festival is not known. We suspect that the WDS, with its Christian ideas of sin and exculpation, was a recent innovation that conservative Seneca such as Henry O'Bail found disruptive of the old ways. Regardless of the conflicts and schisms that followed, the innovations among Handsome Lake's group set the path for changes in the WDS as it developed and spread over the next three decades.

The Reverend Thaddeus Osgood:
His Seneca Account, 1812

In his presentation of data relating to the Indians of New York and nearby Canada, Timothy Dwight (1752–1817) incorporated information regarding the Indians that he had received from several important informants, including Samuel Kirkland and a yet-to-be identified Mr. Deane. Dwight, a Congregationalist minister, was president of Yale College for much of his life. His statement that the Indians arrived in the Americas via the "Straits of Behring" appears to be a logical inference by learned clerics, who at that time were considering the dispersal of the tribes of Israel rather than any of our modern data or interests regarding this thesis of Indian origins. Dwight died before the first publication of his *Travels* (1821–1822) in which these data on the WDS appeared. The work went through several editions, with Dwight's London (1823) edition being the one cited here.

Regarding the WDS, Dwight reported that a Mr. Deane believed that the only form of worship among the Iroquois involved:

> "the annual sacrifice of a dog to Taulonghyauwaugoon, the 'Supporter of the Heavens.' At this sacrifice they eat the dog."
>
> Dwight 1823, IV: 190–191

Mr. Deane may have had a great deal more to say about the Midwinter Feast, but only his remarks on the dog sacrifice were included by Dwight. This selectivity reflects the general attitude that prevailed among outsiders regarding what was "central" to the Iroquoian midwinter festival. The eating of the flesh of the "sacrificed" dog as reported by Deane suggests that his observations were made during the transitional decades (ca. 1800–1820) that seem to include the following Osgood report.

More important among Dwight's few observations attributed to Mr. Deane is his note that among "The Iroquois . . . the house of the principal man of each village was distinguished by a long pole set up at the door" (Dwight 1823, IV: 190). This is the only clue we have to the presence of long poles being a possible general feature in these villages. The location is given as near a residence, not a "council-house." In fact, we could focus on references in these accounts to these special structures and whether they were indeed frame buildings of late date, or post-1800. Frame residences were being used by various Iroquoians by the 1750s, but data on their incidence at any location have yet to be assembled. The many accounts collected by Major General John Sullivan (1887) from his officers provide by far the best indication available of the incidence of frame structures among these peoples in the year 1779.

Following the Deane note regarding the dog sacrifice, Dwight indicated that "The following account of this subject, as it exists among the Seneca, was given me, in August 1812, by the Rev. Thaddeus Osgood" who "was present at one of these solemn festivals." Dwight also added the important observation that in addition to his eyewitness record, Osgood had added data provided by an interpreter (Dwight 1823, IV: 201). The added information probably included the duration of the feast, given as being seven days (see also Tooker 1970: 131).

> "On the evening before the feast commences they kill two dogs, and after painting them with various colours and dressing them with ornaments, suspend them in the centre of the camp, or in some conspicuous place in the village. [There follows feasting and dancing after which the celebrants] proceed to every house in the village . . .".
>
> "On one of the festival days" the celebrants extinguish all the fires and scatter the ashes "with their hands." . . . "Towards the close of the festival they erect a funeral pile [sic], place upon it the two dogs, and set it on fire. When they are partly consumed, one of them is taken off and put into a large kettle, with vegetables of every kind which they

have cultivated during the preceding year. The other dog is consumed in the fire. The ashes of the pile are then gathered up, carried through the village, and sprinkled at the door of every house. When this ceremony is ended, which is always near the close of the seventh day, all the inhabitants feast together upon the contents of the kettle; and the festival is terminated."

Osgood 1812, in Dwight 1823, IV: 201
(see also in Tooker 1970: 131–132)[6]

If this Seneca account is accurate it provides an excellent representation of a transitional phase in which one dog is eaten while the other is cremated. This also may explain why two dogs were strangled, in order to have one consumed and one providing for a new ritual. We are not certain how Osgood transmitted this information on the WDS to Dwight in 1812, but another 11 years passed before Dwight published the narrative. Osgood himself does not appear to have published any of this specific information on the WDS, despite issuing a slim volume of anecdotes (1829?; see also 1851) relating to Indians and settlers in Canada and the United States. Note also should be made that many of the details in Dwight's account of the WDS that he attributed to Osgood are remarkably similar to details found in the Jemison version of the WDS as it was published in the same year, 1823. The possibility that Dwight's version of Osgood's account was available to Seaver, who published the Jemison account, is worth consideration. Comparisons may be noted. In the Jemison account the source of the meat in the kettle is not specified. The Horsford account of 1816 later in this volume specifies that the meat would be venison, as would be expected since these ceremonies followed the winter hunt. The addition of dog to the kettle, however, might be expected during these years of transformation.

Edwin Scranton's 1813 Report from the Rochester Area

Henry O'Reilly (1838: 249, 275–277) reports an account of a Seneca WDS from near Genesee Falls that had been witnessed by Edwin Scranton in January of 1813. O'Reilly (p. 275) proclaimed this as an account of "one of the great pagan festivals" not performed in Rochester for 26 years! During January of 1813 Edwin Scranton witnessed a WDS near Genesee Falls in the area of Rochester. His account, perhaps never written, was related to Henry O'Reilly, who was arranging a collection of "sketches" from western New York. I believe that O'Reilly learned this information at some point soon before 1838. O'Reilly (1838: 275) declared that Scranton's account corresponded with those of the "Rev. Mr. Kirkland [1800] and by the 'White Woman' [Mrs. Jemison 1824]." Some of the Kirkland accounts were published before his death, and the many copies of his diaries deposited at learned institutions made the information widely available (Tooker 1970: 176, n11; Patrick 2009, pers. Com 29 Jan. 2013).

O'Reilly perceived this event as indicating that "as late as 1813 one of the great pagan festivals (the Sacrifice of the Dog) was solemnized publicly at the rising ground beside which the Bethel Church now stands" (O'Reilly 1838: 249). In contrast to Mrs. Jemison's account of a nine-day ritual with two dogs sacrificed, Scranton (1838: 275–277) reported a feast "Curtailed to five to seven days and a single dog was made the scapegoat to bear away the sins of the tribe!" We know where these Seneca were living, and that one dog was sacrificed, but even the length of the feast was not certain. More significant is that no other WDS is known or reported from that area during the next 25 years.

Tooker (1970: 175–176, n5) indicates that the Scranton account as published by O'Reilly formed the basis for an 1841 comment by James Silk Buckingham. Buckingham had toured the United States in 1837 and 1838 but was in Rochester for only 10 days, in August and September of 1838 (1841, III: 51–52). Buckingham clearly cites O'Reilly's version as the source of his information on the WDS. F. Houghton (1920: 130–131) mistakenly believed that Buckingham had actually seen a WDS. Houghton also makes note of the missionary Jabez Backus Hyde who appears to have seen a WDS during the winter of 1811–1812 and included the event in an 1820 account. Hyde (1903: 242) has a single sentence listing the four feasts of the Seneca of which the third is a "feast of atonement or yearly sacrifice," in which no WDS is noted

The Horsford 1816 Seneca Account
from Squakie Hill, New York

Tooker (1970: 132–134) identified an 1816 eyewitness description of the WDS included in a centennial history of Livingston County, New York. Lockwood L. Doty (1876: 63–56) had access to the diary of the Reverend Jedediah Horsford (1791–1875), who had recorded the day-to-day events of the WDS that he witnessed in 1816. Geneseo is located in this county, which lies south of Rochester and east of Buffalo. The Horsford diary, of course, would be the preferred source of this information, but its present location remains unknown.

Horsford settled in Mount Morris "[a]bout the 1st of October 1814" where he had gone to teach the Indians at Squakie Hill in the Genesee Valley. His interest in native customs included reporting on a dance he had seen that was "designed to restore an Indian seriously indisposed" (Doty 1876: 51, 328). Later Horsford served as a U.S. Congressman for many years. While the Horsford diary appears to be the basis for Doty's account, the narration also may have included information reported to him by Governor George W. Patterson.

> "*Hon. Jerediah [sic] Horsford was present at this festival and noted the ceremonies from day to day in his diary. . . . Governor George W. Patterson attended the festival three years later, at the same place, in company with several young men of Groveland, and has given me valuable facts."
>
> Doty 1876: 53

Not clear is how much, if any, of the information given to Doty by Governor Patterson may have been incorporated in the narration below. Presumably the natives were Seneca and the location was one of 11 reservations established by treaty in 1797. Doty's account was the source of Beauchamp's brief note (1889), as both include the error that this group was composed of Erie Indian survivors of Seneca raids who were taken to live among the Five Nations (see also Smith 1881). In 1826, the land in this area was sold to the Ogden Land Company.

The New Year's festival at Squakie Hill, in 1816, opened on the morning of the 7th of February.* A white dog was brought to the council-house and strangled, care being taken not to break its bones or shed its blood, and hanged to a post. Its body was then striped with red paint, and five strings of purple beads were fastened around the neck. A stem of hedge-hog quills was attached to the body, from which hung a clump of feathers, a rag with something like fine tobacco being placed under them. To each leg was tied a bunch of feathers with red and yellow ribbons. The day was spent in short speeches and dream-telling. Near night, two Indians, with blackened faces, appeared in bear skins with long braids of corn husks about their ankles and heads. Keeping time to a dolorous song, they began a tour of the village. Entering a house, they would pound the benches and sides and then proceed to the next, and so on throughout the village.

The discharge of three guns opened the second day's proceedings, when five Indians appared with long wooden shovels, and began to scatter fire and ashes until the council-house became filled with dust and smoke. This ceremony was repeated at each house several times during the day, but to a different tune at each round.

Speeches, exciting levity, and dreams occupied the third morning. About noon the fire-shoveling was repeated with increased vigor. This over, the clothing of the actors and others was changed, their heads were adorned with feathers and their faces with paint. A number of squaws in calico short gowns and blue broadcloth petticoats, ornamented with bead-work and a profusion of silver brooches, joined in the dance, which, beginning at the council-house, was repeated at every hut several times during the day. A species of gambling with a wooden dish and six wooden balls and a like number of white beans was practiced from house to house. In the evening a party of dancers would enter a dwelling, and soon a person dressed in bear-skin and false face would come in, when the dancers, as if afraid, beat a retreat to the next house.

The fourth day was devoted to ceremonies in which false faces and dancing held the principal place.

The maskers [Tooker enters this as "members"] reappeared on the fifth day. They approached every person for a trifling gift. An apple, a plug of tobacco, or a few pennies was enough, in default of which the party refusing was often roughly handled. Two Indians, disguised as bears, came next. On their entering a house the inmates would at once quit it, when the mock bears pretended a disposition to tear everything in pieces or to overturn whatever fell in their way. A number

---

* Seen by Horsford

of Indians followed them, flashing guns, as though forcibly to drive out the simulated bears. Next in order was a game of ball upon the ice, played with great life by a party of seven on each side. Many a hard fall occurred, which always drew forth shouts of laughter. Three Indians then appeared in deer-skins and rags, one of whom, personating the evil one, had his clothing literally torn from his body by his companions, who quickly covered him with skins, and then led him from hut to hut. In each hut he would lie down and roll along the ground, tumble into the fire, paw out the ashes and scatter it about the room, all the while groaning and making great ado. A dancing group next entered the council-house with painted faces, attired in skins, with feathers around their heads and deer's hoofs or pieces of tin fastened about their legs. A large Indian, with bow and arrows, soon came in, bringing three lads. The four enacted a rude drama of hunter and dogs. The boys got down on hands and knees, barking, growling and snapping at whatever came in their way, as they passed from door to door, demanding bread for the final feast, which two girls gathered into baskets.

On the morning of the sixth day, seven lads, one of whom was covered with wolf-skins and used two short sticks for forelegs, went from house to house. The dwellers brought out corn and placed it in a basket carried by an aged female. Next followed a dance at the council-house. 'The female dancers,' says an eyewitness, 'were the most graceful, and, I may add, the most modest I ever saw tripping the fantastic toe upon the bare ground.' An old squaw stepped into the ring with a live pig under her arms. She would strike it upon the head, when the dancers would spat their hands and sing.[*] About noon preparations were made for burning the white dog, which was taken down and laid upon a small pile of dry wood, ornaments and all. An Indian gave three yells. The wood was then placed around and over the dog. When old and young had gathered quite near Jim Washington, a favorite speaker, he applied the fire, and, as it began to burn, he walked around inside the circle, occasionally throwing pulverized mint into the flames, all the while talking as if to some invisible being. The spectators appeared quite solemn, and at length joined in singing. When the pile was partly consumed Jim stopped. After a moment's pause, he put a question which met with loud response from the circle, and then all dispersed.

A general feast was now prepared [6th day] at the council-house. Two brass kettles, filled with squash, corn, beans, pumpkins and venison, which had been boiling for hours over fires in the center of the room, were placed on the ground, and the contents dipped away in

---

[*] Quis-quis, meaning pigs, swine, was a word constantly repeated.

calabashes and eaten with spoons, or from wooden sticks, with the bread gathered the day before. The evening was devoted to dancing, in which all joined. At length, one after another withdrew, and by ten o'clock the council-house was empty and silent. The ceremonial part of the festival was over, and though the seventh and last day was to follow, it was mainly spent in petty gambling and feats of strength.

Horsford [1816], in Doty 1876: 53–56

Tooker's (1970: 134) transcription of the Doty text ends at this point. Two further lines in Doty's text, not included by Tooker, are of interest here. Whether these two lines were added by Doty or if they were part of the Horsford diary account is not evident. These lines specifically link the WDS to Handsome Lake's religion, which included a concept of sin and atonement that had not previously been a part of Seneca religion.

The burning of the dog was designed to appease the Great Spirit's wrath. So were the burnt sacrifice of the ancient Hebrews . . . None but a white dog, the emblem of purity, could be used. . . . Late in the last century a new religion was announced by a native of Canawaugus, . . . Handsome Lake.

Doty 1876: 56–57

A brief note on Iroquoian masks, also called "false faces," and masked dancers may be of interest. The use of false faces reveals a continuity of this part of the midwinter rites with ancient customs. A great deal of recent literature purports to link specific false faces with past rituals, but how their use varied among the several tribes has not been investigated. Some early examples in museum collections, including in the State Museum of New York, derive from nineteenth-century collectors. Earlier examples are rarely reported. During Sullivan's 1779 military action noted earlier, also called the Sullivan-Clinton campaign, only one pitched battle was fought. At the town of Chemung (Newtown) on 29 August, 40 false face masks were discovered prior to the burning of the village. One of these reached Du Simitiere's "museum" collection in Philadelphia by November of that year, and a second was reported sent by George Clinton in October 1781 (Potts 1889: 366, 372). These masks were an integral part of the midwinter rites, as will be seen in most of the accounts of the WDS. The use of tobacco and other forms of "incense" in these rituals also merits review (see Potts 1889).

A Buffalo Creek Seneca Account;
Mary Jemison, Before 1823

Mary Jemison was a 15-year-old colonist captured by Indians in 1758 and ultimately raised by a Seneca group, perhaps those at Genesee (Tooker 1970: 127–128). Others suggest that she lived among the Buffalo Creek Seneca. Her descendants, by two Seneca husbands, still figure in the current generation of this tribe. James Seaver met with her in 1823 and recorded her autobiography (Jemison 1824). Seaver's appendix (Jemison 1824: 91 ff) includes an important early description of the Midwinter Feast and the WDS. At best it is an amalgamation of Jemison's experiences with these annual rituals—but it is a true ethnographic summary from a valid informant. A clue to the accuracy of Jemison's narration is Seaver's note that in 1823 he believed that only one dog was sacrificed whereas Jemison specified the number at two. Seaver also stated that by 1823 he found the feast more commonly lasted only five to seven days, whereas Jemison reported the length at nine days. Tooker interpreted this discrepancy as an indication that the 80-year-old informant was describing events predating 1799. We suggest that the many midwinter rituals of her group in which Jemison had participated since 1799 were more significant to her recall than earlier dog feasts. In fact, the narrative section of her account does not include the WDS, details of which she must have related to Seaver in a context outside her autobiographical reporting. She also refers to the newly introduced Christian concept of sin and to a "council-house"—a structure that also may be post-1800 in origin. The quotes from Jemison's account provided below derive from Tooker (1970: 128–130):

> [On the first day] Two white dogs,[3] without spot or blemish, are selected (if such can be found, and if not, two that have the fewest

spots) from those belonging to the tribe, and killed near the door of the council-house by being strangled. A wound on the animal or an effusion of blood, would spoil the victim and render the sacrifice useless. The dogs are then painted red on their faces, edges of their ears, and on various parts of their bodies, and are curiously decorated with ribbons of different colors, and fine feathers, which are tied and fastened on in such a manner as to make the most elegant appearance. They are then hung on a post near the door of the council-house, at a height of twenty feet from the ground.

Following the hanging of the dogs, the members of the committee, who were all dressed only in breach clouts and each carrying a paddle, extinguished all the fires of the tribe and took up and scattered all the ashes, "and new fire, struck from the flint on each hearth, is kindled, after having removed the whole of the ashes, old coals, &c."

On the second day the committee dance . . . and . . . beg through the tribe, each carrying a basket in which to receive whatever may be bestowed. The alms consist of Indian tobacco and other articles that are used for incense at the sacrifice.

On the fourth or fifth day the committee make false faces of husks, in which they run about . . . smearing themselves with dirt and bedaubing every one who refuses to contribute something toward filling the baskets of incense, which they continue to carry, soliciting alms. During all this time they collect the evil spirit, to drive it off entirely, for the present, and also concentrate within themselves all the sins of their tribe, however numerous or heinous.

On the eighth or ninth day, the committee having received all the sin, as before observed, into their own bodies, they take down the dogs, and having transfused the whole of it into one of their own number, he, by a peculiar slight of hand, or kind of magic, works it out of himself into the dogs. The dogs, thus loaded with all the sins of the people, are placed on a pile of wood that is directly set on fire. Here they are burnt, together with the sins with which they were loaded, surrounded by the multitude, who throw incense of tobacco or the like into the fire, the scent of which they say, goes up to Nauwaneu, to whom it is pleasant and acceptable.

. . . On the last day [ninth?], the whole company partakes in an elegant dinner, consisting of meat, corn, and beans, boiled together in large kettles, and stirred till the whole is completely mixed and soft. This mess is devoured without much ceremony—some eat with a spoon, by dipping out of the kettles; others serve themselves in small dippers . . . After this they perform the war dance, the peace dance, and smoke the pipe of peace; [etc].

They are fond of the company of spectators . . .

Jemison to Seaver (1824: 101–103) (see also Tooker 1970: 128–130)

David Cusick's 1825 Perceptions: An Ambiguous Tribal Affiliation

Before continuing with a first-person, first-hand report of observations of the mature WDS among the Seneca, which dates from 1829, brief mention should be made of a "Tuscarora"-influenced version dated to 1825. This synthetic view was formulated during that significant period of transition among the various Iroquoian people as they were shifting to a stronger focus on sedentary agriculture and also, as a corollary, from a matrilineal descent system, where kinship and inheritance pass through the mother's line, to a patrilineal system. The changes taking place among native cultures in New York may have led David Cusick (c. 1780–c. 1840) to feel compelled to record native tales told to him that he believed might disappear. Cusick's brief work, perhaps the first account of native history and legends told by an Indian in the Northeast, is dated "Tuscarora Village, June 10th, 1825" (Cusick 1848: 3). The first edition (1827) was printed in Lewiston for the author. This 26-page version must have sold very well, as a second edition, of 36 pages, was issued in 1828. The 1848 version used here is widely available.

Whether or not his text was altered in the 23 years between its 1825 dedication date and the 1848 version is irrelevant. The account is both brief and not specifically linked with any particular tribe. In fact, even David Cusick's perception of his own cultural affiliation remains unclear. David's father, Nicholas Cusick, may have been born on Oneida lands. He served as an interpreter for missionaries to the Seneca, but he also has been described as a Tuscarora elder. Nicholas Cusick also is identified as an ancestor of Albert Cusick (1846–?; Sa-go-neh-guah-deh) who is described as an Onondaga elder. Albert was born on the Tuscarora Reservation, but his mother was Onondaga.

Modern confusion in identifying cultural affiliation often derives from a failure to understand matrilineal descent, a pattern that remained strong among many Iroquoian groups into the twentieth century. Thus David Cusick may have been a resident in a Tuscarora Village in 1825, but since his mother's cultural affiliation remains unknown we cannot speculate on her cultural identity and the cultural influences from that important (matrilineal) vector. The proximity of the territory of the relocated Tuscarora to the Seneca tracts in the period 1780–1830 leads us to infer that Seneca rites, including the midwinter rituals, may be what David Cusick recorded.

Some of the many events and behaviors observed by Cusick are, in fact, associated with a named tribe. This is not the case with his limited information pertaining to the WDS, all of which may not be related to a single event or a single tribe. It is not even certain that the "sacrifice" described took place during the midwinter rites. Cusick's few relevant lines on the WDS appear in the middle of a long, rambling paragraph. We believe that Cusick never saw a WDS, but that he is simply retelling part of "the history involved with fables" (Cusick 1848: 3) that he himself had been told by kin and probably by members of other tribes. For this reason we include these brief remarks, including several synthetic accounts (see Table I). Who provided information regarding this event or events to Cusick we do not know.

> They have a certain time of worship; the false faces first commence the dances; they visit the houses to drive away sickness, &c. Each town or district are [sic] allowed to sacrifice a couple of white dogs; the dogs are painted and ornamented with strings of wampum; they throw the dogs into the fire, and some tobacco, and addresses [sic] the Maker. They pretend to furnish him ["the Maker"] a coat of skin and a pipe full of tobacco; after which, [they] have dances for several days.
>
> Cusick 1848: 31

Cusick's reference to furnishing "the Maker" with "a coat of skin" can be best understood with reference to the dog sacrifices so widely reported from the accounts of Major General John Sullivan following his campaign of 1779. The fusion of the traditional bargaining with a deity of the various Long House peoples and the post-1800 sacrifice as repentance for sins can be better understood from this period.

A Seneca Account from 1829, by Mr. Harris

Had the WDS existed prior to 1799, reference or note of the ritual could be expected to be found embedded in missionary or other accounts of native life among one or another of the Five Nations. Between 1799 and 1823 we have five clear published accounts of the WDS as part of these rituals, if we include the Jackson report. In 1829, Harris provided a long, reportlike account of the "Indians" within which he referred to an event witnessed the previous winter. Harris (1829: 90–92) describes events among one of the Seneca groups where the sacrifice of a white dog was reported as part of the Winter Feast. The many details provided suggest that he actually witnessed these events, which included the stirring of the household ashes and other elements that are rarely mentioned in the more cursory descriptions. Four days of ceremonies were followed by the white dog rituals, which possibly took place on the fifth day, during which they

> attend on the great annual sacrifice of the white dog. The dog on being strangled, was highly painted and adorned with ribbons, and suspended to a post previously prepared. The officiating priest, at the proper time, would advance, take down the dog, lay it on the pile of wood already in flames, and throw upon the consuming victim, a handful or two of Indian tobacco.
>
> Harris 1829: 92

Harris indicated that they then prayed to "our son" to whom they offered this present with a request that he send these supplicants various goods. Harris remarked that this was unusual as it was the only time he knew the Indians to pray. Following the prayer there were celebrations that included sexual license.

Harris appears to have been struck by the Christian influence of prayer being merged with what appeared to him to be a native ceremony. The winter feast, and almost certainly the sexual license, may have been traditional, but the act of prayer and the "blood" sacrifice reveal recent introductions to these rituals.

Crowell's Early and Unusually Detailed Account from a Seneca Group Resident in Ohio, 1830

One of the more detailed accounts of the midwinter WDS among the Seneca was recorded by Samuel Crowell, a resident of Fremont (Lower Sandusky?), Ohio. His extraordinary anthropological observations resulted in a record of events that took place in 1830 (Crowell 1877; see also in Tooker 1970: 118–123; and the summary in Oberholtzer 2003). Crowell's record (1944) largely agrees with later Seneca accounts, suggesting that the WDS as practiced by Handsome Lake and his followers became part of a revitalized and Christianized version of earlier Seneca midwinter rituals. A century after these observations were made in Ohio, William Fenton (1944: 162–163) suggested that the people observed by Crowell "were not Senecas at all" but were Mingos living among the Seneca. Fenton's own records negate this claim, leading us to wonder why he proposed a non-Seneca ethnicity for the people observed by Crowell. Fenton's denial of their Seneca origins may have been his attempt to reconcile his early findings of wide variations in the many descriptions of the WDS, together with the very late dates (post-1799) of all the accounts.

The Crowell account first appeared in the *Sidney Aurora* of 1844, derived from records made during or soon after the event and entered into his scrapbook (Fenton 1944: 158, Lang 1880: 98–106). The version offered here derives primarily from the republished edition (Crowell 1877) of the earlier account. A "centennial" version (Crowell 1944), including commentary by William Fenton (1944) and an introduction by F. M. Setzler (1944), differs for the most part in only minimal details. In February of 1830 Crowell was sheriff of Sandusky County, Ohio. A group of Seneca Indians then resident in Seneca and Sandusky Counties had just sold their reservation lands and were intending to move west. On the first of February, Crowell joined his friend Obed Dickinson (?– before 1844), who was a respected merchant in the area. Dickinson had been invited by the three "principal head-men, or chiefs" to attend the ceremonies. Hard Hickory and other natives are named in this account, as are several individuals of lesser rank, one of whom may have been "white" or had no known native ancestors (Crowell 1944: 148). Hard Hickory, whom Fenton (1944: 158) suggests was recognized as leader of this band in 1830, spoke French "fluently" and English intelligibly. He also indicated that this feast was being held because of a dream that Hard Hickory had experienced (Crowell 1944: 152–153). Connections between this group, at "the western limit of Seneca jurisdiction" and other settlements are posited by Fenton (1944: 158–159). Fenton's speculations regarding "Mingo" influences on this manifestation of the WDS reveal an early research error.

On the afternoon of 1 February, Dickinson and Crowell arrived at the Seneca council house on Green Creek bearing as a gift "a quantity of loaf sugar and tobacco." The council house is described in detail, as are the ornaments worn and the gourd and undressed (rawhide) deerskin instruments being played. Rawhide drums are rarely reported, but Lenape drums, of simple rawhide that was folded over into a rough square, are well documented. The Seneca event on that Friday afternoon was marked by dancing by both males and females. Local white residents also participated in the dancing, indicating that Crowell and Dickinson were not the only non-natives invited to attend or who were attending as neighbors. Descriptions of the beds within the native houses, dreams of various individuals, and a six-inch long canoe amulet augment the anthropological record. How long these festivities had been going on before February is not mentioned. When Crowell asked these people when "they intended to burn their dogs" . . . as a "sacrifice to . . . the Great Spirit" (328–329), the answers invariably were vague.

On 2 February, Crowell and Dickinson "rose early and proceeded directly to the council house" where they found a large group already assembled, apparently outside the structure. Amidst them was "a pair of the canine species, one of each gender suspended on a cross, one on either side thereof." Whether this was a Christian (Latin) cross or a "T"-shaped arrangement is not specified, nor is the height of the "cross" given. A functional "T" might reflect a less Christian influence on this Seneca event in 1830 than a Christian cross. More commonly this rite involved the use of long poles to suspend the dog or dogs.[7] The dogs had been strangled that morning, without fracturing a bone or disturbing a hair. "They were of a beautiful cream color, except a few dark spots on one, naturally, while the same spots had been put on the other, artificially, by the devotees" (Crowell 1877: 329).

Although Crowell notes that the "Indians are very partial in the selection of dogs [that are] entirely white, for this occasion; and for which they will give almost any price," it is evident that such examples were not always to be had. Crowell's keen observation demonstrates that cream-colored animals could be used, and that spots were allowed. In this case paint had been used to add spots on one dog so that the dogs would be of the same "color," rather than using paint to cover the spots on the other dog. In addition to the painting of the pelts, the dogs both were decorated in the same manner. Whether the similarity in decoration reflects moiety or gender equality, or if any two dogs of suitable color and available for sacrifice were selected, is not known. The decoration on each of these dogs, or what Fenton (1944: 162) identifies "as dressing the dog which is called *ganiyóndon*, 'a decorated thing'" is described by Crowell as follows:

> A scarlet ribbon was tastefully tied just above the neck [1944: "nose"]; and near the eyes another; next round the neck was a white ribbon, to which was attached something bulbous, concealed in another white ribbon; this was placed directly under the right ear, and I suppose it was intended as an amulet or charm. Then ribbons were bound round the forelegs, at the knees, and near the feet—these were red and white alternately. Round the body was a profuse decoration—then the hind legs were decorated as the fore ones. . . .
>
> Adjacent to the cross, was a large fire built on a few logs; and though the snow was several inches deep sufficient wood was provided.
>
> Crowell [1830] 1877: 329–330

Crowell laments that he did not see the lighting of the fire. He suspected that they did not carry a flame from within the council house but had struck a new "fire from a flint, this being deemed *sacred*" (Crowell 1944: 154). At least this is what Crowell believed would have been involved in a ritual process for this occasion.

A large number of Indians were assembled for this ritual, and as the sun topped the trees they "formed a semicircle enclosing the cross" from which the bodies of the two dogs were hanging. Cath Oberholtzer (personal communication, 2008) notes that the rising sun's "blessing" is an important part of ritual among Algonquian-speaking peoples and some other Native American groups. How this "blessing" influenced ritual on cloudy or rainy days is not known, but the weather may account for variations in selecting the day of the Iroquoian Midwinter Feast chosen for the burning of the dog. Crowell reported that not a single woman was present at this part of the ceremony.

Good Hunter presided over the ceremony, and at a signal "two young chiefs sprung up the cross, and each taking off one of the victims" gave them to Good Hunter, who solemnly laid them on the fire. Crowell states that he could not tell if any preference was given to the male or to the female dog. The sex of the animal may not have been relevant. Good Hunter then gave a long oration during which he held a white cloth in his left hand. At intervals he extracted from the cloth "a portion of dried, odiferous herbs, which he threw on the fire." Tobacco is nowhere mentioned, but mixtures of tobacco, herbs, and bark (*kinickinick*) were often smoked by various native groups. The large number of men was silent "until the victims were entirely consumed." Then they all entered the council house where they sat down and each "recounted his exploits as a warrior." The description of this aspect of the ceremonies parallels that of "counting coup" among the Plains tribes of that period, a form of formal narration common in warrior societies, but they may have been recounting sins.

At the conclusion of these ceremonial parts of the event on 2 February, dancing was renewed and the women joined the men. At the end of this dancing, a young Indian drew Crowell to the door to be out of the way of "an Indian running at full speed to the council house; in an instant he was in the house and literally in the fire, which he took in his hands, and threw coals of fire and hot ashes in various directions, through the house" and apparently all over himself (Crowell 1877: 332, 1944: 156). This individual was wearing a false face and had "horns on his head." The role of this individual, which calls to mind accounts of the pre-1800 midwinter rites among the Huron, may be critical to this ritual, and the goal here may have been to scare off the spirit of the dog. All during these activities abundant quantities of food were available. Crowell left during the afternoon of 2 February, having spent about 24 hours with these Indians. Possibly the entire feast lasted no more than the two days of his brief visit, which would be quite unusual for the midwinter rituals of the Seneca. If this Ohio group held a two-day midwinter ritual, the timing may have led Fenton to suggest that these people were of different ancestry.

The Seneca Reservation near Buffalo, circa 1832 or 1833

Another account of the WDS among the Seneca, which we believe dates from the 1830s but which was not published until 1860, provides data from among those members of this tribe then living near Buffalo. Although the rites appear to have been seen in the 1830s, they were not published until almost 30 years after the event. In 1860 one of the older white residents living on a tract of land near Buffalo that had become the Ebenezer Settlement related an account of "burning the dog" to a certain "BDG" whose name has not yet been identified. We now have only the initials of this person, derived from the published version of the account (G. 1860). The Ebenezer Settlement, then situated four miles east of the small town of Buffalo, occupied an area of the Seneca Reservation formerly known as Jackberry Town. The informant had been interested for several years in seeing the ritual of the WDS but consistently had been given the wrong date by the Seneca. Though the reporter felt that he was being put off in his efforts to witness this event, we suggest that the indeterminate nature of dates associated with these rituals is typical of all non-literate societies. In the 1830s literacy seems to have varied considerably among the various native communities. The absence of calendars and other means of setting ritual events among these peoples appears disorderly to non-native observers who are concerned with fixed dates and clocks. In the case of the observer from Buffalo who later reported to BDG, he felt that he was deliberately given misinformation. There may have been no specific information to give, since the timing of specific elements of these "rituals" may not have been fixed, a view held by Knapp (1837: 3).

The informant recalled that in 1832 or 1833 he and several other interested individuals had gone to the reservation on four or five consecutive days bearing gifts of tobacco and trinkets but not alcohol, which he reported as strongly prohibited. Almost certainly this prohibition was by the Indian participants in these rituals rather than by law. At some point a Seneca identified as Old Captain Billy privately told the informant that the Indians did not wish the whites to see the ritual for fear of being laughed at. Captain Billy must have been the Seneca who revealed the correct day and timing of the midwinter ritual events in that year to the unnamed observer. This non-Indian observer, who later became the informant, appears to have organized a considerable "outing" for many curious whites. Captain Billy may not have wished these outsiders to think that these Indians were disorganized and unreliable. He may have made up a different defensive reason for being unable to communicate a specific time and date.

If over the several days of the feast any of the "white" people had seen singing and dancing or any other activities associated with the ritual, it was not reported. On the "appointed" day, after several sleighs filled with whites were leaving the Ebenezer Settlement, the observer told the two companions in his small sleigh that the burning was to take place that afternoon. The informant and his friends apparently had left with the other outsiders but then returned to witness a twilight ritual. Near the council-house they saw a "large pile of brushwood and logs" and two dogs suspended from a horizontal pole by cords around their necks. The pole "rested on a couple of crotched stakes." The dogs were described as spotless white "bedizened with strings of wampum and a profusion of ribbons of all colors; and were besides adorned with paint of various hues, and in various devices."

The informant claimed that 500 Seneca were present at the twilight rituals. When the fire was "full" the dogs were added. Red Jacket
(c. 1758–1830) spoke, and then the people marched around the fire
"each casting upon it, as an offering, a handful of dried herbs." Musi-
cians played little drums and a war dance followed, then medicine men
(salamanders) rushed at the fire and with their hands, in thick mittens,
scattered the brands like "madmen." There followed an orderly march
around the "sacrificial flame," during which each participant cast more
herbs, which gave off a "pleasant odor." Thus ended the ritual.

In his 1860 account, BDG added that the Cattaraugus band of
Seneca, presumably living somewhere to the southwest of Buffalo,
also sustained "this custom" but offered no dates or further details.
In response to BDG's 1860 publication of this account of the WDS,
another contributor offered two corrections and some comments. The
writer, identified only by the initials CDN, indicated that old Red Jacket
had died on 20 January 1830. The implication is that Red Jacket was
not actually present when BDG's informant witnessed the rituals. CDN
recalled that the ritual lasted "an entire week" and that the "Iroquois"
strangled the dog on the first day (N. 1861: 28). On the fifth day the
"dog is taken down and placed upon the sacrificial altar erected near
the council-house" and then the fire is lit and the assembled chant
while it burns. Tobacco leaves are scattered on the flames. This individual may have been describing a WDS from either of two tribes and at
any year prior to 1861. He believed that the ritual remained the same,
although he suggested that the "dog may be bedecked with a few more
ribbons than formerly" but assumed that it was always the same ritual.

A·"Synthetic" White Dog Sacrifice Near Buffalo, 1837

In 1837, Samuel Lorenzo Knapp (1783–1838), a noted biographer and
historian, reported that he spent "several weeks last winter in Buffalo,
that city of the hither West, which has grown up, as it were, by the
magick of enterprise and industry" (Knapp 1837: 3). While "confined
by a distressing illness for twenty days at Buffalo," he acquired some

information on the Seneca. He heard that some 960 were then living on a 50,000 acre reserve, led by a descendant of Cornplanter named Big Kettle. Although Knapp may have been in Buffalo during the WDS, he does not appear to have actually visited the reservation. He relates that by "the road-side you see the ancient 'council-house,' now in a state of decay." We believe that he had all of his "Indian" information from "the most intelligent people" of whom he inquired. During the period of Knapp's stay, the young Lewis Henry Morgan and others were becoming interested in the lives of their Indian neighbors and were building the foundations of modern ethnography. Whether Knapp met any of these gentlemen is yet to be determined.

Knapp's narration includes a number of disparate bits of information. On the whole, it appears quite similar to the briefer contemporary account by Cusick (1848). Only the more substantive bits of Knapp's narration are recorded here:

> The greatest festival of the Six Nations, and one which is common throughout North America, is "the sacrifice of the white dog." . . . When most, or all the hunters are at home [from hunting], in the dead of winter, one or two white dogs are killed and hung up in some publick place; these dogs are probably strangled . . . men, women, and children, meet in some publick place, dressed in their wildest costume, highly painted, and the men frequently stripped to the waist-band. [much drumming and dancing followed, after which] The carcasses of the white dogs are then taken down; some say skinned, others that their hair is taken off by scalding or singeing, and the flesh roasted to a cinder, when a morsel is taken by each, to preserve him for the season from all harm, and particularly from the sorcerers. This done, the revels begin; [more dancing, roasting of venison, feasting].
>
> The Indians are assiduous in making great preparations for this festival; and they make as much a mystery of it as possible. They have, probably, no very definite idea of what they intend themselves, . . . many of [the Christian Indians] attended when it was celebrated among the Senecas last winter, toward the last of January. This festival is highly relished by the females; and they seem to be treated with more respect at that time than usual. They put on all their finery on those occasions, making no small display of ornamental moccasins, and exhibit in their dress a profusion of beautiful feathers.
>
> Knapp 1837: 3

Lewis Henry Morgan: 1846

Lewis Henry Morgan (1818–1881) made enormous contributions to anthropology, particularly in the areas of social organization and material culture. Morgan's field notes may offer insights into the evolution of the WDS, but his published account (1851, I: 175–179; 1922: 207–213), derived from Tonawanda Seneca longhouse rituals, is a synthesis or composite of information rather than the recording of a specific event. Morgan's generic assemblage foreshadowed those produced by Wallace and by Tooker and others in the twentieth century.

Morgan's account of the WDS, derived from Tonawanda Seneca informants, provides information that Tooker (1970: 177, n14) believes had been secured in 1846. Her reading of Morgan's "Journals" (Morgan N.d.) indicate that "Morgan visited Tonawanda at the time of the Midwinter ceremonial in 1846" but that it is unclear "how much of the ceremony he saw." MJB had reached the same conclusion from the nature of Morgan's reconstruction of the events. Morgan and his fellow students of native culture may have observed and taken notes at one or more of the winter ritual cycles, but what he published is clearly a synthetic account rather than a careful ethnographic description of a single event.

Morgan's "journals for this [1846] trip contain only the information that he saw the white dog hanging on a pole before the longhouse and an account of an interview with Jimmy Johnson on the ceremony" (Tooker 1970: 177, n14). Tooker found that the interview provides the information found in Morgan's published version, which does not include the vital information in Morgan's journal (see Table 1A). Tooker found "similar brief descriptions of the ceremonial" elsewhere in his journals but discounts their value. She believes that Morgan's description is based "on Ely Parker's description of it to Morgan sometime after October, 1846." The vast archives of papers left by Morgan and his contemporaries may yield specific accounts, but to date no one has reported finding among these documents any actual records of firsthand observations of the WDS.

The young Morgan's synthetic narrative of the WDS, apparently derived from Johnson and Parker, states that the WDS took place during the seven days of the winter festival and was seen as a means to "approach *Hä-wen-né-yu* in the most acceptable manner" which was "the end and the object of burning the dog" (1901, I: 208). In Morgan's "narrative" the participants are said to have "hung around his neck a string of white wampum, the pledge of their faith" (Morgan 1962: 215–217, 1901, I: 208; cf. in Schwartz 1997: 83). Morgan appears not to have seen any ornaments on the hanging dog in 1846, but was told that this adornment took place "On the morning of the fifth day, soon after dawn, [when] the White Dog was burned on an altar of wood . . . near the council-house." Morgan states that the dog was borne from the council-house "upon a kind of bark litter." He suggested that, "[t]hey used the spirit of the dog in precisely the same manner that they did the incense of tobacco, as an instrumentality through which to commune with their Maker." The importance or function of the wampum, if any, is not stated.

Morgan saw a single dog suspended from a pole in 1846 but does not appear to have witnessed other parts of the Midwinter Feast or the WDS. Tooker (1970: 177, n14) says that Morgan's Journal records a brief "interview with Jimmy Johnson on the ceremony." His account is not referenced. In his 1851 publication, Morgan (1962: 219, n1) includes an oration, or address, supposedly from a Seneca WDS, said to have been provided "by Hä-sa-no-ań-dä (Ely S. Parker) as delivered by his grandfather, Sose-há-wä, at Tonawanda" at least 25 years prior to 1851. Morgan was more concerned with understanding why his informants spoke of sin than with their recollections regarding the ornaments placed on the dog. Morgan's native informants described the WDS as an offering made to atone for their sins. Morgan found it important to reconcile this Christian idea with his very accurate understanding of "Iroquois" religion. "In the religious system of the Iroquois, there is no recognition of the doctrine of atonement for sin, or of the absolution or forgiveness of sins." Morgan believed that to equate the dog with the "scapegoat of the Hebrews, is also without any foundation in truth" but preferred (wished?) to see the "dog as a messenger to the Great Spirit" (Morgan 1962: 216). Such a messenger, in the seventeenth century, might have been expected to carry a string of wampum, but that custom had ended early in the nineteenth century. Morgan, as many others following him, believed the WDS to have great antiquity, rather than being a Christian-influenced innovation among the Seneca.

The lack of a specific context for any details in Morgan's WDS narrative excludes the possibility of considering expected changes taking place during that period. Perhaps this failing is what led Lloyd (in Morgan 1922: 255) to gather a collection of WDS accounts as well as narratives of Dream Feasts. Lloyd linked these together as a means of examining the WDS (in Morgan 1922: 261–264).

Also unclear at this point is the extent to which Morgan's "record" influenced reports of the WDS made during the decades after 1850. A number of derivative "descriptions" of the WDS were published near the end of the 1800s (e.g., Stevens 1870: 462). Most appear taken from Morgan's 1851 account. Other fictitious variations of Morgan's widely read account include Eleazer Munsell's statement that dogs were eaten at feasts by Indians in central Illinois where the "sacrifice of the white dog usually ended the dance" (Duis 1874: 526). This "record" appears to be Duis's or Munsell's elision of data on the Seneca and other Iroquoian's WDS with a dog feast held in Illinois (see also Morrison 1990).

Horatio Hale (1885) was not the first "anthropologist" to incorporate Morgan's derivative recollections of the WDS among the Seneca (Morgan 1851: 183–216). Two years earlier, G. L. Gomme (1883: 89) had provided a paragraph on the WDS of the "Iroquois" specifically derived from Morgan (1851: 207–221). Gomme proposed that the Midwinter Feast lasted six days, with the dog strangled on the first and burned on the morning of the fifth in a fire kindled by friction. In the Gomme account, the "white dog was borne in procession on a bark litter, until the officiating leaders halted, facing the rising sun, when it was laid upon the flaming wood and consumed." The WDS was even reviewed in a successful freshman prize-winning essay in Clinton, New York (Coventry 1889) that is notable only as an indication that some areas of student research have not improved over the past century.

CATTARAUGUS SENECA, 1886 and Before

In 1886 a major group of Seneca lived along Cattaraugus Creek where it enters the south side of Lake Erie near Gowanda, New York. A brief paragraph is all we have to document the celebration of the "new year of the Seneca Nation . . . on the Cattaraugus Reservation" in that year (Anonymous 1886). "One of the chief features of the celebration is the 'burning of the white dog.'" The anonymous author believed that this "sacrifice assures them of fish and game in plenty and immunity from disease for the 12 months to come." Whether this was inferred by the writer or repeats information derived from a native informant or elsewhere is not evident. This account tells us very little about this WDS, but it does demonstrate that the ritual remained part of the Cattaraugus Seneca Midwinter Feast at this date.

Other, secondhand accounts provide specific details of the Seneca WDS but are derived from observations made before 1886 and only included within a synthetic account by Harriet Caswell in 1892. Caswell's (1892, 2007) relevant ethnographic reconstruction of the feast includes valuable data gathered by the missionaries Asher and Laura Wright in the mid-nineteenth century. Laura Wright, born around 1809, had married Asher Wright in 1833, and they moved to the area of Buffalo, then part of the western frontier. L. Wright worked among the Cattaraugus Seneca, but how much of their ritual she actually observed and how much was related to her by people such as "Old Silverheels, a pagan," we do not know (Caswell 1892: 214; Snyderman 1961: 589). Nor do we know the dates of any events that were described to Wright or if her synthesis represents a collection of pieces derived from more than a single event.

Silverheels, a member of a well-known Seneca family, provided considerable information regarding the "New Year's feast [when] we thanked him [the Good Creator and Ruler] for all his gifts" (in Caswell 1892: 215). The New Year's Feast and the White Dog Dance were believed to be ceremonies "which Ha-wen-ni-yu commands" that in "old" times lasted nine days. A week before they began, the ceremonies were announced by two grotesques (beings of odd or unnatural

appearance, probably men wearing false face masks; see Fenton 1987).
During the nine days of the feast no one could be buried (Caswell
1892: 217–218). Note that Morgan gave the Feast as lasting seven days
and had little to say regarding the ornamentation of the dog.

> On the first day of the feast, a white dog 'without spot or blemish' was
> chosen and strangled, that no blood should be shed or bones broken.
> The body was painted with spots of red and decorated with feathers.
> Around the feet were wound strings of wampum and beads. The dog
> was then fastened to the top of a pole, about twenty feet from the
> ground, where he [sic] remained until the fifth day. Then they built an
> altar of wood, upon which the body of the dog was laid and burned.
>
> H. Caswell 1892: 219

Caswell's 1892 "description" is not an account from a direct observation but rather a version recalled by Silverheels, or another informant, after an interval of some years. The 20-foot pole may derive from
the Jemison account of 1823. The Silverheels account also describes
the use of tobacco in the ceremony. Note also should be made that both
wampum *and* beads were said to have been used to ornament the dog.
The dog is identified as "he," not "it," suggesting that it may have been
a male. The English pronoun "he" used here may accurately translate
the Seneca pronoun.[8]

The information combined within Caswell's Seneca account may
derive from actual observations made in the years just before 1892,
a period during which there was a report of the WDS made to *The
New York Times* (Anonymous 1886). Caswell's version also may be
compared with the Halliday Jackson narration. Perhaps other accounts
may be located in the diaries and publications of the Quaker missionaries who worked among the Seneca during that critical period in
native history. Morgan's (1851, I: 175ff) account of ceremonies from
the Tonawanda (Seneca) longhouse (cf. Fig. 5) as well as the version
of the WDS seen at the end of the nineteenth century are significantly
different. The reasons for these differences may relate to the way synthetic versions are assembled and not to actual changes in the ritual
or errors in reporting.

The Most Complete Report on Burning of the White Dog: Seneca circa 1898 (Boyle 1898: 91–108)

In 2011, as we were making revisions to this manuscript and tracing obscure references, we located David Boyle's extraordinary but generally unknown 1898 account of the WDS. Boyle's extremely detailed eyewitness account of the Seneca Midwinter Festival at which a white dog was sacrificed merits better exposure. The original publication also provides many important photographs, including one of John Buck (Fig. 6; also see Becker, in review A). Since Boyle's work is available online, we have chosen to transcribe only the most relevant portions of the text.

Boyle's (1898: 81–82) account of the New Year Festival "lasting ten days" describes an important part of the Seneca feast cycle. Despite the considerable detail of the observations, there are a number of problematical elements that derive from a lack of editorial oversight. One of the more obvious is this opening statement regarding the length of the festivities. There is no clearly stated date of beginning and no complete narration of events. Thus we have what may be one of several synthetic elements, probably introduced by secondhand reporting. Also unclear on these first pages of this 1898 account is when Ka-nis-han-don (Sand-bar, or William Williams) arrived and whether he had come from Toronto (Boyle 1898: 82) where he had been one of two singers who provided Boyle with the words of various speeches and the music for songs from the Seneca Longhouse (Boyle 1898: 171; also Boyle 1900b; also C. 1900: 136). These were songs that Williams had sung for years (Boyle 1898: 147). These songs were recorded and later published.

Ka-nis-han-don (William Williams) had been asked to serve as the "Head Man of the ceremonies for the year," perhaps based on the recognition of his skills as a native performer. As master of ceremonies for the rites during that Seneca Midwinter Festival, Williams's information on the WDS added to Boyle's 1898 narration was considered to be significant. The inclusion of a photograph of this leader in Boyle's (1898: 84, fig.) publication also reflects Ka-nis-han-don's high status.

Boyle (1898: 84) recounts that the Seneca women attending this feast appear to have dressed especially for the occasion while the men did not. Later in his account Boyle (1898: 89) says that "men appear in fancy dresses" for the War Dances. This may indicate that the men changed their clothes or added specific items for this part of the rite. Also important is Boyle's observation (1898: 87) that the "Head man speaks a short time . . . then sings the song of the Burned White Dog." No previous account of the WDS refers to a specific song being sung in association with these rites, but Boyle (1898: 148–149, 156) recorded and transcribed the music and offered a description. Formal recordings were made at some time in 1898. Years later, Fenton (1942) included a relevant song ("Dream Song of the Creator at the White Dog Sacrifice") among his recordings made in 1941. Whether this song was recorded at the Allegany Reservation in New York or at Canada's Six Nations reserve, and by whom, remains to be determined.

Boyle's long account of the WDS also mentions that the attendees at the feast were "sprayed," an activity not reported in any other WDS record. We suggest that it is a survival of the splashing-with-water recorded for the Midwinter Feast in the Jesuit records and not a baptismal-like innovation of the 1890s. Possibly the spraying reported by Boyle relates to the "Purification ceremony of the Society of Otters [Dawandó], a Seneca women's winter ceremony" (Parker 1912: caption to Pl. 23, and pages 121–122). Also harking back to the Jesuit accounts is the scattering of hot coals and ashes reported by Boyle (1898: 90–91). Boyle (1898: 152, 156) recorded the song "Scattering Ashes" and provides the words. Boyle also identifies a Huron parallel for this part of the midwinter rite that appears in the *Jesuit Relations* for 1640–41 (XXI: 151, 153).

Boyle's title for his 1898 report, "Pagan Iroquois," also explains his emphasis, at two places (pages 91 and 95), on the cooperation between the Christian and Pagan Indians attending this feast. He indicates that "some of the Christians not only took part in the dances, and in the ashes ceremony, but assisted very actively at the sacrifice of the White Dog" (p. 95).

FIGURE 5: Onondaga longhouse, Six Nations Indian Reserve 40, Ontario, showing old longhouse at the right.
Canadian Museum of Civilization, Frederick Wilkerson Waugh, 1915, control number 34690.

To the long portions of Boyle's text transcribed here we have added, within brackets, our own commentary and suggestions for interpretation, as well as the page numbers from Boyle's text. Only those of Boyle's footnotes that we found relevant to the WDS are included here, inserted between curly brackets within the text where Boyle had placed his numbers. Paragraphing also has been altered to conserve space. Boyle (1898: 83) specifically indicates that Williams led the rituals on the Sunday and Monday mornings "preceding the Burning of the White Dog . . ." on the afternoon of the last day, suggesting that these rites were a distinct part of the long festival.

[91] The ceremonies connected with the Burning of the White Dog, which were announced to begin at sunrise on Monday morning, Jan. 31st, were delayed until after noon. Some difficulty had been experienced in procuring a suitable animal, for, as an Indian stated to me, 'It must not be a Newfoundland dog, nor a collie dog, nor a bull dog, only just a nice little Indian dog, all white, you see.'

Perhaps the delay was on account of the dog not having been delivered by the owner before ten o'clock, but the fact that this was in illustration of the good fellowship that exists among . . . the pagans on this occasion [who] were indebted to the services of a Christian Indian, who, not only at some trouble, procured a suitable animal and paid for it, but provided also the beef required for the closing feast, making himself responsible for the payment. In both cases this was made good to him by the pagans.

[92] The dog having been taken to the house of, David Key, some three or four hundred yards from the Longhouse, was there strangled by George Silversmith, and decked with ribbons and painted by Peter Williams. Meanwhile the fire was prepared by We-ho-goh-yeh or Loud Voice (John Buck) a younger son of the late highly respected Ska-naw'-a-ti, the old Onondaga Fire keeper. I am unable to say whether the choice of young John for this duty had any connection with the office formerly held by his father. {Since this was written I have made inquiry and am informed by Ka-nis-han-don that young John Buck was chosen on this account}. John Sugar assisted him. {In former times, on the New York Reserve, it was customary to strangle the dog, (sometimes two of them) on the first day of the New Year ceremonies, after which it was suspended fifteen or twenty feet from the ground until the fifth day when it was taken down and burned. The Cayugas on the Grand River Reserve kill the dog the first day and hang it against the building by its hind legs until the time for burning, five days afterwards.} [This hanging sounds very much the way meat is hung to age it for consumption] After the dog was strangled, fully an hour and a half elapsed before it was sufficiently cold to be removed, meanwhile, however the decoration was going on.

In the Longhouse, which was not at all crowded, Chief Johnson Williams appeared in due time (or rather in over-due time) carrying suspended from his left shoulder, the object of sacrifice, plentifully marked with red spots about the size of a half-dollar. Round its neck body, tail and legs were tied silk ribbons, red, blue, green and white. Its feet were also connected by ribbons to the neck and hips in such a way that the legs remained at right angles to the body as if standing. Another ribbon extending loosely from the fore to the hind feet served as a strap for carrying purposes, the dog hanging body downwards and head forwards. In addition to these ribbons a feather decoration was fitted to the head so as to form a small crest pointing backwards and round the neck was a small string of wampum. {To show that it is an accredited messenger to Ta-ron-ya-wa-gon, the Holder of the Heavens}.

The bearer placed the dog on its right side on the long-bench in the middle of the building, head towards the Four Brothers' end, and near to its tail he set a small old chip-basket containing from half a pound to a pound of home-grown tobacco. Having made an address lasting only a few minutes, most of the men went outside, but the women kept their seats. Standing at the south-east corner of the Longhouse several of the men gave a prolonged whoop which was followed by the firing of two or three rifles simultaneously, the rifles [93] being pointed skywards {The intention of firing towards the sky is to attract the attention of Ta-ron-ya-wa-gon.} and southwards. This was answered by whoops from Ka-nis-han-don and a companion who were now seen standing near the house of David Key to the south, where the dog had been strangled.

The whoop and volley, and the reply, having been repeated, the Head man's messenger, (who had been sent from the Long house to tell him that all was ready) came forward leaving his superior to approach more leisurely, while the men again entered the Long-house and took their seats with uncovered heads nobody smoked, and the air of seriousness that pervaded the assembly reminded one of a good old Presbyterian country congregation on the occasion of "fencing the tables."

In the meantime Ka-nis-han-don was leisurely approaching the Longhouse, singing plaintively. On opening the door at the Two Brothers' end, he paused before entering, and ceased his song as his eye fell upon the white dog. {According to the tenor of his speech (which follows) he is not supposed to see the dog, but this is how his appearance struck me at the time.} He then walked slowly and with downcast head to the song-bench, looked for a second at the dog, again began to sing, and continued to do so while he walked three times round the song-bench, when he was stopped at the starting-point by Chief Johnson Williams. After a brief address from this chief, he goes round the bench again, singing, and is this time stopped by Louis Dixon, who delivers to him a short address, at the conclusion of which the male portion of the audience gives a whoop.

Ka-nis-pan-don [sic] then indulged in a brief soliloquy, the men giving another whoop at its conclusion. He next sang for a little while, the audience accompanying him with "Heh-heh-heh," the syllable being uttered fifty times, by actual count on my part.

After another monologue, he again sang, walking round the dog as before. This time he was stopped and addressed by John Silversmith. When Silversmith was done, the audience again whooped. Once more Ka-nis-pan-don [sic] talked as it were to himself, in a low tone, and was answered by another whoop from the men. He then walked back and forth on the north side of the song-bench, singing in a more lively tone than formerly to a general accompaniment of "Heh-heh-heh," and as soon as he stopped, the men set up a "Wah-h-h-h-h!" Indulging in another monologue, he once more sang as he walked sorrowfully-looking, round the dog, and on completing the circuit he was stopped and addressed by Jacob Hill. When this warrior finished, Ka-nis-han-don uttered a loud "Hooh!" which was the signal for a general whoop.

Standing on the north side and looking towards the Four Brothers' end he again spoke, as it were, to himself, and at last broke out into a song, walking as before, on the north side. In a short time the men gave the whoop "Wah-h-h-h-h!" and as he continued singing, they all accompanied him with "Heh-heh-heh-heh." At the conclusion of this song someone gave a loud "Hooh-h!" and immediately all joined in "Wah-h-h-h!" Once more he indulged in another soliloquy or monologue* then took to singing as he walked around the white dog, and left the room by the Two Brothers' door. Singing all the time, he marched slowly round the Longhouse, proceeding along the north side westwards, and back by the south to the same door, which he again entered, and (still singing) walked round the dog for the last time.

Having finished this song he proceeded after a brief pause, towards the Four Brothers' door, followed by Chief Johnson Williams carrying the body of the victim suspended from his left shoulder, and the basket containing the tobacco in his right hand. {This, I have since learned, was a mistake. The dog should have been carried over the right shoulder, and the tobacco in the left hand}. Three or four warriors accompanied them to the fire which all this time had been burning on the south side of the building, and within fifteen feet of it near the Four Brothers' end. Here the dog was laid upon a small platform of pine boards that seemed to have been made on purpose for its reception. Its head was in the same direction as when the body was lying on the song-bench, and as in that case also, the basket with the tobacco was set down at the animal's tail. After the dog is outside, it is said to be immaterial how its head points, but inside it must be directed towards the west.

Ka-nis-han-don said a few words as he stood beside the dog on the south side of the fire, and he was followed by Chief Johnson Williams who first gave three subdued whoops, after which he made a long speech. Within ten minutes from the time of beginning he placed the dog on the fire, and after another short interval he threw on the fire a small gift of ribbons in a loose bunch {All the decorations used on the dog were gifts from the pious, and the bunch of ribbons here mentioned came too late to be arranged on the dog, and was therefore thrown on the fire that its "heart" might accompany that of the dog}.

Afterwards, at each of [95] six intervals he threw a handful of tobacco on the burning dog, and last of all he placed in the fire the basket [Nota Bene] itself with the tobacco that remained in it. At the conclusion of his speech he gave three whoops. Next, four "warriors," one at a time, sang doleful songs as they walked slowly back and forth across the west end of the fire, while those who were gathered round kept up the constant "Heh-heh-heh-heh!" and thus ended the Burning of the White Dog.

Ka-nis-han-don, the Master of Ceremonies, during the celebration of the sacrifice was dressed in white, having a dark blue sash across his shoulder, and a blue cap ornamented with numerous feathers. {The Leader or Master of Ceremonies is permitted to dress as he pleases, so long as he wears nothing that is red. As all the Leaders or Speakers must be buried in ceremonial costume, and as red is a forbidden color in grave clothes, it is easy to see why it is objected to in the dress. A Leader may officiate in ordinary garb, but at his death, his people must provide a suit of official garments.} Five others, (one chief and four warriors) were similarly dressed in white, but variously diversified with spangles and ribbons. All of them had their faces painted with

FIGURE 6: (L. to R.): Joseph Snow, Onondaga Chief; George Henry Martin Johnson, father of Pauline Johnson, Mohawk John Buck, Onondaga; John Smoke Johnson, father of George Henry Martin Johnson, Isaac Hill, Onondaga; John Seneca Johnson, Seneca.
Reference: Electric Studio/Library and Archives Canada/C-085137, Mikan no. 3193501.

vermilion. Ka-nis-han-don's face was merely highly colored as if to give the appearance of rosy cheeks, while that of Chief Johnson Williams was marked by three bright lines about one-fourth of an inch wide and three inches long running obliquely downwards from his nose across his cheek. {So marked because Williams is a chief.} Of the others I failed to make note. [Etc.]

Boyle 1898: 92–95

Boyle Asks: Why Is the White Dog Burned?

At this point in his long and detailed description, Boyle (1898: 95–96) poses a basic question: "Why is the White Dog burned?"

> Even if we accept the earliest date, 1790, as that of the year in which Ska-ne-o-dy'-o is said to have received his revelation from the Four Persons, or Angels, the ceremonies connected with his teach[96]ing are scarcely more than a hundred years old, yet there are numerous evidences that during the century many changes have taken place in the ritual, the body of which is no doubt mainly an adaptation, and to some extent, a modification of still older rites and ceremonies.

Boyle 1898: 95–96

Boyle's footnote, which appears after the date 1790, cites "J. Clark's History of Onondaga [in which] 'The "preacher" in all his addresses refers to the time that has elapsed since the revelation to Skaneyodyo.'" We cannot determine if Boyle meant to refer to Joshua Clark's (1849) *Onondaga* or W. W. Clayton's (1878) *History of Onondaga County*, as we have not yet located reference to a native preacher in either of these works. Boyle then continues with a number of important observations regarding the variability in the native rituals that were performed during the midwinter rites:

> Originally it was taught that all religious performances must come to an end at mid-day, and while it is true that the "preachers," so-called, observe this injunction very strictly, no regard is paid to it by others who perform offices that are considered quite as sacred as are those of the preachers. The reason assigned by the latter both here and in New

York, for this prohibition is that the Great Spirit rests during the afternoon, but the pagan laity in both places seem to credit him with being more wide-awake. On the Grand River Reserve they do not appear to think He needs much sleep at all, or perhaps they only think, as I heard an Indian say with apparent seriousness, that if they can stand to be up the greater part of the night performing acts of worship, the least thing He can do is to keep awake and listen. One of their preachers, himself, did not appear to know of any injunction respecting night performances, and when assured that this was the case, he professed to explain that the night doings here were not a part of the real religious ceremonies, but were intended only for the amusement of the people. Others equally well-informed, insist that he is in error on this point.

There can be no doubt that the Burning of the White Dog is not only a part, but a very important part of the purely religious ten days' ceremonies, yet, we have seen that in connection with the Seneca observances last New Year, the sacrifice was not offered until after one o'clock p.m. It was news to our Ska-ne-o-dy'-o that So-se'-ha-wa, the Founder's grandson, and successor in the preacher's office, wholly ignored the burning of the dog, and that the practice had been distinctly forbidden by Hoh-shah-honh, the Omar of our Onondaga Mahomet.

Boyle (1898: 96–98), citing several sources regarding the eating of dog meat at feasts, concluded that "the burning of the dog as a religious rite long antedates the revelation of Ska-ne-o-dy'-o." But the use of dog meat at the feasts cited was to ward off spells or the ill fortunes of a dream. Boyle cites Colden (History of the Five Indian Nations, p. 6, London), Le Jeune (in the Jesuit Relation for 1637, p. 229, vol. 13 of the Cleveland edition), the Jesuit Relation for 1640–41 (Cleveland edition, vol. 21: 161), and a Huron example of eating dogs in the Relation of 1642 (p, 173, vol. 23). Our review of dogs as a food source as well as dog burials appears later in this volume. The pre-1800 examples do not include the cremation of dogs, but do reveal the preparation of dog for feasting.

Boyle also provides an account by the Reverend William Hamilton, a Presbyterian missionary to the Sacs and Iowas of Nebraska during the years from 1837 to 1853, who saw dogs hung by their necks to trees, or to sticks planted in the ground. Hamilton was told these dogs were offerings to Watanka; and an Indian named No Heart telling him about a smallpox epidemic, said, "'We threw away (i. e. sacrificed) a

great many garments, blankets, etc., and offered many dogs to God'"
(from Dorsey 1894: 426). The "hanging" of these dogs has similarities,
in some cases, with the WDS, but that dogs were sacrificial animals
in 1800 does not appear surprising. Boyle also cites the tale told in
1894 by an "old Ojibwa Indian" resident on the west bank of the Flint
River in Michigan in which a monster told a man to go home and
bring him six white dogs as a sacrificial offering (Smith 1897: 325).
Smith also stated that "[A]mong the very Indians from which this myth
was procured, the white dog sacrifice was practiced as late as 1819."
Iroquoian people who had entered that area after 1800 and interacted
with the Ojibwa may have brought elements of the then-formulating
WDS with them.

Harlan Smith may have been mistaken in associating the WDS
with the Ojibwa and certainly erred in suggesting that it was, in 1819,
an old tradition. However, during seven weeks of field work among
the Ojibwa of Parry Island during the summer of 1929, Diamond Jenness appears to have been told important information relating to the
WDS. Possibly this information entered Jenness's monograph from
other sources, or his informants offered bogus information, as is the
rule when people ask silly questions. Clearly Jenness did not witness
the Ojibwa yearly ceremony that he reported took place in the autumn.
They reported to Jenness (1935: 32) that they "bound a white dog"
and burned it as a sacrifice, to both "manidos" (also *manitus*, gods),
"and offered up thanks for their care of the people during the past
year." On the following page, Jenness (1935: 33) discusses the origin
of the "white dog sacrifice" and says that it takes place about February, indicating that this information came from sources other than his
informants. Quite probably the Ojibwa had exposure to the WDS from
Seneca or other practitioners, but little more.

Boyle (1898: 99) also quoted from Horatio Hale's report (1895).
Hale recognized "that the dog was selected merely as being the animal
most prized by the Indians, and therefore most suitable for a sacrifice
to their divinity." Boyle (1898: 100) suggested that recent dog offerings,
or those from recorded history, were vestiges "of a ceremony when the
dog was burned along with his deceased master." Boyle did not indicate

that cremation burials had not been used anywhere in the Northeast for perhaps a millennium, but cites Harmon (1820: 335–336) regarding tribes west of New York among which the bodies of deceased dogs were cremated in the same way that they would the "bodies of their relations." Boyle (1898: 101) had written to Daniel G. Brinton regarding "the philosophy of this ceremony." Brinton "very courteously replied. 'I am fully persuaded that the sacrifice of the white dog among the Iroquois had a deeper symbolism than was suggested by our late friend, Mr. Horatio Hale.'" Brinton then cited examples of dog sacrifice from Central and South America but could offer nothing from the Northeast or anywhere east of the Mississippi. None of the dog rituals from other times or other locations relate in any known way to the Iroquoian examples. Boyle (1898: 101–102), referring to this,

> the last sentence of Prof. Brinton 's letter, I had made an effort to secure as much as possible of the ritual in the Mohawk [sic] dialect of the Iroquois tongue, and it is satisfactory to know that the plan commends itself to so high an [102] authority. {Too much praise cannot be given to Ka-nis-han-don [William Williams], who acted as Master of Ceremonies at last New Year's Festival in the Seneca long house, for the great trouble he has taken to repeat word for word the most important parts of the ritual in the Seneca dialect. I have to thank him also for numerous personal favors by way of explanation, afforded to me before and after the Sacrifice of the White Dog}.
>
> Boyle 1898: 101–102

Boyle's review of cremation as an aspect of the WDS then turned to some ideas offered by General John S. Clark (1823–1912) of Auburn, New York. Beauchamp (1908: 14) reports that Clark held the field notes of early surveyors in Onondaga County and that these never-published records include a great deal about the Indians. These records may be with General Clark's papers that now reside at the Auburn Historical Society. Note should be made that Clark had taken photographs of the Onondaga wampum belts before 1898.

> General J. S. Clark, who has given much thought to this and kindred subjects connected with the social and religious customs of the

Iroquois, writes to me respecting their religious beliefs, more especially as these seem to have a bearing on the Burning of the White Dog, that while he has some difficulty in harmonizing the material in his hands relating to the Great White Wolf, the Infernal Wolf and the Devil, he is of the opinion that these refer "to the God of war, Agreskoui, as known to the Hurons and Iroquois." [Boyle then points out that] "Megapolensis makes a clear distinction between Tharonhiawagon and Agreskoui of the Mohawks, making the latter represent the Devil, and the former the Supreme God," because "sacrifices were never made to Tharonhiawagon" whereas "they did worship and present offerings to Agreskoui."

In proof of this the General cites Jogue's account of the burning and eating of a woman and two bears; and Brebeuf's story concerning a similar horrible feast in the Huron country, to placate Agreskoui. After pointing out that Parkman believed Agreskoui to be identical with the sun, General Clark proceeds.

"There is much to warrant this conclusion[.]"

[Clark also cites Parkman, who] says also that Agreskoui was the same as Jouskeha, but with different attributes. . . . Now as the Jesuit missionaries among the Hurons identified the 'Infernal Wolf' as the veritable *devil*, and the early writers respecting the Mohawks describe Agreskoui as the same character, it appears highly probable [103] that the Infernal Wolf was also the 'Great White Wolf' the prototype and original of the Wolf gens of the Hurons, Iroquois and kindred tribes. We know that the white animals, such as the buffalo, deer, bear and wolf, are held at the present day as having peculiarly close relations to their Pagan deities, for the reason that the deities themselves and all their subordinates are supposed to be white. The representative tribe among the Iroquois, having closer relations with the deities than any other, was the Mohawk, from whom all the others descended—the most eastern of all, where the sun rises—"the white land," "the bright land."

The great divinity of the Algonkins was "the great White One," or the *White Hare*, and Jouskeha was also white, as were all the other of the great and beneficent gods whose residence was in the Sun, or, as often expressed, was the Sun itself. This idea ranged over both continents. All the Iroquois were sun-worshippers . . . [and] Charlevoix says that all the Huron sachems were accounted Children of the Sun, and the relation of the Iroquois sachems could not have varied materially from this. [and] the beliefs of the Hurons and Iroquois were not far removed from those of the Natchez, whose principal chief, as claimed, was the Sun itself. . . . I am very much inclined to the opinion that the burning of the White Dog was not a sacrifice in any sense, but simply a special preparation as a message-bearer or messenger to the power above. {[in a footnote Boyle adds] Some such idea exists among the pagans, now-a-days, one of whom informed me that Ska-ne-o-dy-o wishing on a certain occasion to send a message to the Great Spirit, when he could not go himself, strangled his dog for this purpose. Some time afterwards when 'up there' on very important business, he not only saw the dog, but the dog recognized him, by its fawning upon him and licking his hand.

Boyle 1898: 101–103

Boyle's publication of John S. Clark's communication provides the general's only known comments on the "Great White Wolf" among the Iroquoians. This beast remains unknown from any previous printed source. Boyle (1898: 103) continued his narrative with an extremely important reference to the importance and function of the wampum used in the WDS:

That strings of shell beads are burned with the dog is but carrying out the idea that credit should be given only to messages accompanied by wampum. The relations of the white dog to the originals of the animal kingdom above were of the closest character, as were their relations to the people below.

[104] Hale gives Rononghwireghtonh as the Great Wolf of the Onondagas who alone formed a distinct class or clan, and apparently was a subordinate of the White Wolf of the Mohawks, which, in turn was a subordinate of The Great White Wolf above, whose residence was in the Sun, if, indeed, it was not the Sun itself. It is not to be expected that anything of importance can be learned at the present day from the myths among the Iroquois, beyond possibly some hints throwing light on the ancient customs and beliefs . . . .

Cuoq gives (p. 32) Okwari as white bear, and Okwaho as loup or wolf [probably Cuoq 1882], and I am confident that both should be rendered white, i.e. White Bear and White Wolf. . . .

Boyle's (1898: 104) discussion then returns to General Clark's letter and to passages relevant to Clark's theories regarding the ceremony of Burning the White Dog. Boyle found them based "mainly or wholly on the assumption that Indian forms of religious belief were the outcome of Sun worship, to the study of which General Clark is devoting much time . . . In a former communication the same gentleman reminded me that 'the burning of the dog, and a spotted dog at that, was certainly [105] practiced by the Mayas, and apparently was substituted for human sacrifice under the reformation of Quetzalcoatl." We agree with Boyle and find General Clark's data base to be faulty and Clark's conclusions unwarranted.

Of considerable interest to us within Boyle's impressive report is his inclusion (1898: 105–106) of a translation of the song sung "by the Master of Ceremonies at the fire, when the dog is burned." Presented here are only those portions of this Seneca supplication that specifically reveal aspects of the WDS. Comparisons with Fenton's (1942: iii, 18) text of the "Dream song of the Creator at the White Dog Sacrifice," sung by Chief Joseph Logan (Oneida of Canada), reveal the absence of actual reference to a sacrificial dog by 1942 (see also the following text). Boyle's transcription of this Seneca song, dating from 1898, reveals a close connection between the song and the traditional white dog and the important role of the song in the midwinter rituals, a connection that had vanished by 1941. Portions of the song as transcribed by Boyle follow:

> Great Master, behold here all of our people who hold the old faith, and who intend to abide by it. By means of this dog being burned we hope to please Thee, and that just as we have decked it with ribbons and wampum, Thou wilt grant favors to us Thy own people. I now place the dog on the fire that its spirit may find its way to Thee who made it, and made everything, and thus we hope to get blessings from Thee in return.

> He throws the dog on the fire and proceeds:

> Although, Great Master, there are not so many of us who worship Thee in this way as there were in old times, those who are here are as faithful as ever now, therefore, listen to us Thou who art far away above us, and who made every living thing. We ask that the sun will continue to shine on us and make all things grow. We ask that the moon may always give

us light by night. [106] We ask that the clouds may never cease to give us rain and snow. . . . We ask that these blessings may help us through life, and that we may remain true to our belief in Thee, and we will make Thee another offering like this next year. . . .

May the scent of the tobacco I have thrown on the fire rise till it reaches Thee to let Thee know that we are still good that we do not forget Thee, and that Thou mayest give us all we have asked.

Boyle 1898: 105–106

Following the presentation of the text of this song in Boyle's account he offers a description of the "Scattering of Ashes. (Ro-non-wa-ro-rih.)" This refers not to the ashes of the white dog, but to ashes gathered from the hearths of the many families of the village. This aspect of the Midwinter Feast also is recorded in the pre-1800 Jesuit accounts. The absence of a dog sacrifice from the pre-1800 Iroquoian records reveals that the burning of the white dog is a later inclusion. We offer only the most relevant paragraph from Boyle:

On the day following the Burning of the Dog [31 Jan. 1898], two runners appointed by the Old Men (Ro-dik-sten-ha) summon the people to stir, or scatter ashes at the Longhouse the following day. On entering each house the runner himself scatters ashes, after which, addressing [107] the heads of the household he informs them that according to the wish of Niyoh (the Creator) they are to appear at the Longhouse the following day, and to be sure to take the children with them. He then sings:

Boyle 1898: 106

Tooker (1970: 174–175) recognizes that there was a chronological error in Boyle's discussion of the scattering of the ashes. She convincingly indicates that the scattering took place on 25 and 26 January 1898, not after the "burning." In a footnote that offers another clue to decoding this long narration, Boyle proposes that the words in the five lines that he recorded:

at one time had some significance. At present Mr. Brant Sero informs me, there is none beyond what may be extracted from the first two

syllables "Ka-weh," or Ko-we, used until somewhat recently as an
expression of self-satisfaction on the accomplishment of any unusual
or desirable act, and even this maybe but a coincidence. (Compare with
Gen. Clark's reference to Icoue, or go-weh, ante p. 104.)' Ashes also are
scattered the following day.

Boyle 1898: 107–108

Earlier in his long account, Boyle (1898: 101) had noted an interest in securing an account of the WDS "in the Mohawk dialect." That
appears to have been when the Seneca William Williams (Ka-nis-han-
don) and a second Iroquoian had come to Toronto to provide data and
to record songs. The second Iroquoian acting as a cultural informant
for Boyle was the Mohawk named J. Ojijatekha Brant-Sero. At the time
Boyle probably assumed that Brant-Sero would be able to provide information on the WDS as Boyle erroneously *assumed* it to be practiced
among the Mohawk. As we reveal later in this volume, the WDS never
spread as far east as Mohawk territory, who often were seen as marginal
to Five Nations activities (cf. Campisi and Starna 1995). Brant-Sero
must have been completely unfamiliar with the WDS and unable to
provide data on the subject to Boyle. Similarly, Brant-Sero was able to
provide only limited data on the first two syllables of a song.

Boyle's study also provides the text, in Seneca, of a standard feast
oration, along with an English translation. Boyle then offered a description of the exchange of newly made paddles and other rituals. Boyle
also indicates that "the leader (this year, He-es-gonh, John Silversmith)"
made an address in Seneca, presented in full by Boyle, who adds an
English translation. The close of the address suggests that the entire
ritual is basically a new-fire rite such as would be expected at this
season of the year. We also note that unlike some accounts of the WDS
in which there is a mention made of a deer-hide drum, Boyle offers
no commentary on what appears to be a single drum used in this rite.
Rattles are often noted by Boyle, with some being specified as turtle
shell. Details of the rich material culture are few, but the more elusive
aspects of this ceremony have been preserved by Boyle's extremely
important efforts.

SENECA 1901: Brush's Account from Cattaraugus

Edward Brush's brief account may be a bit thin, but he includes some excellent photographs and drawings of a post-dog WDS. Brush recognized that all Iroquoian feasts were "thanksgivings to Hä-wen-né-yu" and that "Often an entire week is devoted . . . [to] a single festival" (1901: 63, 67). Given the complexity of these events, he chose to focus on "the exercises of a single day" of the New Year's festival, or dance, at the Long House on Cattaraugus Reservation in 1901. He identifies the first day as coming five days after the first new moon in February, which was a Friday in 1901. Though he says this is the "only festival not varied to accommodate circumstances," Brush is a bit vague about how the starting date is calculated. On that Friday, the first day, "the announcers, two in number, wearing buffalo robes and masks of corn husks, and carrying corn pounders . . ." went forth from the Long House to begin the feast (Brush 1901: 67, ill. 48 and esp. 51). An interior view of the activities of the "Indian New Years First Day" was "Drawn by Gar-nos Dr-yan-oht, Jesse Cornplanter [a] Seven Year Old Seneca Boy." The day chosen by Brush as the focus of his account was the following Thursday, the seventh and last day of the event. At noon, one of the keepers of the faith apologized for not having begun earlier so that they could "end the ceremonies at noon" (Brush 1901: 68). A long description of the activities follows, focusing on dancing, but clearly reflecting the former rite that had once included a burning of a dog.

The feast ended with the Big Feather Dance, once associated with "the ancient ceremony of burning the white dog" (Brush 1901: 71, 57). By 1901, that aspect of the ritual was "no longer carried out on the reservations of New York State," but they were said to survive in Canada on the Grand River Reserve. Brush was familiar with Boyle's 1898 report. Brush's estimate that it had been about 20 years since the last WDS in New York is overestimated. Brush's brief account makes no mention of baskets in any context, reflecting the many synthetic versions of this rite.

Parker's Narration of the 1906 Seneca Feast at Cattaraugus: Another Seneca Burning of a Basket, Not a Dog Sacrifice

Arthur Caswell Parker (1881–1955), the son of the Seneca Frederick Ely Parker, was born on the Cattaraugus Reservation and became an archaeologist and director (1924–1945) of the Rochester Museum of Arts and Sciences. In 1912, Parker published a complete account of the Code of Handsome Lake, the Seneca Prophet. In this account there is a "preliminary translation of the ceremonial prayer at the Seneca Indian new year's [sic] ceremony" (1912: 85) as recorded in February 1906 among the Seneca at Cattaraugus (Parker 1912: 85–94). Also included here is his important "description" of the entire Midwinter Feast (Parker 1912: 85–93). This volume also includes Harriet Caswell's (1892) account of the WDS. Was his middle name bestowed to honor Harriet Caswell?

Parker's (1912: 81–104) brief summary of the entire ritual cycle of the Newtown (presumably *Ganûn'dase:'*) Seneca longhouse, within the Cattaraugus Reservation, provides another variation of the Midwinter Feast of which the WDS was a part. Parker's account, however, dates from the period when the use of sacrificial dogs in the Midwinter Feast was fading. How much his report reflects Harriet Caswell's earlier distillation of events and how much reflects the realities of the rituals as performed in 1906 remains unclear to us.

The activities of the first three days of the ceremonies are summarized, suggesting that the White Dog *prayer* was offered on the fourth day. The prayer includes what we now know to be telling references to burning of tobacco and to "that basket of sacred tobacco" (1912: 87), but the rituals and an actual burning of the dog are not mentioned. The burning of this basket recalls Boyle's (1898: 95) observations of the Seneca burning tobacco as well as the "old chip-basket" in which it had been carried. The significance of the basket in these rituals will be discussed in a later chapter.

Parker (1912: 66, note 2) refers to "Chief John Jacket who wrote out the Gai'wiió in Seneca in 1860" but no direct reference is again made to that account. The illustration of the WDS on Parker's Pl. 20, captioned "Sacrifice of the White Dog on the Grand River reservation of the Six Nations, Canada," depicts 19 or more men standing behind the fire. We do not know the date of the photograph, obviously pre-1912 in origin, or which of the Six Nations is represented by these people. A "string of wampum, ot'go'ä" is mentioned as evidence of repentance (Parker 1912: 57), but no wampum in any form is spoken of in relationship to ornament or sacrifice associated with the WDS.[9]

4

Onondaga Accounts

hanks to William M. Beauchamp's interest in all things relating the Native American people in New York, we have available direct or indirect references to a great deal of information from the latter part of the nineteenth century. Beauchamp's insightful studies are particularly rich in accounts from among the Onondaga. The earliest account of the WDS was made the year after Beauchamp was born and published eight years later. Why Beauchamp almost totally ignored this record remains unknown.

Onondaga 1841

The earliest account of the Onondaga WDS was published by Joshua V. H. Clark (1849: 65–66) from notes taken at Onondaga Castle in January of 1841 "by the author on the spot, and explained by the late Abraham La Fort [sic]." La Forte is best known for assisting Henry Schoolcraft in compiling a vocabulary of the Onondaga language, but details of his life and his interactions with Clark remain unknown. Clark notes that the entire ritual as he observed it was conducted in Onondaga, but that "the Indians . . . seem pleased with the company of visitors and strangers who are disposed to treat them respectfully" (1849: 66).

Clark's monumental two-volume history of Onondaga County, New York provides a particularly important record of the Onondaga people. Why any mention of this printed record of 1849 is absent from Beauchamp's publications remains an interesting question. Only at the age of 78 did Beauchamp (1908: 325) make reference to Joshua Clark's observations at Onondaga Castle in 1841. The citation of the date 1841 in Beauchamp's account, but not the date of 1849, suggests that he may have held Clark's original field notes.

Clark's long and detailed record narrates events related to the WDS as it took place more than two generations prior to the even longer Seneca account of these rituals provided by David Boyle in 1898. The details of the rituals specifically pertaining to the dogs and the baskets that were central to the expiation of sin are transcribed here, while elements of the songs and dances are excluded from this presentation.[10] Clark (1849: 53) emphasizes that this festival, in late January or early February, was the last and most important of the five that comprised the Onondaga ritual cycle. A specific name is not provided. The focus of the event was on Ha-wah-ne-u, who held several titles including Creator of the World and Holder of the Heavens. Clark (1849: 55–56) provides a great deal of information on the organization of the festival, at a period in time when traditional social organization was still important to the Onondaga, and the elaborate costuming that was part of this feast. The ceremonies involving extinguishing the old fires, the cleaning of the hearths (and gathering of ashes?), and the use of flints to strike new fires are detailed as part of the first day of this feast. On the second day the two

> managers are fantastically dressed, and proceed from house to house with baskets, collecting the gifts of the people with which to grace the festival. These gifts consist of pork, beef, bread, beans, peas, ears of corn, tobacco, savory herbs, small handfuls of straw nicely bound, and every article is received, that is useful for food, for incense or for sacrifice. Every one is bound to give something, or he is not to be included in the general absolution.
>
> Clark 1849: 56–57

These activities continue "for several days according to the time allotted for the continuance of the festival" (days three to five?). Here Clark provides information that is important to us as it suggests that he knew there was no set number of days allotted to this feast. This is supported by his observation that "On [the] first of last three days" the committee members dress in garish fashion and run about "crying, 'give, give'" (Clark 1849: 57). The materials that they gathered appear to continue a collecting of materials representing sins to be expiated, a form of indulgences.

"The last day, and the one to which most consequence is attached, being the great day of sacrifice . . ." involves the dogs acting as scapegoats. Whether this was the sixth or seventh day of this Midwinter Feast seems to have been irrelevant. A house "near the council-house

is selected as a place in which to make preparation." The involvement
of a second structure in these rituals appears to be a feature that is
critical to the particular celebration described by Clark. Though this
appears unique to this specific description of a WDS, it is also known
from Blau's (1969) account of an Onondaga Midwinter Feast that took
place over 100 years later. Blau's event involved baskets in place of
dogs. What may be of importance here is that the Onondaga Castle
at that time was basically a small village with somewhat traditional
layout. Subsequent accounts of these sacrifices appear to reflect a later
decentralization of residences, leaving the council-house as a structure
somewhat removed from the heart of the community.

"The grand master of ceremonies or high priest, takes his station at
the council-house . . ." while the helpers, including several well-dressed
women, get ready for later events. What transpired in these preparations was not seen and is not recorded, but it obviously involved painting and ornamenting the living dogs.

> About nine o'clock, the managers rushed out of the house of prepara-
> tion, and two white dogs fantastically painted with red figures and
> adorned with small belts of wampum, feathers and ribbons tied around
> their necks, legs and tails, followed them. A long rope with a single
> knot [loop?] in the centre was instantly passed over the head of one
> of them, when some eight or ten of the managers seized the rope on
> either side . . . [and] suffocated [the dog which was then] hung up on
> a ladder which leaned against the house.
>
> Clark 1849: 59

The second dog then was subjected to the same treatment, after
which guns were fired into the air. After a half hour the "dogs were
taken down and carried into the house of preparation."

Clark states that the sacrificial dogs, which "are always white, or
as nearly so as they can procure them," are carried from the house of
preparation by two persons. The dogs' "legs being tied so as to admit
of their being slung like a pack" (Clark 1849: 60). We suspect that the
small wampum bands had been removed from the dogs in the house of
preparation, perhaps along with feathers and ribbons. The procession
ultimately leads to the council-house. Inside, the master of ceremonies

holds up each and every gift, arrayed on display, while the giver stands in front of him. This appears to be a transfer of sins, after which the dogs were brought in, and additional ceremonies are described. An altar of wood had been built outside, and when it had burned sufficiently the dogs were cast into the fire.

> "Different individuals now brought forward baskets of herbs, tobacco, and such like, which were at intervals thrown upon the fire. And with the consuming dogs produced a variety of scents, not easily comprehended."
>
> Clark 1849: 61–62

There followed a great variety of activities that included an enactment of the ritual slaying of a captive (Clark 1849: 63–64). The feast ended with the elders only, smoking a "pipe of peace" (Clark 1849: 65–66).

Onondaga 1846

The next known account of the WDS as practiced by the Onondaga is the Isaac Hurd narration of 1846. Hurd apparently recorded this account while visiting among the Onondaga, but the specific circumstances are not provided. The records of the Onondaga midwinter ceremony held in January of 1846, as reported by Hurd, have been examined by Robert Bieder (1980: 357) but otherwise have not been studied. The Hurd account (Hurd, manuscript A), covering at least two days of the WDS, provides one of the longer and most detailed descriptions of this ritual but without even a reference to the other parts of this long feast. Clark's 1841 account, not yet published in 1846, mentions "small belts of wampum" among the dogs' adornments, but only five years later we find no mention of these ornaments.

The absence of any wampum in the 1846 Onondaga account, as with the earliest complete account from among the Seneca, may simply be a matter of faulty reporting rather than reality. Since wampum was clearly noted in Clark's report of an Onondaga ceremony from 1841, the entire Hurd manuscript should be reviewed for any possible references to strings of wampum that may have been employed anywhere during this festival. The Hurd narration provides a description of native ritual in New York at a point in time (1846) when culture change was accelerating at an extremely rapid pace. Diplomatic wampum was no longer being employed by 1846 (see Becker 2002, 2006). By 1846 the meanings, or past functions, of the surviving diplomatic wampum belts were all but lost (Becker 2013). Decorative uses for traditional wampum were becoming more common on the Great Plains than among the acculturating native peoples of the Northeast.

Before documenting the next known account of the WDS among the Onondaga, dated to 1872, we present briefly a recent verbal recounting of a possible reference to the WDS. Whether this recent narration refers to an actual publication or represents modern myth making has not been determined. Arthur Einhorn (personal communication, 27 January 2013) believes that his files contain a magazine article written by a supposed descendant of a young man who crossed New York State on foot in the 1840s. During that period the advice to young men to "go west," commonly attributed to Horace Greeley (1811–1872), indicated frontier locations including places such as Rochester, New York. During his journey, the young man of the story was said to have spent a night among the Onondaga, known to be hospitable people. According to Einhorn's recall, the lad left the following day, taking with him "a white dog slated for sacrifice."

The cultural disrespect of this young man that is "documented" in this tale is of use within this larger review of the WDS for what it indicates of a non-native perspective. The sacrifice of dogs by native peoples might be compared by Christians to the sacrifice asked of the biblical Abraham. An impulse to rescue a selected canine victim may have been strong, and the "barbaric" act seen in many different lights. However, as we stated earlier, the numbers of published reports of the WDS must be far fewer than the numbers of accounts that may appear in letters or diaries.

An 1872 Onondaga Account

Following the 1846 record by Hurd, the next known eyewitness report of the WDS among the Onondaga dates from 1872 (Anonymous 1872a). This third-earliest known Onondaga account, dating from 26 years after the Hurd report, offers an extremely important indicator of change during that period. These inferred changes, of course, depend upon the accuracy of the reports that are now available to us. Also possible is that normal variations that may have appeared had been allowed in the rituals, with particular note given to Fenton's (1936) observations. Fenton recognized the variability in the order of events and timing of the ceremonial calendar among the several Iroquoian villages, which reflects traditional flexibility rather than any deterioration of the processes involved (see also Snyderman 1961). The Onondaga accounts, both American and Canadian, should be compared with Blau's (1969) review of calendared ceremonies as they were held by the Onondaga of New York. Blau also recognized the variations that were normal features of these activities.

The anonymous reporter's 1872 description of the ritual strangulation and cremation of a white dog by the Onondaga focuses on this single feature of the midwinter rites. This report suggests that the actual sacrifice of the dog took place on either 17 or 18 January of that year, although this may have been the beginning date of the festival with the sacrifice and/or burning at a later date. The day is identified as that of the (full?) "moon preceding our month of February." The location of this Onondaga community, with its two churches and council-house, was given as eight miles south of Syracuse, along Onondaga Creek where it flows through the present Onondaga National Indian Reservation. The reporter of this well-illustrated account believed, or at least stated, that the Onondaga were the only member of the Five Nations to have survived, and that this ritual was among the last "traces of paganism" (Anonymous 1872a). At an "early hour of the forenoon" the sacrificial dog was strangled and the body carried into the council-house and presumably placed on a bier. At two in the afternoon, the cremation ritual began.

Captain George, who, as head chief of the nation, acted as high priest, entered the council house and proceeded to array himself in a white tunic, the sleeves of which were bound up with white ribbons. He then girded himself with a belt of beads, and placed upon his head an adornment that might excite the admiration of the most fashionable of milliners—it was so light and feathery. Taking his seat in the center of the room, he waited in solemn silence for a long time. At length the solemn moment arrived, and so impressive were the proceedings that the only white men permitted to be present felt themselves compelled to uncover their heads and cease their labors. Rising slowly and majestically, bearing a long white wand in his right hand, Captain George commenced to chant in the Onondaga language; passing slowly around the typical dog from his position at the east he proceeded to the south, west, and north, and then returned to his former position, where he consulted with one of the chiefs. This proceeding was repeated three times; and then, as if he had gathered all the sins of the people, he approached the dog and uttered a pathetic lament, after this the body of the victim, which was laid upon a rough bier, was gently lifted up and borne to the place of sacrifice by the hands of the chiefs of the nation. The high priest then, standing at the east side of the altar of sacrifice, solemnly committed the victim to the flames. The sacrifice was completed; the atonement made.

(Anonymous 1872a, copied verbatim by Bruce 1896: 1061, and also by Beauchamp 1908: 325–326)

At some point after the cremation process had begun, guns were fired and congratulations exchanged. The anonymous reporter makes no reference to any wampum or baskets being used at any point in this ceremony at Onondaga (Anonymous 1872a). This absence of commentary regarding ornamentation or other details may reflect the limited concerns of the reporter. There is no indication of painted designs on the body of the dog lying on the pyre, designs depicted in the engraving by "G.S.R" (Fig. 7). The several lithographs illustrating this anonymous account vary in quality, with the largest and poorest in quality being that depicting Captain George and several people assembled around the pyre. Captain George wears a feather headdress set into a silver or cloth headband. We cannot tell from the illustration if the beaded sash donned for the ritual was a wampum band, a glass-beaded strap, or a woven band of the type that had become common among the Five Nations during the contact period (assumption belts, or *ceinture fleche*). All relevant illustrations (e.g., Brush 1901) indicate that no wampum was used in 1872, but that glass-beaded sashes may have been worn across the chest of Captain George.

The reporter implies that this might have been the last performance of this ritual, perhaps due to the growing influence of the two Christian churches that also are depicted in engravings. The passing of this ritual, predicted by the reporter, lay several decades in the future. Burning the basketful of collected sins, possibly the central element of these rites, continued for some time and was still performed into the 1970s. For many of the Onondaga, the ritual meal of the body and blood of Christ, another sacrifice for human sins, appears to have

FIGURE 7: "Offering the Sacrifice." Woodcut engraving by G.S. Ranger published in *Harper's Weekly* on February 17, 1872.
Reference: Anonymous, 1872. The Onondaga Indians [From Photographs by Ranger and Austin]. Harper's Weekly XVI (No. 790, for 17 Feb.): 141–142.

replaced the strangulation of a white dog and the burning of a basket of sins.

This long, illustrated account of the 1872 WDS (Anonymous 1872a) was paralleled by a very brief report of this same event that appeared in the *Syracuse Journal* for 18 January, and was repeated in *The New York Times* three days later (Anonymous 1872b). The *Journal* account, as reported in the *Times*, suggests that the "ceremony always takes place during the old moon nearest to the month of February" and had taken place on 17 January. Of interest is that here we find Captain George described as "the only person present arrayed in full Indian costume." The "perfectly white" dog is "supposed to have the sins of the whole nation cast upon him" in order to be "acceptable to Ha-wah-ne-a, who is the creator of the world." According to this reporter, the dog was strangled about noon, and only after

> "the whole tribe had marched around the lifeless dog three times, the priest of the occasion faced the east and solemnly devoted the body to the flames. While the dog was burning a solemn chant was kept up by Capt. George."
>
> Anonymous 1872b

The timing of this strangulation and burning, both taking place on the same day, is reported slightly differently in the *Times* account as compared with the other anonymous report (1872a) that appears to be of the same event. Not known is if the Captain George who supervised this 1872 ritual is the George Silversmith who is a significant figure in Boyle's (1898) account 26 years later.

An 1878 Onondaga Account

In 1880, Asbel Woodward presented a paper, later published, that supposedly describes an 1878 viewing of the WDS. Whether Woodward actually saw a ceremony in 1878 or took his information from Morgan's (1851) account (or both) remains uncertain. Woodward's note of a

pole being used suggests that Morgan was not the only source for the
following statement:

> "A string of white wampum was hung around the neck of a white dog
> [that was] suspended to [sic] a pole and offered as a sacrifice to the
> mighty Haweuneyn. The wampum was in pledge of their sincerity, . . ."
>
> Woodward 1880: 32–33

Two 1884 Onondaga Accounts?

Two separate newspaper accounts published in 1884 recorded that
the WDS had taken place, apparently among two separate groups of
Onondaga. One reports the event from the Syracuse area while the
other appears to be from the Grand River in Canada (presented later
in the section of Canadian examples of the WDS). From the very brief
"Syracuse area" account, it is difficult to determine what information
came from informants and what derives from the perceptions of the
reporter. The report with the dateline "Syracuse, N. Y., Jan. 21" is captioned "Burning the White Dog. A Sacrificial Ceremony By The Onondago Indians." Because the body was burned in a stove, presumably in
the longhouse, we infer that the size was quite small. The full Syracuse
text is as follows:

> The ceremony of burning the white dog was observed by the Indians
> on the Onondago Reservation to-day. The Indians were all dressed in
> bright colors, and the chiefs and braves were adorned with feathers
> and ribbons. The dog to be burned is first hanged till it is dead by a
> delegation of sagamores appointed by the chiefs and warriors of the
> tribe in council. This is done in secret. The carcase of the animal is
> then daubed with spots of red paint signifying a sacrifice of blood. Blue
> and red ribbons are tied about the animal, and the legs are fastened
> together with a long band of blue ribbon. The dog was laid beside a
> stove, while the squaws set up a howling, and the chiefs and braves
> uttered incantations in a low monotone. Chief Webster made the sac-
> rificial address. He wore a silver crown, and asked that the sins of the
> Six Nations be forgiven. A short chant by the Indians followed, when

the dog was placed in the stove, together with baskets of tobacco and herbs. The Indians then departed to their homes.

Tomorrow forenoon dancing and feasting will be indulged in, and on Wednesday the New Year's ceremonies, which last three days, will end in a grand fantastic pow-wow, consisting of dancing and feasting.

Anonymous 1884a

This 1884 account from Syracuse was far from a report of the last burning, but it relates to Beauchamp's later, and erroneous, assertion (1888a: 195) that "the animal sacrifice has ceased at Onondaga" soon followed by his note (1888a: 199) that the last burning took place in 1885. Beauchamp also offers a discussion of possible reasons.[11] Beauchamp's (1888a: 199) description of a 14day midwinter ritual that supposedly took place at Onondaga in 1885, at which the white dog was killed and also burned on day nine, should be considered in light of Beauchamp's (1888b) statement that no dog was burned in 1888 or during the previous year. Clearly Beauchamp did not witness the 1888 WDS, which was reported by Converse. Tooker's (1965, 1970) findings (see also Beauchamp 1908: 325–326) offer clues to this cloudy reportage.

In January of 1888, Harriet Maxwell Converse was a witness to what may have been the final sacrifice of a dog among the Onondaga living near Syracuse in New York. Her immediate reporting of this sacrifice of a single dog to a newspaper in Elmira, New York was followed by publication of her more detailed account in the *Journal of American Folk-Lore*. Together they provide us with important evidence for these activities.

The Converse report of 1888 and its variations were published only three years after Horatio Hale issued an account of the WDS among the Canadian Iroquoians (see below). The Converse account (1930) provides a view that can be compared and contrasted with accounts from among the more conservative Canadian Onondaga of the same period. Converse noted that the solitary dog was "decorated with ribbons and red paint, and ornamented with feathers," but wampum does not seem to be used in the basic decoration. The gifts of individuals who "hang upon its body trinkets and beads of wampum" (Converse 1888: 84) provide an important view of the immediate sources of the wampum used in this rite. This difference suggests that wampum beads may have been as common in the hands of individuals as in the hands of "Sachem Ha-yu-wan-es (Daniel Lafort, Wolf), [or] Oh-yah-do-ja-neh (Thomas Webster, Snipe), hereditary keeper of the wampum belts, [who] were masters of the religious ceremonies" (Converse 1888: 84–85; see Becker, in review A). We do not know anything about the roles played by any of the "actors" in these rituals. Perhaps the masters of these ceremonies asked for offerings of wampum and other gifts from the participants, or these guests may have known that giving was part of the ritual and included no beads.

The New York Onondaga "wampum keeper" named Thomas Webster had given testimony in July of 1888 before a New York State Legislative Committee specifically studying the "Indian question" (New York [State] Assembly 1889). By 1888, Thomas Webster had no recall of the origins or any functions relating to the wampum belts in his charge. Because he did not know what these wampum belts meant, Webster was strongly criticized in public by his kinsman in a manner alien to traditional Onondaga culture (Becker, in review A). Beauchamp (1888: 201) confuses the issue regarding Webster's testimony and the testimony of others regarding wampum belts and strings. Beauchamp at that time held in his personal collection, through purchases, a great number of Onondaga "strings," including several sets that were bound together and called "hands" or "branches." Beauchamp offered (1888a: 201) a long paragraph on their functions or meanings (for illustrations, see Beauchamp 1901). The use of wampum with the WDS will be addressed shortly, but at this point some notes on Harriet Converse and William Beauchamp are in order.

Beauchamp cannot have been ignorant of Converse's work. However, in a letter to the editor of *Science*, dated "Baldwinsville, July 12," Beauchamp (1888b) repeats what could be Daniel La Fort's perjured testimony as follows:

Daniel La Fort testified before the legislative committee this month
that the Onondagas burned no white dog this year, because the Indian
breed had run out. He told me soon after the feast, which occurred as
usual [in January], minus the dog, that it was a sacred breed and no
others could be used; and I think none was burned last year. Of course,
this is partially an excuse for letting the custom die out, as Indian dogs
could be procured from other Iroquois if so desired.

Beauchamp 1888b: 36

We believe that Beauchamp became annoyed when he discovered
that Converse had seen the 1888 WDS and he had not. He may have
been deliberately excluded from the event. Many accounts of the WDS
suggest that notice of a dog burning was not always made public in
advance. We suggest that the specific day and time of the event was
highly variable, perhaps depending on the weather or other conditions.
La Fort may simply have not informed Beauchamp, who missed the
event in 1888 and possibly the previous year if a WDS had been held
in 1887. In his letter, Beauchamp (1888b) states that "Forty years ago,
two dogs were burned" and that the ritual had been in decline since
then. This letter appears to refer to Clark's observations of the WDS in
1841 and published in 1849. Beauchamp also noted that "The last feast
[January 1888?] attracted some antiquarians from a distance, who were
much disappointed at the omission" of the sacrifice. But Converse was
there, and she reported the event very differently. We suspect that the
brilliant Reverend Beauchamp had been left off the "guest list" and was
annoyed that he was scooped—and by a woman!

In 1892, Beauchamp (1892: 85) again reported that white dogs
were no longer burned among the New York Onondaga, but that two
had been sacrificed only a few years ago. This directly contradicts his
earlier statement (1888b) that two dogs had been burned 40 years
before, unless he was citing a change in the number of dogs used 40
years previously, as distinct from the "solitary dog" burned in 1888
as reported by Converse (1888: 84). Also of interest in Beauchamp's
1892 account is his specific identification of the "day" of the burning
as "Koon-wah-yah-tun-was," translated as "They are burning dog" (see

Hewitt's letter, Figs. 8 and 9, for the term used). In most descriptions of the WDS, the day of the burning is identified by a day-count from the beginning of the Midwinter Feast, without recognition of the specific day name. Assigning a name to the specific day of the burning is in

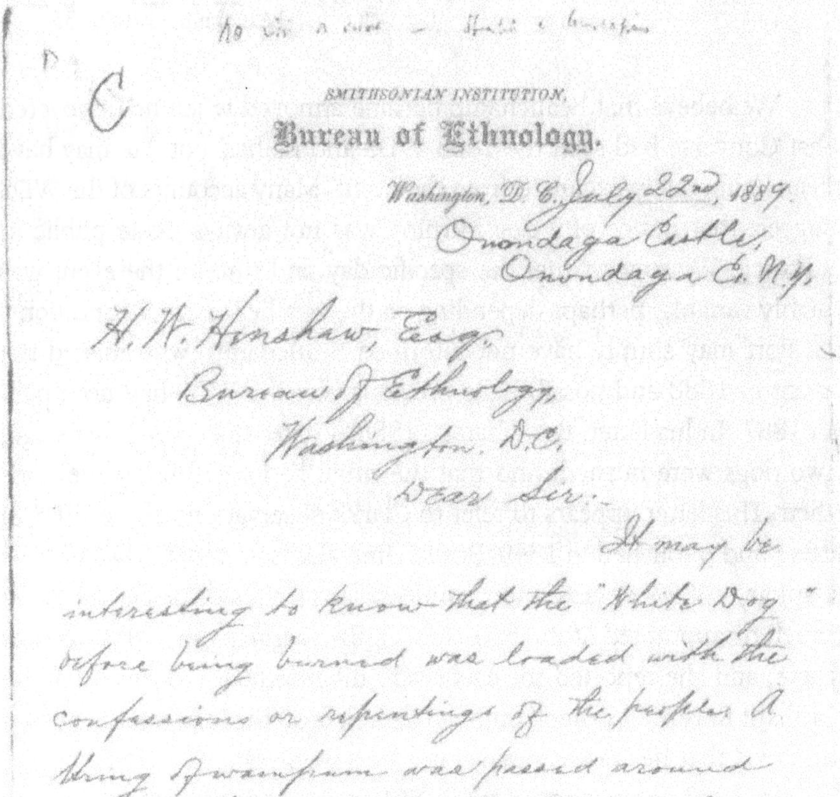

C

SMITHSONIAN INSTITUTION,

Bureau of Ethnology.

Washington, D. C. July 22nd, 1889.

Onondaga Castle,
Onondaga Co. N.Y.

H. W. Henshaw, Esq.
Bureau of Ethnology,
Washington, D.C.

Dear Sir:

It may be interesting to know that the "White Dog" before being burned was loaded with the confessions or repentings of the people. A string of wampum was passed around among the assembled people & each & every one would repent of some sin or failing while holding the string of wampum. When all had repented the string was fastened about the neck of the dog which

FIGURE 8: J.N.B. Hewitt's letter (1889)

Reference: National Anthropological Archives, Smithsonian Institution, Suitland Maryland, Records of the Bureau of American Ethnology, Correspondence, Box 10.

accord with the idea that there was no particular day for that rite, or specific length of time allotted to the feast. Beauchamp's 1892 publication, however, provides a good indication that the New York Onondaga had abandoned the sacrifice of dogs after 1888.

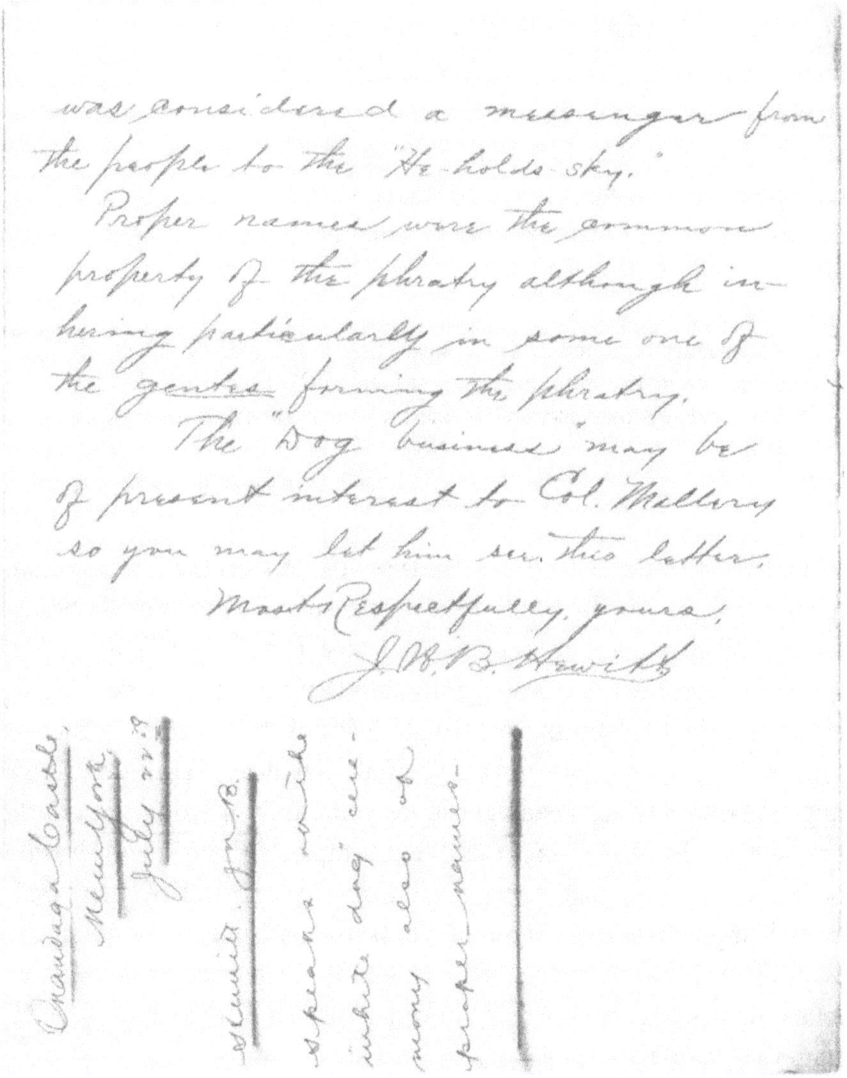
was considered a messenger from the people to the "He-holds-sky."
Proper names were the common property of the phratry although inhering particularly in some one of the gentes forming the phratry.
The "Dog business" may be of present interest to Col. Mallery so you may let him see this letter.
Most Respectfully yours,
J.N.B. Hewitt

Onondaga Castle,
New York,
July

Hewitt. J.N.B.
Speaks of white dog' ceremony also of proper names.

FIGURE 9: Reverse side of Hewitt's 1889 letter

Beauchamp's "Reflections" on Wampum Use
and the Onondaga White Dog Sacrifice

The Reverend William Beauchamp began his studies of American Indians, including the collection of wampum and other artifacts of shell, in
the 1870s. In his classic study of wampum and shell artifacts (1901),
Beauchamp illustrates a vast array of wampum belts and strings, many
loaned to him for his study (cf. Becker 2007c, 2007b). Included in this
compendium, Beauchamp provides a list of 12 wampum belts as well
as some strings that he had seen in the hands of the Onondaga in 1878
(cf. Becker, in review A). Included is an important suggestion regarding
the use of strings at that time. Beauchamp made specific note of certain
wampum bands, especially the

> "fragmentary ones now at Onondaga. These last, I imagine, are slowly
> disappearing. Wampum is in request [demand?] at the white dog sac-
> rifice, and this may account for the broken condition of some of the
> belts."
>
> Beauchamp 1879: 230

Whether any of the several old bands or strings then held in common
for the Iroquois by the Onondaga were dismantled to provide beads
for the WDS remains unknown. We suspect that Hale (1897: 237)
accepted this idea from Beauchamp, and that neither had eyewitness
evidence for this assertion but simply inferred the process. Examination of the present state of the 12 belts that Beauchamp described
might reveal if white beads are more commonly missing than dark
beads. Regarding the strings that Beauchamp (1879: 230) was shown,
he reported that he had been given a "minute account of their use."
Beauchamp's 1879 account appears to be the basis for five pages in his
magnum opus (Beauchamp 1901: 345–349). Of particular note is the
following passage that relates to information that Beauchamp gathered
from the Oneida.

> The Oneida chief, Abram Hill, gave the writer some wampum in 1878,
> with explanations of much that he had. Most of the large collection of

strings and loose wampum was his own. There were no belts, nor were these [strings?] often used in recent years on public occasions, many writers to the contrary notwithstanding. Most of his wampum was the black or purple, the white being now [in 1878?] quite rare.

Beauchamp 1901: 345

Beauchamp (1901) continues his narration with a long description of the various strings of wampum that he saw when he visited among the Oneida as well as other groups, and the varied uses that were served by these strings. Some were said to have been used as symbols representing each tribe, others for presentation in condolence and mourning rituals (Beauchamp 1895), and still others as greetings and in announcing meetings (Beauchamp 1901: 345–349). Presumably one or more of these strings was used in confessions by the end of the nineteenth century (see Speck and General 1995: 51, for Cayuga beliefs about the use of wampum strings; also Becker 2008a). Beauchamp's data are followed by a long discussion concerning the volume of wampum that survived in the latter part of the nineteenth century. The actual amounts of loose and strung wampum available among the Five Nations Iroquois around 1880 remain uncertain. Since 1999, Becker has heard numerous verbal reports that packets and even bags of loose beads were available in central New York as late as the 1950s, and that the Heye foundation held a large number of loose beads. The colors of these undocumented examples of loose beads were not reported by the commentators.

No observers of the White Dog ritual offered any specific indication regarding how many wampum beads were destroyed during each ceremony in which beads were involved. W. H. Holmes (1883: 252) accepted Beauchamp's conclusion that the surviving bands were being dismantled by the 1880s, pointing out that "Mr. Beauchamp, states that they [the 12 belts at Onondaga in 1883; there may have been others] are yearly wasting away, as a little wampum is annually caste into the fire at the burning of the 'white dog,' and these belts are the source of supply." Whatever Holmes's actual source of information in 1883, the WDS and perhaps other ritual activities may have been very slowly eroding the supply of traditional wampum beads still held among those native peoples who were maintaining old traditions. The sale of belts and strings of wampum to people outside these native communities was a much more rapid cause of the decline in the available supply.

During the nineteenth century, diplomatic wampum that was communally held in a native community provided a source of wampum beads for rituals such as the WDS. Offering wampum to the collection plate at Christian churches had long been common to all religions (Becker 1980). In Catholic Churches this had been the traditional means by which wampum was accumulated to create ecclesiastical belts (Becker 2001, 2006a), at least since the 1640s. A similar "tithing" may have generated the bands and necklaces worn by white dogs. While many of the 12 wampum belts held at Onondaga in 1879 may have been missing some beads, we doubt that the major wampum bands were then being dismantled to provide beads for ritual purposes. The recycling of diplomatic strings and small bands had always been common among native holders of wampum (Becker 2008). The possibility that some white beads were stripped from large belts cannot be discounted, as perhaps only 20 to 25 beads would have been needed for a small necklace worn by a sacrificial dog.

Beauchamp's long and detailed studies of various Five Nations customs became increasingly sophisticated through time. Perhaps his recognition of the flexibility of these rituals led him, in 1908, to repeat a much earlier anonymous report regarding the WDS rather than to attempt an updated statement. In his history of Syracuse and Onondaga counties, Beauchamp (1908) simply repeated an account that had appeared 36 years earlier (Anonymous 1872a) and had also been used by Bruce in 1896.

Hewitt's Onondaga Commentaries

John N. B. Hewitt (1859–1937), whose mother had Tuscarora origins, became an important scholar working for the Bureau of Ethnology of the Smithsonian Institution (see Swanton 1938). His studies among the Five Nations reflect his vast personal knowledge plus his desire to decode the various perspectives on language and culture to which he was exposed while growing up. As is so common among compulsive collectors of data, the ability to sort and publish his records became overwhelming. Hewitt's (1910) published work on the WDS barely reveals his growing understanding of the wide diversity of reports on this ritual, many of which appear to have been incorporated into his ideas. Thanks to recent research by Kathryn Merriam (2010a), a number of Hewitt's letters that include references to the WDS, as well as a related document written in Onondaga, provide information not available elsewhere. The earliest and perhaps the most important of his observations dates from July of 1889, perhaps 18 months after the 1888 burning reviewed earlier. This July letter suggests that there was a summer event related to the WDS, but it may refer to the documented 1888 event. In 1889 Hewitt had some wampum belts "read" for him at the Grand River reserve, but why he drafted this July letter from New York, with its odd concern for wampum and the WDS, is not yet known. It's hand written on Smithsonian Institution letterhead, as follows:

July 22nd, 1889
Onondaga Castle,
Onondaga Co. N.Y.

H. W. Henshaw, Esq.,
    Bureau of Ethnology,
    Washington, D. C.

Dear Sir:—

It may be interesting to know that the "White Dog" before being burned was loaded with the confessions or repenting of the people. A string of wampum was passed around among the assembled people & each & every one would repent of some sin or failing while holding the string of wampum. When all had repented the string was fastened about the neck of the dog which was considered a messenger from the people to the "He-holds-sky."

Proper names were the common property of the phratry although in-hering [sic] particularly in some one of the <u>gentes</u> forming the phratry.

The "Dog business" may be of present interest to Col. Mallery so you may let him see this letter.

Most Respectfully, yours,

J. N. B. Hewitt

Hewitt's 22 July 1889 letter tightly links the confession of sins with a string of wampum passed among the confessors that then was said to have been "fastened about the neck of the dog." This information may have been reported to him during his summer visit to the Onondaga and not part of his own observations. We suspect that Hewitt never witnessed an actual sacrifice of a dog but only used the term to describe the Midwinter Feast. Despite Hewitt's several mentions of plans to attend a WDS, there has never been any evidence found that he actually witnessed the burning of a dog. Even his specification of the future date on which the dog would be burned seems at odds with the many accounts collected here in which the day of the burning seems to be highly flexible and may depend entirely on the weather. Hewitt may have used the term "sacrifice" to describe the entire Midwinter Feast, with the burning of a basket of offerings having replaced the dog by the time that Hewitt witnessed the ceremony. The fact that by 1902 Hewitt identifies the event as the White Dog Festival rather than as a Midwinter Feast (Merriam 2005: 6) suggests a peculiar focus on an aspect that may have been transformed at an earlier date.

Note should be made of the synthetic account of the WDS that appears in an 1896 history of New York's Onondaga County. This note includes well-reproduced engravings depicting the 1872 WDS and also uses some of that earlier text. Bruce reports that:

> Among the Onondagas feasts, sacrifices, and dreams formerly held an important place in their tribal ceremonies, and although a number of these ancient practices are still observed many have passed wholly into oblivion. The Dream feast occurred in January or February and intensified all the follies of the ordinary dream. The False Faces described by John Bartram, form a sort of secret society and are still a prominent body. Green Lake, west of Jamesville, was the reputed ancient resort for their greatest mysteries. . . .

The sacrifice of the White Dog in point of time corresponds to and takes the place of the old Dream feast, and even retains some of its features. It is the most important of all the Pagan usages. The white dog is now seldom burned among the Onondagas. It is an ancient custom whereby the sins of the people are supposed to be gathered by the chiefs, who by some vicarious mystery lay them upon the head of a perfectly white dog, without spot or blemish, and organically sound. A single black hair would destroy the efficacy of the victim. The dog is strangled; not a drop of blood is shed; it is then fancifully painted and carried into the council house. In the afternoon the sacrificial ceremonies commence. The accompanying engraving represents the sacrifice which occurred at Onondaga Castle on January 18, 1872, when Captain George was the great chief, arrayed in all the splendor of his office, standing in the foreground.

[Engraving from Anonymous 1872a]

The feast, when fully carried out, lasts 14 days, the first 3 being devoted to religious services and the confession of sins. Then follow three days of gambling, on the last of which the false faces visit houses and poke in the ashes; on the seventh and eighth days the false faces come to the council-house in a body. These are known as medicine men, and their function at this time is to go through the ceremony of chasing out witches and devils. On the ninth day, called Koon-wah-yah-tun-was (they are burning dog), the white dog, now strangled and painted, is carried out and burned on a pile of fagots. This proceeding is best described by the following extract from a contemporary [1872] periodical:

[Description of Captain George from 1872a]

"The sins of the people were expiated, and general joy was manifested by the firing of guns and mutual congratulations. Formerly two white dogs were burned, but now only one is sacrificed. When the full ceremony is carried out the tenth day is given up to dancing by the children, who with adopted persons are named; the eleventh is for the dance for the Four Persons, Ki-yae.ne-ung.qua.ta-ka; on the twelfth are held dances for the Holder of the Heavens, and on the thirteenth occurs the dance for the Thunders. The next morning the men and women take opposite sides in gambling, and if the men win it will be a good season. Between seven and ten days later the False Faces search houses, receive gifts, and dance at the council house.

This feast was formerly attended with ceremonies of the most indecent character, but within recent years it has been shorn of its excessively objectionable features and materially shortened in the period of its observance. Even many of the rites previously mentioned have been dropped. Since the celebration of 1872 but few burnings of the white dog have occurred at the Reservation. The last one, and the only one of the kind in several years, took place on January 18, 1896. New Year's dances, however, are still continued annually."

Bruce 1896, II: 1061–1063

No confirmation has been secured to indicate that a burning of a dog took place among the Onondaga in 1896. Bruce may have misstated the year of the last documented WDS or recorded an undocumented report. However, his account may offer an accurate reference to a little known event. A possible clue to the accuracy of Bruce's 1896 date appears in a letter written by J. N. B. Hewitt in January of 1900. Hewitt's incidental remark indicates that he had missed a WDS among the Onondaga on 10 January 1900, but that he had crossed into Canada and planned to be present at the Midwinter Feast of the Seneca in February and there to witness a WDS. A further record of the possible survival of the WDS in New York appears in a 12-page document, "Notes on Iroquoian Cosmology," that had been "collected" by Hewitt and dated to 1902 (National Anthropological Archives, MS 3693). Among these 12 sheets is a single page written in Onondaga said to relate to the WDS. The space for recording the place on the catalogue card has been left blank. In fact, this single page, as translated by Hanni Woodbury (July 2013) relates to the dream guessing part of the Midwinter Feast and not to the WDS.

5

Canadian Onondaga Accounts

Converse's account of 1888, presented earlier, is the last known description of the WDS among the Onondaga within the United States. The earliest record of a WDS in Canada is an extensive description from among the Onondaga at the Six Nations Reserve in Canada. This description appeared in a newspaper account based on C. A. Hirschfelder's 1884 observations (Anonymous 1884b). There is no dateline to the anonymous version in THE MAIL, but the observer mentioned was almost certainly Charles A. Hirschfelder of Toronto. The article begins with a list of eight captions that serve as section headings:

> GI-YE-WA-NO-US-QUA-GO-WA. Solemn and Impressive Ceremony of the Iroquois Indians. Sacrifice of the White Dog. Annual New Year's Jubilee Lasting Seven Days. Thanks Offered to the Great Spirit. Song of Lamentation and Prayers for the Dead. Petition for the Fruits of the Earth. War Dance in Honor of a Pale-Face Visitor.

Hirschfelder, who had provided his notes for the 1884 anonymous article, subsequently published a serialized account under his own name in "The Indian" (Hirschfelder 1886a). That piece is nearly identical to the anonymous report of 1884. Also in 1884, this American donated a huge collection of artifacts to the Canadian museums. The full text of his account incorporates a great deal of ethnographic information. For the most part, both texts are identical except for an occasional word and some punctuation. Where the differences are of note, we have included the variation within parentheses. The latter part of this report derives from the 1886 publication, a copy of which can be found with ease.

> Mr. Hirschfelder, the well-known archæologist, received a letter from Chief Johnson, interpreter for the Six Nations or Iroquois Indians on their reserve on the Grand river, inviting him to go up and witness the ceremony of the sacrifice of the white dog . . . . A reporter of THE MAIL called upon Mr. Hirschfelder, who kindly gave his copious notes and account of the festival to be published. [one of their six principal annual feasts]. . . . the Christianized Indians take no part now in the events which, what we now denominate, the pagan Indians celebrate

. . . the sixth and last event celebrated {in their annual feast cycle} was the New Year's festival, the great jubilee of the Iroquois, at which the sacrifice of the white dog takes place.

There are regularly appointed officers who take charge of the various festivals. They are elected and occupy the position for life,. . .[but] have no power except during the celebration of their various events, . . .[and] no particular costume . . .

. . . The Indian name for this {Midwinter} festival is Gi-ye-wa-no-us-qua-go-wa, which literally means "the most excellent Faith," or "The supreme belief." [The dog] must be a spotless white, as that colour is the emblem of purity among them; . . .

The ceremonies in connection with the festival lasted seven days. [describes wooden blade, *Ga-ger-we-sa*, for stirring the ashes] In ancient days the killing of the white dog took place upon the first day of the ceremony, but they do not kill it now until the day of the sacrifice, which is the fifth day of the festival. . . .

The fifth day, the sacrifice of the white dog took place {before dawn?}, and it was the principal day of the festival. The proceedings on this day commenced by all assembling in the council-house, which is situated as in ancient days in the Onondaga section. When I arrived the council-house was filled with men, women and children, of all sizes, ages, and appearances. Some faces were exceedingly pleasant while others had that peculiar look of the Indian which gives them an awe-inspiring expression. The dresses of the women were very striking, they, of course, having all the colours of the rainbow represented. [But bright scarlet predominated.] The women took their places at one end of the council house and the men at the other. About eleven a.m. a chief arose and addressing the keepers of the faith said that the time had now arrived for the day's proceedings to commence, and he trusted that the people would behave themselves, as became proper on such an important occasion. [ ] The principal orator of the festival was an Onondaga chief known by the name of Buck, but whose Indian name is Shan-ah-wa-tee (the other side of the swamp). He is a perfect specimen of an Indian, of the average height, has a face which is exceeding handsome, and is one of the most fluent speakers I have ever had the pleasure of listening to. On arising he asked the attention of those present, congratulating them upon retaining their rules and customs and being able to offer universal praise to the Great Spirit. They ought all to join with him in regret at those absent and taken away during the past year. [Etc., including a slight variation in these texts, plus the following information that appears much later in the published account] He then left the council-house going outside singing at the top of his voice, and walked some distance away. After being out some time he returned again, never having stopped singing. Immediately on entering he walked up to the bench upon which the dog lay when all arose to their feet, and one of the officers stepping foreward took the dog and threw it over his shoulder, while another took the basket containing the incense and carried it in his hand. The trio then walked around the bench twice, when they left the council-house in Indian file, followed first by the men and then by the women, and went straight to the place of sacrifice, which was situated at a short distance from the council-house. When they arrived at the place of sacrifice all present bared their heads and kept them uncovered during the whole time occupied in delivering the address to the Great Spirit, which lasted nearly half an hour. [Etc.] A chief then arose and gave the rules which were to be observed while carrying the {body of the} dog to the place of sacrifice . . . {for burning}.

The white dog was then brought in and placed upon a bench in the centre of the council-house. . . . Immediately the dog was placed upon the bench all the Indians arose to their feet, and, going to where it lay, tied ribbons of every colour to different parts of the body. It had previously been daubed with red Indian paint, and had a bunch of pure white feathers fastened to the centre of the body and another around the neck, so that by the time it had all the ribbons fastened to it[,] it was almost impossible to see anything of the dog. The two front legs were tied together by themselves, and also the two hind legs. The four were then attached together with a ribbon, which represents that the dog had no other power than only that message entrusted to it, and could not walk away. There was also a string of wampum attached to the body, which is the ancient way of addressing a message to the Great Spirit. At the head of the dog was placed a basket containing a mixture of bought tobacco and tobacco of their own growing, which is thrown into the fire and ascends as an incense in the open air [to the Great Spirit Who dwells] on high.

After the dog has had all the offerings fastened to it, another short address was delivered, asking the Great Spirit to send them fruits, grain, &c., for their livelihood . . . . At the conclusion of this speech all the men left the council-house, the women remaining inside. An Indian was sent for by a messenger, who arrived all bedecked in feathers, paint, and other aboriginal paraphernalia. This Indian came to take the place of the absent dead. While all went into the council-house again, this messenger of the dead stood outside and sang a song of death lamentation. He then came in . . . and while singing he walked half way around the dog. . . . He again walked around the dog singing, but was stopped repeatedly by all those who had lost a friend addressing him. They did so, however, in turns, and as nearly as could be gleaned from this part of the ceremony, every time he walked around the dog, which he did a great number of times . . . it represented some dead relative for which he offered up a special prayer to the Great Spirit. . . . After this part was over he again started walking around the dog . . . He then commences to sing again, while all the men kept up a guttural noise . . . After he had finished—He then left the council-house going outside singing at the top of his voice,

Anonymous 1884b

Excerpts from the latter part of this 1884 narration are provided below, derived from the transcription taken from Hirschfelder's (1886) version, to which he signed his name.

and walked some distance away. After being out some time he returned again, having stopped singing." {Here the 1886 account repeats ver-batim the activities listed above, regarding picking up the dog and carrying it out to the "altar of sacrifice" (the term "place" appears ear-lier)}. . . . The dog was then put upon the fire with solemnity [and] the whole assemblage, amounting to several hundred, keeping perfectly motionless, the orator then continued "we send up to heaven on high, on behalf of all mankind an offering according to Thy will and orders, which Thou hast given us, that we should adhere to Thee . . . We send now direct unto Thee through the air (some tobacco was now thrown in the fire) an offering."

Hirschfelder 1886

In Herschfelder's account, there follows a long prayer of supplica-tion that is very different from the prayers of traditionalists who "return thanks" for that which is given to them. Traditionalists never beg for anything in advance. "After seeing that the dog and tobacco had been reduced to ashes, they left the place of sacrifice" (Hirschfelder 1886: 87). The basket is not mentioned.

Hirschfelder's account then turns to records of past feasts, none of which he witnessed. Hirschfelder believed that the natives "returned thanks for every object which was of the slightest value, but the sixth day is of more consequence now, ..." Hirschfelder's final section focuses on the events of the sixth day and the larger number of attend-ees and the focus on dancing. Near the close, Chief Buck, identified by Hirschfelder (1886: 86n) as "the hereditary holder of the wampum belts" among the Onondaga at the Six Nations Reserve in Canada (but, see Becker, in review A, manuscript D), indicated that he hoped Hirschfelder would follow up on this, his first visit to the Midwinter Feast, and that he would enjoy the real "war dance" given in his honor. "Chief Johnson" acted as interpreter for Hirschfelder. Readers should be aware that 1886 was at the end of the Plains wars and during a period of serious repression of native rituals in Canada.

Horatio Hale's Observations at Six Nations, Canada

Horatio Hale's observations of Iroquoian rituals in Canada (1883) led to his important and careful description of the WDS among the Onondaga residents on the Six Nations reservation. He did not provide the precise date of his observation, but Hale (1885: 7) says that it was "on a recent occasion" at the "Council-House of the tribe, on the Canadian Reserve of the Six Nations." Regarding the sacrificial dog, Hale notes that "a string of the precious wampum encircled its neck." Ribbons of various colors and colored feathers were attached to the dog, and other objects (offerings) "lay near it" (Hale 1885: 8). Hale's comment (1886: 298) that the sacrificed white dog among the Onondaga "was enveloped in strings of wampum" appears to be a distortion, by elaboration, of his own observations as published elsewhere the previous year. This distortion in his own publications suggests that we should be careful with Hale's other observations. Hale's commentary regarding the Iroquois League reveals that he recognized that many adjustments had been made to their epic "Book of Rites" that "suggests that important aspects of the League epic have changed over time" (Starna 2008: 298).

Hale's (1885: 8) report that the "sash adorned with beads" was worn by the Onondaga named Abraham Buck leads us to believe that wampum was not included among Buck's ornamental beads. Buck was not a chief but was related to two men identified as "chiefs": John Buck and his brother (see also Beauchamp 1888: 196). Hale says of Abraham Buck that a "string of wampum surrounded his neck, and lay

upon his breast." Hale also provides a transcription of the brief invocation associated with the actual burning, noting that it is "repeated
among the Senecas—substantially the same" in the version provided
by L. H. Morgan, but that the Onondaga in Canada around 1885 were
more conservative than the Seneca of New York around 1850 (Hale
1885: 12).

Hewitt's WDS Comments from Canada: 1900–1903

Hewitt's many trips to New York and Canada were in search of wampum
and other ethnographic items for the Smithsonian collections. Other
major collectors at that time included George Heye, who was willing
to pay much more than the Smithsonian could expend for native artifacts. On 21 January 1900, Hewitt wrote, in longhand, to Mr. Lund
at the Smithsonian, mostly to discuss the shipping of his typewriter,
problems with the ticket costs at the Niagara Falls Suspension Bridge,
and stationary. Within the few paragraphs of this three-page letter is
the following:

> "I have the opportunity to see the ceremony I missed on the 10th
> instant. The Senecas will have a dog-burning on the 8th proxime,
> beginning on the 5th. I hope to attend all the ceremonies."
>
> Hewitt to Lund: National Anthropological Archives, BAE,
> Hewitt Collection Box 10, Ms 20b–c (1-21-1900)

We interpret this as indicating that Hewitt had been in New York
but had missed a WDS (or equivalent?) held among the Onondaga
on 10 January 1900. Hewitt then crossed into Canada and expected
to attend the Grand River Seneca Midwinter Feast, beginning on 5
February, with the burning of the white dog to take place on 8 February. Assuming that a dog was actually burned, that would place the
cremation, but not necessarily the strangulation, on the fourth day
of the feast. An actual report about this activity in 1900 has not yet
been located.

Exactly one year later, on 21 January 1901, Hewitt again wrote to Mr. Lund. In this extremely brief and mostly typewritten note offering a box number in "Niagara Falls, N.Y.," Hewitt informs Lund that "After this date my address will be Tuscarora, Brant Co., Ontario, Canada." The very last line reads "I leave for the burnt dog feast," (unreferenced photocopy, Merriam to Becker). Once again, any notes or description of this event are not known.

During 1902, Hewitt had begun corresponding with Laura Miriam Cornelius (later Kellogg: 1880-ca. 1949), a young Wisconsin Oneida woman. Cornelius was extremely manipulative and was later arrested a number of times for fraud (Merriam 2005; see also the polite account by Hauptman 2008). In his letters to her, we learn a great deal about politics at the Smithsonian as well as some ethnographic details with which his extensive field notes must be filled. On 19 July 1902, his four-page typed letter to Cornelius, then in Seymour, Wisconsin, declares his hope of attending the September Green Corn festival of the Six Nations. If he cannot leave:

> until the winter time I will go to attend the [1903] New Year festival of the 1,000 pagans still resident on the Grand River reservation in Ontario, east of Detroit, which lasts 15 days, beginning on the 5th day of the moon called Disgóná' by the Onondagas, and at which time they customarily burn the white dog as an offering to their ancient god of growth and life, Thaěⁿʰiawǎ'gǐ, or in Mohawk, Te'haroⁿʰiawǎ'koⁿ'. If you have never seen this festival, you should do so before it is forever gone.
>
> National Anthropological Archives-Ms 4271 Box 2,
> JNBH to Laura M. Cornelius 7-19-1902, p. 4 (The
> accents as reproduced here are not exact)

A Gap in the Canadian Record?

Hewitt's letters plus other accounts of the WDS from Canada suggest that the custom persisted for some years after it had ended in the United States. This timing, however, may be an artifact of the available records. We consider the possibility that Canadian government concerns with "pagan rituals," stimulated by Christian churches, may have led to attempts to suppress the WDS or to exercise efforts to prevent outsiders from witnessing these rites.

In 1941 Chief Joseph Logan, Senior (Thadodaiho?: 1878–1961) told noted American ethnographer William Fenton that as a boy he had participated in the last WDS among the Onondaga in New York (Fenton 1998: 163). The date of Logan's participation was not specified, but it would seem to be during those rites of the 1880s. A description of the WDS as well as the narration regarding the song sung with it were provided to Fenton by Chief Logan and should be considered as Onondaga. William Fenton's recording of the "Dream Song of the Creator," supposedly sung by the Oneida at the time of the WDS, was sung by Chief Joseph Logan with the "assistance of Simeon Gibson at Six Nations Reserve, Canada, 1941" (Fenton 1942: iii). Fenton (1952: 2) used the terms Dream Feast or Midwinter Festival interchangeably, but as with most of his informants, he had never seen a dog sacrificed. Thus the WDS described by Fenton as taking place in an Oneida context and in the present tense is actually a synthesis, not applicable to any particular place or time. His failure to report a Midwinter Feast at which baskets were filled with sins and sacrificed is unfortunate. Most of the focal paragraph offered by Fenton on the WDS, a synthetic account filled with many unlikely elements, is transcribed here:

> The white dog . . . is a dream token from all the people to the Creator. On the fifth day . . . they burn the decorated dog. The dog must be pure white, although the breed, which survived until it became hybridized in recent years, sometimes had spotted ears. Children who are requested to give up a dog are told they will meet it in the skyworld. The dog must be strangled before sunrise [of the fifth day] by pulling two ropes in such wise that no blood is spilt. When the dog is dead, two appointed dressers decorate its body with a carrying loop which passes from the hind feet to the neck, wampum strings are placed around the dog's neck, and they daub both cheeks with three fingers of ceremonial red paint, with a half circle toward the ears. Then the dog is borne into the longhouse and placed on a litter in the center of the room.
>
> Fenton 1942: 17

Fenton reported that "Chief Logan remembered the last time the Onondagas burned a white dog because he [had] participated as messenger to announce the Creator" and "walked about 200 yards ahead of the appointed singer" to the longhouse common where "he cries to attract the attention of the people waiting in the longhouse" (Fenton 1942: 17). The singer "nears the longhouse singing, enters the building, and circles part way around where the dog has been laid out on a singing bench in the center of the room." There follows a description of the singer's interactions as well as the text of the song in Onondaga and English: "This is said to be the death chant of the Holder-of-the-heavens." The decorated white dog is described as a "token" presented to the Holder, "sent up to the skyworld on a column of smoke, together with a burnt offering of tobacco" (Fenton 1942: 18). No mention is made of wampum in this account or of any use of or burning of a basket.

Tooker's report regarding the WDS among the Onondaga at the Six Nations reserve in Canada in the 1950s appears to rely on Fenton's synthetic account rather than the Morgan account that is the basis for her generic version. She does not specify when the dogs in her version were said to have been strangled but reports that the modern Onondaga reported that, on the ninth day,

> "anciently, white dogs [were] burned. Now, two baskets of ribbons and two baskets of tobacco, one for each moiety, are burned in place of the two dogs."
>
> Tooker 1970: 81

This statement appears to be taken directly from Blau's (1969: 204–206) account, which is based on his observations from 1953 into the 1970s. If Tooker's description actually represents an independent observation, it is not clearly stated nor is it compared with Blau's dissertation data.

For some years, interest in the WDS, or its post-dog transformation, was centered on speculations regarding when the last strangulation was performed. These speculations included those of Speck (1949) for the Cayuga, who never had a WDS. Blau (1969: 217) considered only the Onondaga, among whom he began work in 1953. At that time his oldest informants were in their eighties and might have seen a WDS as children. More likely they recalled discussions of dog sacrifices or were confused about the nature of the rites as they saw them. They may have seen baskets burned but still called the ritual a WDS. Ethnographic descriptions of the WDS vanish from the literature, with Blau's observations during the period from 1956 though the 1960s representing the only written firsthand account of basket burnings (Blau 1969). Blau produced a synthetic account based on his own observations of "the WDS several times from 1953–66 and then again in the 1970's" (Blau, personal communication, 19 February 2013). Blau did not retain relevant field notes, but his sound recordings (Blau 1972; personal communication, February 2013) may include useful data. The account of the WDS assembled in his dissertation, however, provides further evidence of flexibility in this aspect of Onondaga ritual, and certainly adds to other interpretations of the Onondaga midwinter rites.

Onondaga, 1956

Blau (1969: 121–124) indicates that the first three days of the midwinter rites were given over to individual confessions, followed by a chanting of the Code of Handsome Lake (pages 125–129). Blau's observation that by 1955, the time needed for these confessions had dwindled to only one day suggests that his narration of the WDS is a combination of what he saw and what he was told (Blau 1969: 204–218). Blau states that the rite *hadiyadúntwas*, "they are burning the dog," took place on the morning of the ninth day of the feast. "Two baskets are placed on the floor in the center of each house" (the longhouse and the adjacent mudhouse). One "contains Indian tobacco" while the other, "painted white to symbolize its substitution for the white dog," contained colorful ribbons. The baskets with tobacco held a gift from each household of the moiety (Blau 1969: 206); the longhouse moiety and the mudhouse moiety (Blau 1969: 20–25). The four baskets were carried from the two structures in a specific order and taken to the "east end stove of the Longhouse" (Blau 1969: 207–209). Blau's interpretation of the various details (1969: 212–213) can now be amplified using comparative data from the earlier reports gathered in this volume. The source of the idea that a "wampum belt [was] laid over the body of the animal" has not been identified. Use of the term *hadiyadúntwas*, "they are burning the dog," for the basket burning ritual helps us to see linguistic conservatism as well as to help understand why Hewitt's records suggesting that a dog was burned probably referred to the ritual, not what was being burned.

6

The Oneida Accounts: Not a WDS

Three accounts from within the Oneida homeland, situated far to the east of Seneca territory, appear related to the WDS. The most extensive of these was recorded by the Reverend Samuel Kirkland (1741–1808): a report that describes a feast involving the meat of two dogs combined with the ritual sacrifice of a third dog. This account provides the only evidence for the presence among the Oneida of a ritual somewhat resembling the WDS. Important to our basic understanding of Oneida rituals is Kirkland's record of his personal observations that actually suggests the absence of the WDS. The single most significant record of a transitional ritual appears in his journal for 1800. Nine years earlier Kirkland had *recorded* another clue to the origins of the WDS but reveals that it was from among the Seneca, and not the Oneida. The 1791 record documents an observation made some 27 years earlier, when Kirkland had gone to live in the area of the Five Nations in 1764, as a young Presbyterian missionary, and took up residence among the Seneca. Kirkland relocated to an Oneida village in 1766.

During his very brief Seneca period, Kirkland made no reference to anything resembling the WDS. In 1783, however, he recounted some details of the Seneca midwinter rituals to Ezra Stiles (an account that has been presented earlier in this volume), together with the Seneca data on the WDS. During the 44 years between 1764 and 1808, he recorded only three observations that might relate in any way to the WDS among the Oneida.

Kirkland's 1791 account appears in some ways to be ancestral to the WDS, a ritual that never entered the Oneida midwinter ceremonies. The year 1791, just following the end of the War for Independence, was significant because the Oneida were notable for their general support during the war of the emerging United States. The stresses suffered by the other Five Nations affiliates following their defeat were considerable, but the problems were magnified among the Oneida. The Oneida, being significantly distinct in offering their support to the Colonists during the Revolution, may have expected far better treatment than they received from the new federal government. In 1791, Kirkland recorded a narration that reflects a vision that may relate to the origins of the WDS.[12] The WDS became a feature of the midwinter rituals among the Seneca, emerging between 1798 and 1800.

The Pilkington (1980) edition of Kirkland's writings offers a limited view of the many versions of these accounts. Christine Sternberg Patrick's research (2009) has revealed at least 35 previously unpublished journals or early copies of Kirkland's diaries that were not mentioned by Pilkington. The following transcription was kindly provided by Dr. Patrick (personal communications, 11 October 2009, 13 March 2012), who is compiling the many copies of the Kirkland journals for a definitive publication. Dr. Patrick's records of Kirkland's journal for 13 June–14 October 1791, of which two copies are known, include the following, from "Copy, Papers of Samuel Kirkland, Dartmouth College, MS-867." A contemporary copy examined by Patrick is cited as "Copy, Society for Propagating the Gospel Among the Indians and Others in North America, Massachusetts Historical Society, Ms N-176, Box 1." Patrick found the Dartmouth College version to have no significant differences from the version at the Massachusetts Historical Society.

> 22d [August 1791]. Monday; Last evening the Oneida Chief gave me an account of a vision, which one of the professed Pagans declared he had the day before yesterday; his story of which commands the attention of the whole village. The substance of the vision I transcribe, as related to me by this Chief, which he declares he had from the Pagan, whom he found sitting by the river side, naked & painted in the Indian stile.
>
> "My friend, are you surprized to see me here? My eyes have been opened into the true light. I have seen the path, in which our forefathers walked. T'halonghgawagen (i.e. Upholder of the skies) the God of the Six nations has appeared to me in a vision, as he formerly did to our forefathers; & said to me that we were a ruined people, unless we revived the ancient customs, & paid him the homage & sacrifices, which were his due as their protector: he told me, he wished for the sacrifice of a white dog, mingled with the incense of tobacco; the herb, which was given to their ancestors by his Grand mother; he also told me, that the ancient feasts, religious dances & ball plays must be revived, or no good should come to the six nations." This Chief endeavoured to convince him of the fallacy of his vision; but to no effect: he had sitten by the river side nearly 24. hours in expectation

of further revelation from their quondam God, but he never made his second appearance. This Chief told me that several of the Pagen party were much alarmed; & expressed an earnest desire that the whole village would agree upon making the sacrifice of a white dog, perfumed with tobacco. I am also told by this one that several Chiefs will come on soon to get me to accompany them to Whitestown, alias Jigaghgwate, on business in which they request my aid.

23. Tuesy. This day returned to my lodgings, after a tour to Jigaghgwate;* & having part of yesterday & most of this day in a Conference with the Indians before a Civil magistrate, respecting some intruders on their land; proper measures were taken to remove them. I am told that the late seer of visions is very much disconcerted; for after waiting near thirty hours naked by the river side, no further revelation was made agreeably to promise; Some have been so imprudent, as to laugh him to scorn; others compassionate his credulity, & endeavour to conciliate his affection to the Christian faith.

(Samuel Kirkland 1791; Transcription by Christine Sternberg Patrick, used here by permission)

Some insight into the nature of Christian influences among the various Five Nations peoples, and how it related to the complex native pantheon, were discussed by the observant David Boyle more than a century ago (1900). Boyle held that the native pantheon did not include "a Great Spirit" of the type commonly invoked at the WDS. Boyle narrates the tale of the Onondaga known as Ska-ne-o-dy-o, who lived:

> "(in 1790 according to some), [and] declared himself a prophet and claimed to have had intercourse with divine beings. His congeners, by this time, knew enough about Christianity to be in some measure prepared for a message from the Great Spirit" . . .
>
> It is somewhat remarkable that although this revelation is of such a comparatively recent date, there is [now] a good deal of confusion respecting what is known of the circumstances by the friends and relations of the prophet; but this only goes to show us how extremely difficult it is to get at the truth in such matters, and how little confidence we may place in tradition, if we demand exactitude. . . .

---

* "Whitestown" is used in the copy at the Massachusetts Historical Society (MHi).

[agreed upon is] "that Ska-ne-o-dy-o's revelation came to him while
he was in a trance."

Boyle 1900: 266

A Mohawk Revelation to the Oneida, 1798

Kirkland's record (1980: 364–365) describes an event among the
Oneida dated to "the autumn of 1798." A "young Mohawk Indian of
Grand River fell into a kind of *trance* for 24 hours or more" and in
that state he experienced "a dream & had many visions" and met with
Thauloonghyauwangoo, Upholder of the Skies. The deity complained
about the "neglect of the five Nations (the Senekas excepted)" in with-
holding homage and offerings due him. We note here that the Seneca,
or at least Handsome Lake's followers, had originated the WDS about
the time of this Mohawk's dream and thus were not perceived by this
dreamer as guilty of any lapse in making offerings. The power of dreams
among the Five Nations has been well documented, so this account
"immediately gained almost universal credit in the [Oneida?] settlement." The sacrifice was arranged; "Christians & Pagans all attended,
tho' none but the Pagans partook of the feast" (eating of the dog). Supposedly this "dream" and related rites spread among the Oneida during
the spring of 1799, but in fact the WDS as seen among the Seneca and
Onondaga never caught on.

Several other observations relating to the WDS, recorded by Reverend Kirkland, have been published, among which may be the critical
diary accounts of 1800. These include Kirkland's earliest (31 March
1800) description of what seems to be an Oneida ritual entirely based
on traditional feasting and propitiation. Kirkland (in Pilkington 1980:
360) observed that "eating the flesh of the roasted dog in that *ancient
rite* was a transaction equally *sacred & solemn with that* which the Christians call the *Lords feast*." Deardorff (1951: 92, 102) calls this a "White
Dog Feast, of which all partook." A sacrificed dog was roasted and
eaten in a feast that may have been a transitional event between dog

feasting (celebration at which dog was eaten) and the WDS, in which the bodies of the sacrificial dogs were cremated.

Kirkland's 31 March 1800 account, derived from the records now in the archives at Hamilton College, appears in Pilkington (1980: 364–367). Tooker (1970: 176, n11) specifies that her transcription of the Kirkland description of the WDS, which appears "at the end of the journal" derives from that identified as "1800B." This "account of the ancient *pagan sacrifice & religious festivals* of their forefathers performed here last fall; & what occasioned their revival after a total neglect of them for more than thirty years" appears in Pilkington (1980: 364; see also Deardorff 1951: 101). Kirkland had come to the Oneida in 1766 and never saw this ritual, yet he erroneously assumed that it was an ancient and traditional rite that had gone out of use among the Oneida prior to 1766 but was resurrected in 1800.

Did Kirkland believe that the single Oneida feast involving dogs that he witnessed was a resurrection of an earlier practice of the WDS, supposedly dating to a time before his arrival in 1766, or just a feast with dog meat? There is no evidence from the Jesuit relations or elsewhere to indicate any antiquity for the WDS, but there is evidence for hanging dogs on poles as part of rituals of protection. Kirkland was the first outsider to project the origins of the WDS back into the past: a creation of "tradition" rather than recognition of an innovative introduction that was part of Handsome Lake's revitalization movement (Wallace 1956). Kirkland's record of the ritual from 1800 is similar to earlier dog feasting and ritual offerings, rather than a WDS. How this event relates to the Mohawk dreamer's tale of 1791 remains to be examined in detail.

Three Dogs Strangled: 1800

What Kirkland described in 1800 links an Oneida feast incorporating two dogs plus a traditional dog sacrifice with a fall (harvest) festival. As Pilkington transcribes it [errors included], Kirkland states that:

> The requisites & preparations for the *Offering*, feast, & subsequent amusements, are three Dogs, a basket of tobacco, & a bowl curiously

wrought, with a dozen dies with which the game of chance is performed at the close of the ceremonies.

The Dogs are previously strangled or choacked without breaking any part of the body, the fire kindled, & at a small distance, perhaps 20 or 30 Yards, a hole is dug in the ground for supporting the pole (answering to an Alter) upon the top of which one of the Dogs is to be hung up, tied by the neck fast to the end of the pole with a new & well wrought *Mattump line*, the head curiously painted with vermillion, two small belts of the choicest wampum round his neck, One of unmarred *white*, denoting the *Sachem* or *Counsellors* who are always for peace, the other of *black* wampum, with red streaks of paint, characteristic of Warriors, who ever stand ready to defend their liberties & resent any injuries offered them. The pole is then raised up about twelve feet long with great caution & solemnity & fixed in the Ground & well fastened & secured against any blasts which might overset it; for it must stand with the Dog. (or offering) tied or laced on the top of the pole 'till the next annual sacrifice or 'till it moulders away to atoms. The other two Dogs are thrown into the fire, & shortly after the basket of tobacco.

The Priest of old Sachem then [offers prayers and thanks, continuing as follows]. We now by this Offering intreat thee to continue this protection to us. Give us a fruitful season, a plentiful harvest. Defend us from pestilence, from hurricanes, thunder & lightning, from all serpents. Give us success in hunting, & if our liberties should be invaded, we depend upon you (*gyanse*) fellow Citizens, to animate & inspire our Warriors with skill & courage to drive the enemy from our Country with shame & loss [etc.]. Next a Dog is taken out of the fire. The Priest cuts a small piece & eats & by the assistance of his aids, the multitude are all served with a piece, & profess themselves to be the dutiful subjects of the *Upholder of the Skies*, expecting to enjoy his protection & favor. Lastly the War dance, with a rehearsal of military achievements, a social dance by males & females through the night, a game of Chance & a generous repast the next day closes the scene.

On this occasion, the use of ardent spirits was forbidden for the term of *ten days*, but was not observed more than *ten hours*.

> Oneida March 31. 1800 Saml Kirkland
> (From Pilkington 1980: 365, 367)

Several points in this narration are noteworthy.[13] Perhaps the burning of a "basket of tobacco" is the most important element in terms of its allowing us to demonstrate ritual connection with the WDS. The burning of a basket of tobacco during this ritual appears to be a crucial element, from the earliest records, that has only now been recognized.

We point this out as an indication that baskets had significance in the ritual of 1800, and that their use and their ritual burning continued until the 1900s when it became the more prominent feature of the WDS rites among the Seneca and Onondaga but not others (see Tables I and II). In Kirkland's specific mention of one black and one white small belts being used, he also provides details that these are clearly related to Oneida moieties, the external and internal halves of the society (see Becker 1975).

Also important are the elements of the ritual that appear derived from Christian sources. The eating of the dogs, a carryover from earlier feasting involving dog meat, here seems to be more like taking communion rather than feasting. The prayers and supplication of the elder are very different from returning thanks in the native tradition. No specific color is specified for the dogs, suggesting that in 1800 among the Oneida it was irrelevant as it was the sacrificial meat that was of concern (cf. Body of Christ). The rite was closely related to eating dogs at feasts rather than using white dogs as messengers to carry away sins. The third dog was ornamented with "two small belts of the choicest wampum round his neck" (cf. Becker 2008) and hung on a pole using a new tump line (burden strap), examples of which are known from many ethnographic collections (cf. Becker 2011b). By 1800, both traditional tump lines and wampum belts were less frequently made, having come to be considered as elements of traditional native culture. Their use in this ritual suggests revivalistic aspects of this ritual. Laurence Hauptman's brief review of the literature he associates with what he imagines to be the Oneida white dog ritual states that the officials in charge "decorated [the dogs] with ribbons and a wampum collar" (Hauptman 1999: 28, 35, n33–34). A direct quote of the evidence reveals the errors involved.

In later years the use of ribbons for the WDS among the Seneca and Onondaga became more important if not essential to the ornamentation of the dogs, but they are not mentioned at this 1800 Oneida feast. What became of the two belts of the finest wampum used to ornament this dog hung by the Oneida or the surviving beads from those belts as it rotted away is nowhere mentioned. MJB is tempted to

compare the eventual falling of these beads, as the carcass and ornaments rotted, with the ritual scattering of wampum for children to
recover as reported among the Oklahoma "Delaware," around 1900.
The attempt to suppress alcohol use, a modern and deleterious introduction to these peoples, was not particularly successful at that time
but appears to have become fundamental to the ritual in later years. No
ball game (lacrosse) was played, but traditional gambling is noted here.
Gambling also seems to have faded from later versions of this ritual.

An interesting and perhaps important historical perspective is provided by the narration of the "Oneida WDS" by Jim Antone on 10 May
1939 (see Oneida Elders 1999: 112). Antone makes no reference to the
use of wampum in this ritual, supporting Beauchamp's (1885, 1888)
observations regarding the end of wampum use in the ritual at Onondaga. By 1900 many of the surviving wampum bands and strings had
found their ways into museums, and many others reached the safety
of museums during the years from around 1920–1940. In many cases
these transfers were specifically meant to protect them from being cannibalized for ritual purposes, as well as to prevent them from being
sold "out" of the native communities. Loose beads, many strings, and a
great number of belts, however, were still held by native-descent individuals who by 1900 had come to claim them as personal property (cf.
Becker 2013). The cash value of these items, and de facto ownership
by individuals, may have led these "keepers" to resist "donating" beads
to communal rituals such as the WDS, or to donate beads in numbers
no different than any other participants rather than in proportion to
the numbers that they held.

William Fenton's (1942) recording of the "Dream Song of the Creator," sung at the time of the WDS but sung for Fenton's recording by
an Oneida, has information about the actual sacrifice that we believe
derive from an Onondaga. Therefore, this information is placed with
the Onondaga.

7

Not Among the Cayuga or Mohawk: Various Inferences

The only possible contemporary evidence that any Cayuga may have been involved in the WDS can be found briefly mentioned in Boyle's account of the Seneca rites, provided earlier. In a footnote, Boyle (1898: 92) states that "The Cayugas on the Grand River Reserve kill the dog the first day and hang it against the building by its hind legs until the time for burning, five days afterwards." This must have been reported to Boyle, but by whom and when remains unknown.

Fifty years later, Frank Speck and his colleague, the Sour Springs Cayuga named Alexander General (1889–1965), reported on the events of the midwinter rites of the Cayuga (1949: 49, 1995: 49). Speck may have seen these rites in 1933 and again in 1936 (Speck and General 1949: 2). Speck described how the various events were arranged over a period of seven days, but he certainly did not see a WDS. There has never been an eyewitness report of the WDS among the Cayuga, but Speck and General imposed the WDS into the rites that supposedly took place at the Cayuga longhouse. Alexander General, who held "the title and office of Deskáheh in the Council of Chiefs" had the personal name "Sohyówa, 'Great Sky.'" Shimony (1978: 178) presents the name as "Shaǒ-hyowa" and offers an important biography.

There is no known kinship between Alexander General and Levi General (1873–1925), who had held the title Deskáheh at an earlier date and is widely known. Alexander was the youngest of eight children of an Oneida mother and Cayuga father. He grew up in a Cayuga milieu and his primary language was Cayuga, but he retained the matrilineal descent that linked him to his mother's people (Shimony 1978; Speck 1949: 185).

We doubt that either Speck or General knew of Boyle's 1898 publication, or knew of any informant who years before may have provided Boyle with information regarding the Cayuga in Canada. Quite possibly the Cayuga on the Grand River Reserve had adopted some form of the WDS from their neighbors at a very late date, but no firsthand account supports this inference. Speck's confusion of information in his own field records, if he generated any notes at all specifically regarding matters relating to the WDS, is becoming increasingly well known (Becker 2007c, 2012b).

Speck's study of the midwinter rites at the Cayuga longhouse at Sour Springs (Speck, with General 1949) was based on fieldwork conducted in 1933, a period during which no WDS was observed. Speck's inclusion of a discussion relating to the WDS has led some reviewers to believe that the Cayuga were practitioners. The authors (1949: 145) acknowledge that Alexander General "has never seen the rite" that they present as called "burning dog" by the Cayuga. General claimed that it had been performed "about fifteen years prior to the time of writing" or around 1918 (Speck and General 1949: 145–146), when General was about 45 years old. It is very unlikely that General would have missed this important part of the Midwinter Feast!

Speck never claimed that he had ever witnessed a WDS. Wallace Chafe provides an insightful observation that may help explain General's input into the 1949 discussion of the Midwinter Feast. Chafe's study among the Seneca (1961: 5) describes a third ritual similar to the Seneca Thanksgiving Speech and Thanksgiving Dance that he had previously presented, which relates to rituals of the burning of tobacco. Two Seneca terms used to describe tobacco burning translate easily, but a third, "kajíyothwe:?" literally means "dog burning" that Chafe describes as "a ritual now long extinct." Quite possibly this Seneca term is what General, a Cayuga, discussed with Speck, who merged all these details into a synthetic account of Cayuga rituals.

Snyderman's (1961: 589) belief that Speck had actually seen a WDS among the Cayuga is but one of the errors he introduced to the understanding of these rituals. Snyderman also erred in accepting General's report that the rite had been discontinued at the Sour Springs Longhouse only because the Cayuga ran out of white dogs! General clearly had invented the ritual among the Cayuga and then made up a reason for its discontinuance. General's reason contradicts Snyderman's own important assertions regarding the resourcefulness and flexibility of the various Iroquoian peoples. The evidence attests to the use of dogs for the WDS whose coats were far from albino or even pure white. Where the WDS was practiced, non-white dogs commonly were used, supporting Snyderman's thesis of flexibility but contradicting General's report regarding the supposed reason for the end of this ritual among the Cayuga. Speculation regarding the reduced availability of pure white dogs after the 1930s (Cooper 1936: 10, in Oberholtzer 2003) are not supported by the historical record. Pure white dogs, perhaps albinos, were always rare. The dogs used in the WDS were commonly noted as ritually painted before strangulation, suggesting a concern with cosmetic alteration of the coats. The colors of the spots or patterns of painting used may have varied as needed, as in the Crowell account of 1830.

Speck's work at the Six Nations Reserve began around 1914, with a focus on the Delawares resident there. His work in conjunction with General began by 1931. Yet, Speck's description of the WDS is a generic account obviously taken from one or more of the records that we have transcribed. John Buck, an Onondaga, is cited as saying that among the Seneca, the dog's windpipe was cut. This may have been a remark to disparage the customs of the Seneca rather than an accurate recounting of an event actually witnessed. No first-person account of a Cayuga ritual has been produced, nor do we think that one would be possible.

A description (Speck and General 1949: 174) of the Cayuga "Midwinter Ceremony (New Year's Festival)" of 30 January to 5 February 1933 indicates that the first two days of the "Midwinter Festival," preceding the "stirring ashes ceremony," related to confession of sins using one or more strings of wampum (p. 51). Speck and General believed that the stirring ashes rite had been discontinued at Sour Springs about 1890 (p. 53). The confusion, contradictions, and borrowing without citation found in this 1949 account are typical of Speck's work (see Becker 2007c). As Fenton (1950: 521) indicated in a review of this Cayuga volume, Speck's "retrospections on Iroquois religion and society are quite muddy." In these areas, Speck's volume is far less reliable and less well organized than is found even in the journalistic accounts that we have collected.

Speck, as others, realized that confession among the Cayuga and the other Iroquoian people was a Christian tradition that had become part of the midwinter rites through the teachings of Handsome Lake

(Speck 1949: 53). Soon after Speck published, Deardorff (1951: 101) provided carefully documented evidence supporting the proposition that "in the practice and conception of confession" we find the widest variations among the many communities of the Five Nations. Deardorff, as well as Snyderman, understood the considerable differences that existed in ritual and other behaviors among the peoples of the Five Nations. Yet Speck was not alone in his ideas regarding the importance of these differences in confession rituals and in the concept of sin as innovations that emerged as part of the new religion together with the WDS (cf. Abrams 1967). The general assumption was that the WDS was an ancient ritual, rather than a transformation of a feasting behavior into an aspect of confession.

That the WDS did not spread to the easternmost of the Five Nations is revealed by the absence of evidence for these rites among the Mohawk. A possible corollary may be found if the Mohawk also eschew rituals of confession. There may be a number of reasons why the Mohawk never incorporated the WDS into their Midwinter Feast beyond the simple fact of distance from the Seneca. Arthur Einhorn has kindly shared with MJB various reasons why he believes that the WDS remained absent in the eastern part of the Confederacy. Suffice it to say, the Mohawk did not sacrifice dogs of any color.

Transformation of the WDS

Our discovery of Boyle's observations, recorded and published in 1898, came during the process of making final revisions to this manuscript. The difficulty in tracing Boyle's publication reveals how even skilled researchers such as Wallace and Tooker might miss what is the most complete eyewitness account of the WDS. More telling is that William Fenton, a diligent scholar whose research covered much more Iroquoian data, could have missed being informed of Boyle's landmark research.

William Fenton's 1936 recounting or reconstruction of the WDS, at a time when the legend of the rite was barely if at all recalled by members of the Cold Spring Seneca longhouse, has two very different forms. Fenton's earlier narrative indicates that the White Dog

> had been strangled on the day when the heralds went around [Day 2, and], anciently was burned on the fifth morning. This is at present the weakest day in the festival. Further, it would elevate it to the importance of the eighth day, of which it is an abbreviated complement. No informant now living has witnessed the White Dog Feast at Coldspring, for no burning has taken place within their memory.
>
> Fenton 1936: 11

Fenton's belief that the strangulation took place on the second day and the burning took place on the fifth day may derive from his reading of Morgan's synthetic account. Tooker (1970: 69–70) reports that her informants at Cold Spring claimed there was a WDS at both their Green Corn and Midwinter feasts. She did not pursue the matter.

Fenton's Cold Spring account continues with a review of various reports from among his informants, none of whom had ever seen the WDS. The reports of these individuals reveal a complete lack of agreement as to how the WDS was conducted. Fenton (1936: 13) then noted that "a tobacco burning invocation to the Creator . . . was once used over the white dog" (see also 1936: 14). Fenton (1936: 6, n8) also lists the rites of the Canadian Seneca of the early twentieth century but does not report on the ethnographic data gathered. Fenton seems to have been ignorant of Boyle's important (1898) account. The Canadian Seneca were more conservative and therefore perhaps less susceptible to adopting any modern innovations.

Fenton admitted that the passing of "the White Dog Feast at Coldspring" was before anyone who was alive in 1936 had seen it. This is echoed from reports of Seneca legends and lifeways as reported from the Allegheny Reservation in Warren County, Pennsylvania, around 1944. Among the varied recitations of Seneca ritual events are three that reflect on the WDS, affirming that it was long gone. In commenting on the New Year Dance, Florence Crouse (1944a: 81) reported that it "always lasts one whole week," but makes no mention of any element that might be related to the WDS. Crouse (1944b: 57–60,

94–95) also reported that a Ten Day feast for the dead was a "new" rite, having developed from Handsome Lake's teachings. This is a rare linkage between rituals practiced in the middle of the twentieth century and aspects of significant culture change dating from around 1800 CE. In effect, Crouse provides support for our inference that the WDS as a ritual event derives from the teachings of this prophet. Possibly related, although perhaps somewhat distantly, to the WDS is an element of "The Great Snake Ritual" reported by Clara Red Eye (1944: 61–62). Within this rite, a white chicken was sacrificed and the body thrown in the river. The sacred color and the sacrifice rather than consumption of the meat parallel aspects of the WDS. Seven years later, in 1951, Harold Conklin and William Sturtevant were invited to attend the midwinter ceremonies at the Allegheny Seneca longhouse. Their publication (Conklin and Sturtevant 1953) focuses on the musical instruments employed. We are certain that their field notes include no rites relating to the WDS.

By 1953, Fenton's report of information from his Seneca work, around 1930, has but one oblique reference to the WDS. The housemother where Fenton boarded told him that "Snorer is the best speaker, he knows the origin legends, and you will have to pay him" (Fenton 1991: 8). In discussing tobacco invocations, "Snorer (Hawk)" or "the sage of 'High Bank'" stated that "[t]he only time when one should really talk is when he is burning tobacco and making invocations to the Creator at the time the White Dog is sacrificed. They no longer burn the dog" (Fenton 1991: 8, 15, 146). We suggest that by 1953 Fenton came to realize that tales told to him regarding the WDS were all synthetic narrations and not reliable indicators of any actual past events.

8

Were Simple Baskets Always Central to the WDS?

Putting All Yours Sins in One Basket

The Onondaga "Transition," by
1894, from Dogs to Baskets

In what may be the prototype of the WDS among the Oneida in 1800, presented earlier, Kirkland described ritual killing of three dogs, one of which was left to decompose. "The other two Dogs are thrown into the fire, & shortly after the basket of tobacco" (Pilkington 1980: 365–367). Baskets had been burned for as long as white dogs, and probably before, but external observers have continued to focus on the death and cremation of the dogs. An important note on the antiquity of basket burning, and its link with the WDS, is an unreferenced note made by Elisabeth Tooker. In her effort to place the origin of the WDS *before* the period of Handsome Lake, Tooker (1970: 110) presents an account of a dog feast that she dates to the time of the American Revolution. She offers no reference, but we offer here her narration of this report:

> ". . . others went round to every house with a basket, in which each individual was required to deposit something. This basket, with all its contents, was first cast into the fire. Afterward the dog was laid on and thoroughly roasted, and was then eaten. This was followed by . . ."
>
> (Tooker 1970: 110)

other events typical of a midwinter feast at which a dog was eaten. Note that the basket and its contents were burned first. The later transformation to a white dog that was sacrificed without its flesh being eaten was part of the development of the rituals of the WDS. If anything, the basket sacrifice predated the WDS. This gathering of sins in the form of offerings to be burned is distinct from another collection noted in Tooker's synthetic Seneca account in which Tooker (1970: 138) describes an "old woman carrying a huge basket" who, on the third and fourth days (of seven), went from house to house and gathered "materials for a feast."

By bringing all of the detailed descriptions of the WDS together, we can shift our collective gaze to one element of the ritual that previously had seemed relatively minor. The most visual, intense part of the WDS involved the ritual killing, ornamentation, hanging, and burning of the dog or dogs. The low level of concern with the presence of baskets at the midwinter rituals is clearly demonstrated by the many synthetic accounts of the WDS. Not a single synthetic example includes a mention of the burning of baskets. This lack of attention to the baskets as part of the ritual appears to be a function of ethnographic blind spots.

In 1884, the pyre at Onondaga was used for burning the dog "together with baskets of tobacco and herbs" (Anonymous 1884a). The Canadian Onondaga in that same year carried a basket of incense in the procession and presumably burned both (Anonymous 1884b; Herschfelder 1886).

Not long after, William Beauchamp declared that the actual sacrifice of dogs at the Midwinter Feast had ended, he attended "the concluding ceremonies of the White Dog Feast at Onondaga, N. Y., January 18, 1894, under the escort of Daniel La Fort, head chief" (Beauchamp 1895: 209). While the term white dog remained associated with the name of the Midwinter Feast among outsiders, in 1894 a white basket or baskets and perhaps their contents had come to replace the sacrificial dog as the principal offering (cf. Becker manuscript A, regarding baskets and wampum).

Recorded as being in attendance at Onondaga in 1894 were a dozen women as well as some 30 men, including "Thomas Webster, keeper of the wampum, [who] wore a feather headdress" (cf. Becker, in review A). This headdress was of the *gustawa* type. The procession of the elders from the "short house" to the council-house, also known as the longhouse, consisted of three men, "the last of whom bore the white basket, which represents the dog."

The Seneca group observed by Boyle in 1898 (1898: 95) placed "a small old chip-basket" with homegrown tobacco near the tail of the sacrificial dog. At various points during the procedure, they threw tobacco into the fire and lastly the basket with the remaining tobacco. Parker's (1912: 85) account of the Cattaraugus Seneca WDS in 1906 repeats the process of burning tobacco and lastly the entire basket of tobacco. Tooker (1970: 57) reports that the leader of the midwinter festival women's dance among the Tonawanda in the 1950s carried a basket, but the contents are not indicated.

Native-made baskets became a significant source of income in many Indian communities. The market-oriented skills of native makers yielded cost-effective containers throughout the Northeast. Black ash (*Fraxinus nigra* Marsh) and other preferred woods were harvested and converted into an array of containers to meet widespread demand (see Lismer 1941 for Seneca examples; also Lyford 1945: 59–61). The craft of basketry production received little documentation until recently, thus allowing connections with ritual to be lost to memory. We suspect that baskets were a central element in the Midwinter Feast since before the WDS. Perhaps it was the contents rather than the container that were the important agents. With that idea in mind, we turn our review from the scant information relating to baskets to equally rare reports of the use of ribbons in these rituals.

Ribbons and/or Tobacco Collected in the Basket

Ribbons were used to ornament the two sacrificed dogs at Onondaga Castle in 1841, but no ribbons were then listed by Clark (1849) among the items collected as offerings. At some point ribbons were added to tobacco as gifts given by Onondaga individuals as offerings at the WDS. Hale (1885: 8) recorded the use of ribbons and feathers of various colors used to decorate the dog at the Six Nations Reserve. Hirschfelder (1886; Anonymous 1884b) records the use of ribbons as offerings. The strangled dog was carried out to the pyre and then back into the council house where it was placed on a central bench. All the participants tied ribbons of every color to different parts of the dog's body, along with two bunches of white feathers. The dog was difficult to see. At the head of the dog they placed a basket containing a mixture of purchased and homegrown tobacco "which is thrown into the fire." The wampum ornament on this dog was clearly stated to represent the traditional means of addressing the recipient of the offering, to verify the sincerity of the gift.

Whether tied to the sacrificial dogs or collected in a basket, by the end of the nineteenth century ribbons had become a significant part of the WDS. Ribbons were employed as ornaments for the dogs as early as 1841, being purchased or provided by the organizers of the WDS. When they became small offerings made by individuals is uncertain. As a commercial product, ribbons were more valuable than commercial tobacco, which in turn had a greater value than homegrown varieties. By the 1870s all these items had become acceptable offerings at these religious gatherings, but how and when they were given is not well described in most of the later accounts.

Beauchamp (1895: 210) reported that in the 1840s it was common that two dogs were burned. The offering then was reduced to one dog (Beauchamp 1888: 199). By 1894 the offerings were focused on three white baskets. La Fort suggested that this progression was "because the sacred breed of dogs is extinct, but others simply say that the present practice [using baskets] looks better" (Beauchamp 1895: 210). In 1894, three baskets were burned in the stove at the longhouse, along with other offerings (Beauchamp 1895: 211). Later Beauchamp (1908: 326) recalled having "seen the ceremony since the basket was substituted for the dog. Except the procession through and around the council house all was performed indoors, the basket being thrust into a stove." Wampum was not mentioned as part of the 1894 ritual or thereafter, suggesting that the prior use of wampum was purely ornamental and not part of the ritual or of the process of verifying the message carried by the sacrificial dogs to the deities.

The White Dog Feast (Vanesse 1907), and related ritual sacrifices, had continued to attract popular attention among non-native peoples for their "exotic" character well into the twentieth century. Whether acculturative processes or normal processes of cultural change led to variations through time, the many elements of native tradition gradually transformed the Midwinter Feasts. We suspect that the transition from the eating of dog meat at feasts shifted to the sacrificing of dogs, and finally to the burning of baskets, made of "white" materials such as splints of ash, or any basketry painted white. In each phase of these transitions there may have been some greater conservatism among some Iroquoians in Canada. The only clue to traditionalists in Canada sacrificing dogs into the 1930s appears in the reprint of Horatio Hale's 1885 study of Iroquois ritual which includes an *inserted* photograph of poor quality (1989: 322, Plate 19) with the caption "THE LAST BURNING OF THE WHITE DOG, Onondaga Longhouse, Ohsweken [near Branford, Ontario], c. 1931–33." No verification of this date or any details have appeared in our search, but at least three scholars have accepted this account as factual. Speck (1949: 45), Shimony (1994 [1961]), and Tooker (1965: 130, 1970: 46) all believed that the WDS survived into the 1930s among the Seneca living on the Six Nations Reserve or elsewhere. We believe that they misunderstood references to the WDS as referring to the actual dog sacrifice rather than to a ritual burning of baskets.

Ohsweken may well have been the location of the last burning, but the date remains unknown. Any use of wampum as part of this ritual may have ended by 1900, 30 or 40 years before even Speck and others implied that the actual sacrifice of a white dog continued. Long before the 1940s, however, even those Canadian groups still practicing midwinter rites may have come to see the WDS as a cruel activity and possibly incompatible with their rising Christian sentiments. Continuity in the offering of baskets, however, was perfectly compatible with Christian concepts of sacrifice and giving.

Hints of the gradual demise in the use of sacrificial dogs in the Midwinter Feast were offered by Fenton (1942: 17, as cited in Shimony 1994: 186; also Blau 1964). By the 1940s, Fenton recognized that dogs had been replaced by other offerings. Neither Fenton nor any other scholar have previously recognized the long, traditional use of baskets as part of the offerings at the WDS, or the important continuity of this aspect of the midwinter rites after the use of sacrificial dogs had ended. Shimony (1994: 184–189) began her field work at Ohsweken (among Onondaga?) in 1953, a full generation after the date for the WDS suggested in the photograph inserted into the Hale reprint. She erroneously places the last WDS "at Seneca Longhouse in the late thirties, though some informants thought it was 1941" (Shimony 1994: 185). Shimony's description of the WDS is a typical synthesis that selectively blends comments from her informants' recall and information from the literature. In her account (Shimony 1994: 186): "None of the ribbons may be red in color, since bright red is considered inappropriate on a dead person, and the dog was treated just as if he were a dead person." Yet we have eyewitness accounts from the previous century reporting that red ribbons decorated the dogs (e.g., Anonymous 1884b).

In her synthetic reconstruction of the WDS, Shimony (1994: 187) devotes a paragraph to the belief that "Attenders ought to be costumed in 'Indian' dress, since it is respectful to 'dress' for the sacred rites of the Great Creator." What is meant by Indian dress is not clarified, and Shimony does not acknowledge that the 1950s was the decade of native revival in the Northeast, with its attendant efforts to reinvent what then was believed to be native costume. Much of the costuming was imported from the Plains. Shimony does not distinguish between what she saw at Sour Springs (Cayuga) in 1954 and other variations reported to her

As reported earlier, the actual sacrifice of a white dog had ended in the United States by 1890. David Boyle (1902: 117–120) offers a review of dog burning among the "Iroquois of Ontario" as if the rite were still part of ceremonies at the beginning of the twentieth century. The sacrificial dog was bedecked with ribbons and beads, but the type of dog was not specified. According to Boyle, the six requests in the prayers connected with the New Year Festival began with one addressed to Rawen Niyoh, the Great Spirit. Boyle quotes this as, "We acknowledge that the sun will continue to shine on us and make all things grow" (Boyle 1902: 120). Boyle also offers views of other scholars. Boyle states that the cardinal directions were associated with specific colors, and that white was "always associated in the Indian mind with the East, and, in time, with goodness, success, and health." This generic statement has not been confirmed in any of its aspects among any specific native peoples. Boyle notes evolutionary changes in these customs as well as the considerable extent of Christian influences, but the tone of his review seems superficial rather than detailed, as in an ethnographic narrative.

Tooker's studies at Tonawanda in the 1950s led her to conclude that cash and tobacco had become central to the WDS, with the burning of tobacco believed to have replaced the dogs (1970: 41–43). She also found that in the 1950s homegrown tobacco was perceived as a more valuable gift than commercially purchased varieties ("store-bought"). This may have been a function of the rarity of homegrown plants by 1950, or simply continuity from the past. We suggest that purchased tobacco may at one time have been considered more valuable but that nativistic aspects of the Indian revival movement had its influence on the midwinter rituals. Perhaps Tooker's focus on tobacco was related to her being a very heavy smoker. Tooker's generic account of the WDS attaches little importance to baskets, which are first mentioned on page 81. In a similar vein, Blau (1964: 111) provides no explanation for his suggestion that the Onondaga used a basket of ribbons as a "modern substitute" for the white dog, with emphasis on the ribbons. He seems to have had no idea how the various small offerings, that we consider tokens of sins, were collected during the course of the Midwinter Feast. The evidence for these aspects of the ritual that have been gathered here reveals that ribbons and other small offerings collected by functionaries into a basket could have been items representing personal sins that were given as part of the process of atoning for sins.

Quoting at length from all the known firsthand accounts of the WDS enables us to make suggestions regarding its origins and transformation, despite the wide range of variation among the many villages where it was found. Details regarding overall changes in the WDS remain uncertain. The oppressive efforts of Duncan Campbell Scott, superintendent of Indian Affairs in Canada during the early twentieth century, may have extended beyond suppression of the potlatch ceremonies of the peoples of the Northwest coast and the Ghost Dance on the Plains, but Snyderman's suggestion (1961: 573) that some Iroquoian "rites, such as the WDS, were discontinued because of [the] white man's legal and other restrictions" is not supported by specific citations. Snyderman disregarded the possible significance of the transition to the use of painted baskets in his efforts to further his own political agenda. Elsewhere Snyderman (1961: 590) states that the WDS faded because wampum became scarce, an assertion that contradicts his own depiction of flexibility in Iroquoian cultural forms. Snyderman (1961: 590, repeating Fenton 1936: 11) states that the "cessation of the rite [WDS] has made the fifth day of the Midwinter Festival the weakest day of the ceremonial."

The recent historical record offers little indication of how white baskets came to be used in place of dogs for this sacrificial event. The sacrifice took the form of a confession for sins (cf. Speck and General 1995: 51), with a sacrifice made to carry them away. The basic concept of sinning is, of course, a Christian theological belief. The burning of baskets that are painted white, and other vessels used to contain offerings that carry away the sins of the participants, provide a ritual far less attractive to thrill-seeking, non-believing outsiders than witnessing the strangulation of a sacrificial animal and smelling the acrid fumes from its burning flesh. Outsiders were not "burning" their sins, and probably had little interest in these modified rituals among their native neighbors. The burning of baskets also may have been less attractive to the traditionalist native participants as well. Answers to questions regarding who made these baskets, how they were used, and other important questions regarding the evolution of the rituals of the WDS remain to be answered. The continuing transformation of these activities in the recent past suggests that some of the elders now may recall having seen these events in the 1930s and 1940s. Their recall of these rituals, regardless of changes in perception through time, should be recorded.

9

Distribution of the Ritual:

Dog Feasting and the White Dog Sacrifice

Dogs, when available, were a favored food among many if not most North American natives (Delâge 2005). The members of the Lewis and Clark expedition came to enjoy and prefer dog meat. Reports of natives using dogs as pack animals and also eating them are known from the colonial period (Browne 1890, VIII: 515). In their superlative study of every aspect of the use of dogs by native peoples in the Northeastern Woodlands, Butler and Hadlock (1949) provide an unsurpassed review of the literature. The absence of any evidence for the sacrifice of dogs in New England is notable. Beauchamp's (1888: 203, n1) note referring to Cotton Mather's *Magnalia*, implying that a WDS is noted therein, is incorrect. Mather describes the native killing of dogs, supposedly as a sacrifice to the devil, but actually only to silence the dogs of the colonists to prevent them from warning of an attack (Mather 1855 [1702], I: 560, Butler and Hadlock 1949: 22–23, n67). Mather's observations in New England is remarkably similar to a 1642 account in the Jesuit Relations in which a dog was "publicly offered to the Demon of war" then killed and eaten. As we can see in the foregoing compendium, Tooker's belief (1970: 84, 102) that human (prisoners) and dog sacrifices for the New Fire were related to war is in no way supported by any aspect of the evidence

Consumption of the meat of the dog, or dogs, sacrificed in the WDS is nowhere reported, except as part of the ritual during a transitional phase just after 1800 CE. Later reports of the WDS represent a specific and evolved ritual with a very limited distribution among tribes of the League of the Iroquois. The direct evidence suggests that, like so many customs among the Five Nations Iroquois, the custom of ritual sacrifice, as distinct from simple consumption of dog meat, was specific to only two tribes: the Seneca and Onondaga.

Popular accounts commonly confuse the eating of dog with the WDS (Fig. 10). An illustration by William Thomas Smedley (1858–1920) that appears in a popular Canadian tourist book depicts a group of Native men gathered around the bodies of two dogs. The caption reads:

> 59 The Feast of the Dog is celebrated once a year when the Indians meet to receive their treaty money. Conducted with the utmost gravity

by the principal medicine man, a dog is slain, cut up, cooked and eaten. White dogs are preferred, but a dog of any other shade will answer the purpose

(Grant 1882: 340)

Smedley depicts a simple dog feast or meal. The common disjuncture between an illustration and its caption is evident in this figure. Two dogs are shown but only one is specified in the caption. The preference for a white dog suggests the writer was aware of the WDS, but that is irrelevant to this meal. The caption to this same illustration as it appears in a reprint of this volume (1975) is entirely different.

What appear to be true dog sacrifices are seen in two photographs generated in 1920 by Frederick Wilkerson Waugh (1872–1924) during fieldwork among the Ojibway on the Whitefish River, Lac Seul, Ontario. Both are described as "Midewiwin deposits in bush round trees, with dog sacrifice: Photo CD file numbers CD96-631 (PCD no. 5798-1631-0110-010 [& 011]) 48871." The dog in each photograph appears to have been left on the ground to decay.

FIGURE 10: "The Feast of the White Dog." Illustration by W.T. Smedley for Grant's *Picturesque Canada* (1882:340).

Archaeological Evidence

The documentary and historical evidence demonstrates that few of the Haudenosaunee, and none of their near neighbors, practiced the WDS. Consideration of the evidence for these rites from an archaeological perspective provides us with no single trait that might be discovered through excavation. Archaeological finds of dog burials, however, are common throughout North America (see Oberholtzer 2003; also Delâge 2005), but there is nothing to associate the remains of dogs recovered through archaeology with the WDS.

Of some interest is what may be the few finds of dog burials in the Core Area of wampum use (Fig. 2), but they also are known from numerous locations in surrounding areas. George (2011: 7–8) pointed out that complete dog burials are rare at Monongahela sites (late prehistoric period), but one was found at the Wylie 3 site in southwest Pennsylvania, and another from the Duval Site in West Virginia (Dunnell 1980).[14] At least 105 dog burials have now been recovered from the Hatch Site (44PG51) in Virginia, dated to around 1600 CE (see Gregory 1980). Jennifer Fitzgerald's survey of dog burials from several Native American sites in the Chickahominy River area of Virginia (2009) relates them to a practice widely known throughout the native Northeast (see also Pierard, Cote, and Pinel 1987). None of the dog burials tell us anything regarding the WDS.

Butler and Hadlock (1949: 18, 22, 27–29) review the ethnographic literature noting burials of dogs with humans and also list several archaeological finds. Strong (1985: 33), in a review of data on dog burials from Long Island, makes note of two ethnographic references to the strangulation of dogs and suspension of their bodies on poles, both from distant locations: One comes from among the Fox Indians (Underhill 1965) and the other from the Chukchi-Koryak of Siberia. This attests to a wide geographical distribution, but one clearly not continuous through space. Beauchamp, in a review of the WDS literature (1888: 203, n1), refers to a journal in which a dog feast is noted among the Miami, a people living to the west of the Five Nations and close to the Fox. Eating dog meat and making a sacrifice of a dog without consuming the flesh are very different activities. Schwartz (1997: 85) errs in his interpretation of Michelson's (1925: 39) comments on the subject. Schwartz thought that Michelson stated that the Illinois and Miami had a WDS similar to that of the Iroquois, which cannot be demonstrated.

At any site the discovery of the intact skeleton of a dog, and in at least one case a fox, reflects a burial rite that is far removed from what can be expected to survive in the archaeological record from the WDS. If any animal is eaten, the bones become disarticulated and scattered and might become part of an ordinary midden. If these remains were part of a sacrificial meal, they might have been segregated from ordinary trash, but we have no evidence for any such procedure. If the white dog was burned (cremated) rather than roasted for consumption, the cremated remains also might be segregated (kept as a ritual unit) and might be subject to archaeological identification (cf. Thomas 1966).

These various data relating to feasting on dogs and the evolution of the WDS have been linked quite effectively by Cath Oberholtzer (2003). Her study facilitates archaeological interpretation of materials even where the cremation has significantly reduced both dog bones and any associated wampum (cf. Thomas 1966). Oberholtzer's (2003) important review of the literature regarding dog feasts and dog burials from the Great Lakes region includes valuable insights regarding possible prehistoric origins of these rituals. Note that Oberholtzer's target area, after 1600, was in the periphery of the Core Area of diplomatic wampum use (see also Schwartz 1997: 82–91). Oberholtzer discusses finds of scattered dog bones at Iroquoian sites, suggesting butchering and consumption, as distinct from the intact dogs buried in Algonquian areas, an observation that she (2003, n3) attributes to Beverly A. Smith (SAA paper 2000: 7–8). Butchering and eating of dogs at Iroquoian sites has been confirmed by recent studies at the Late Woodland Englebert site. Dog remains recovered from the Engelbert Site along the New York–Pennsylvania border suggests a primary use as food, although two intact dog burials are noted from this site (Biesaw 2006: 3, 13–14). The possibility should be considered that these forms represent two different cultural traditions from two different periods of occupation. Oberholtzer also notes an interesting account from Manitoba in 1848 in which a native woman, awakened from a trance state, was seen to be holding "a large white bead." The large size of this shell bead indicates that it was not an example of wampum, but a cognitive equivalence between her object and the importance of wampum now might be inferred.

Lacking from these few firsthand accounts of the WDS is ethnographic data specific to the location of the burning that might be of importance in archaeological recovery. We suspect that there was no specific location relative to the ritual buildings involved. If fact, the post-Contact evolution of the Iroquoian "Big House" or ritual building remains to be investigated from the perspective of location within or near the village. B. Powell (personal communication, 23 May 2009) points out that fire both purifies and terminates, yet we have little archaeological evidence for ritualized burning in Iroquoia and none at all for the ritual burning of wampum beads other than those associated with the WDS. Nor do we have any evidence of wampum being used for or incorporated in rosaries, or interred with Roman Catholic dead (but, see Lainey 2004: 129, n127). In the 1630s, the Huron had been reported as washing a prisoner and dressing him in the best beaver robe and wampum bands before torturing and burning him. The costly decorations almost certainly were removed before the ordeal began.

10

Wampum and the WDS

The possibility that the wampum strings sometimes recorded as ornamenting the white dog were solely ornamental rather than conveying any symbolic meaning may be considered. The use of wampum strings to validate a message sent by or to people in the Core Area suggests that their function in the WDS may have been the same. Wampum, which became an important commodity in some native trading systems (Becker 2008b, 2010), had a variety of uses that became culturally embedded within each of the Iroquoian and other Core Area tribes soon after 1600 CE.[15] Wampum was used as ornamentation, for wergild, and in diplomacy. Diplomatic wampum presented or received by colonists was carefully described, being an important aspect of treaties and interactions. Wampum exchanges were diligently recorded in the minutes that were essential parts of these meetings. The native view from this period is found in treaty minutes, and their statements and claims were often, at best, contradictory.

The claimed use of wampum in any rituals among any of the Five Nations Iroquois is a subject of growing interest. In 1875, Horatio Hale began to collect data at the Six Nations Reserve at Grand River, Ontario. Fortunately for our study of the WDS, much of his information concerns death rituals. Hale (1883: 73) states that after a death, a delegation goes to the "dwelling of the deceased, bearing in a pouch some mourning wampum" (see Becker 2013). Mourning and condolence wampum, generally in the form of short strings (see Fig. 12), are often noted in the records. A case of a colonial emissary shortening the mourning period through the presentation of a large condolence gift (Becker, manuscript D) reveals much about the function of wampum in the context of condolence rituals. In research parallel to that of Hale, William Beauchamp (1888: 195) suggested that "the public confession of sins upon a string of wampum" reflects "an introduced religious custom." Similarly, Beauchamp (1895b: 314) observed that the use of wampum strings in condolence activities is a late (post-1800) innovation. The use of wampum, while ancillary to death rituals after 1800, is certainly not an ancient nor essential aspect of these rites.

Recent studies of how wampum was used in the past reveal patterns of innovation and change, along with some ideas regarding how

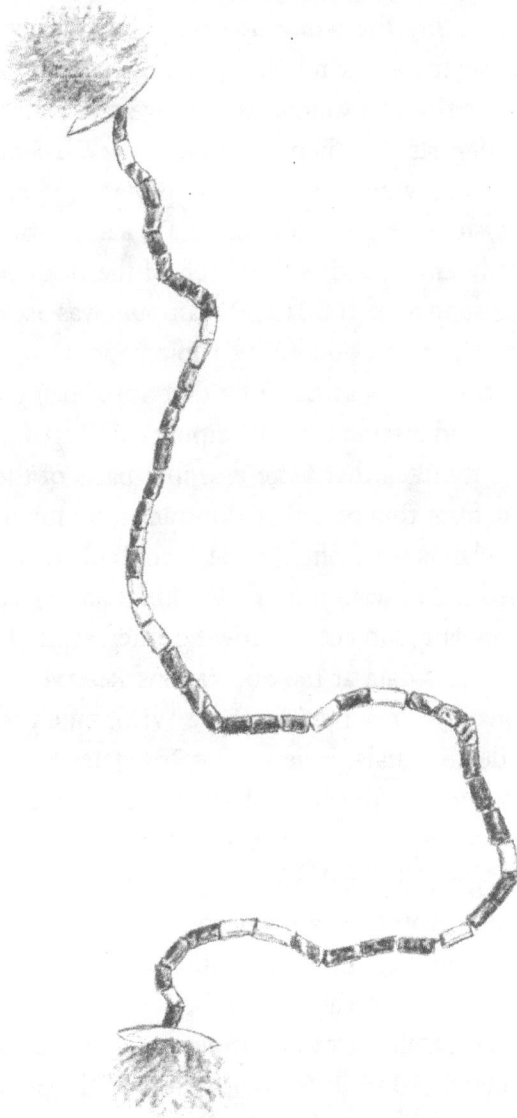

FIGURE 11:This string of wampum was preserved among the Hurons of Lorette (Wendat of Wendake) in 1846. The author of the drawing notes in his manuscript: "A single string of Wampum used as a letter or the credential of an Envoy. [. . .] the string is tufted with beaver fur." The Wendat never performed the White Dog Sacrifice.

Reference: Huyghue, Samuel Douglas Smith. "Some Account of Wampum." Dec. 1879, Hawthorne. Museum Victoria, Indigenous Cultures Department, Ethnohistoric Materials, Melbourne, Australia, 14 pages. Ms XM1495.

and why these changes took place. These transitions and transformations of the past may provide significant insight into present processes of change involving the use of tobacco and tobacco smoke in native rituals and modern uses of wampum, both new and old.

Lewis Henry Morgan (1852: 73; see Holmes 1883: 241) stated that "White wampum . . . was hung around the neck of the white dog before it was burned." The early reports, however, make no mention of wampum being used in the WDS. This suggests that both wampum and the concept of the removal of sin became part of this ritual at some point after 1800.[16] All of the later reported examples of this ritual note that the sacrificial victim's body, as well as all ornaments placed on it, were burned.[17] The confession of sins at the Midwinter Feast and the use of wampum in this ritual remained strong into the 1960s. Tooker found that the Tonawanda Seneca continued to talk about the white dog during the Midwinter Feast, at which they placed a string of (white?) wampum on a bench in the Council House. A confessor picked it up to confess sins, "replacing the wampum on the bench when he has finished" (Tooker 1970: 42; Fenton 1941: 161).

Beauchamp (1895: 211, see also 1888: 198) recognized at an early date, about the time when the ritual sacrifice of dogs was ending, that the WDS had been a late innovation among the Seneca. The projection of this ritual into the native past was a part of inventing tradition for these natives on the part of the outside population that came to surround them (cf. Hobsbawm 1992). The assumption that native "customs" that may be quite new have a long history may be a false inference. The native Midwinter Feast, or at least an aspect of an "ancient" ritual cycle, may be very old, but the details of rites may change at an extremely rapid pace. Is it only the Europeans who project these customs, such as the WDS, into the deep past? Are those native-descent peoples who accept these external realities revealing their acculturation and with it the need to associate what they do with great antiquity as a legitimizing force?

The essence of tradition may involve making up rituals and songs on the spot. The general outline of various rites may be sufficient to allow an elder to improvise an adequate semblance of the ritual without regard to specific details. As George Abrams recalled when a ceremony was created for the removal of the longhouse on the Allegheny Reservation in 1965, the earlier removals "on the Allegheny Reservation, were either not recalled or were not accompanied by any elaborate rituals . . . and the ritual had to be recreated" (1967: 23). Even the dates of those earlier relocations, about 1913 and about 1921, were unknown. Unmentioned was the early history of these lands in Cattaraugus County, New York which had been the homeland of the Wenro, a tribe exterminated by the Seneca in 1638.

Sixty years after Beauchamp recognized the relatively recent origins of the WDS, George Snyderman reported the beginnings of the sacralization of wampum belts. Snyderman recognized this process as the invention of a tradition on the part of descendant natives and concluded that "[t]he religious basis for present-day [1951–1961] use of wampum is to be found in Handsome Lake's Code" (1961: 607). The codification of the Deganawidah epic in the years around 1800 is best summarized by Starna (2008: 294–296), who points out that the process, and related religious transformations, was part of the developing interest in literacy among the Seneca.

The evolution of the WDS, as distinct from simple consumption of dog meat, began during the decline in the use of diplomatic wampum among the Five Nations Iroquois, about 1790 to 1800. The aspects of the WDS that today appear less humane were transformed long ago among the traditionalist native communities. Only the recent horror film *White Dog Sacrifice* (2005), written and directed by Michael Flaman, revives images that now are associated, erroneously and unfortunately, with these ancient ways.

Information regarding various ritual uses for wampum within native communities, as well as any ornamental functions, is surprisingly limited. Earlier, we had noted the possibility that differences in the quality and/or accuracy of the reports now available may have influenced our interpretations. This is unlikely. Becker (2006) has suggested that activities involving the use of wampum in ritual, as well as other traditional rites, were retained by the various Iroquoian groups in Canada for a decade or more after they had ended in New York State.

Perhaps relative isolation slowed the adoption by these Iroquoians of the languages and complete range of material culture from non-native communities. Traditional native customs and the uses of special artifacts, however, remained largely unrecorded even in Canada, unless they were observed by outsiders in an ethnographic context. Rituals such as the WDS, or even the recall of any elements of these practices, no longer survive even in the oral tradition. The confusion between an oral tradition and spontaneous creation of stories for verbal reports leads some naive scholars to believe that they can elicit evidence from the past. Anthropology has spent a century in negating the idea of racial memory only to find the subject generating a great deal of discussion in the popular press.

Particularly interesting regarding the survival of the WDS is the observation that it does not appear among any of the 138 Seneca folktales collected by Curtin and Hewitt (1918). Neither the WDS nor midwinter rites appear within any of the traditional tales, although the power of dogs and their aid to humans is well confirmed (Curtin and Hewitt 1918: 193–195). Snyderman's later ethnological study (1982) that focused specifically on Allegheny Seneca folklore relating to wampum notably makes no mention of any use of wampum in the WDS or in any other ritual context. The very absence of wampum from these traditional contexts suggests that the appearance of wampum in conjunction with the WDS in the 1800s was a late innovation related to the teachings of Handsome Lake. Not surprisingly, the WDS also is absent from Oneida folklore (see Wonderley 2004). The innovation of dog sacrifice to native activities and rituals without consumption of its flesh never penetrated traditional telling of folktales. The WDS appears to represent a specific moment in the process of culture change, one associated with the adoption of Christian concepts of sin and confession that had not existed in Iroquoia.

The ethnographic records may hold other clues to the transformation or multiple evolutionary paths of the White Dog Ritual, but the observations that have been noted here suggest that the use of wampum in association with this event began only after 1830 and had ended at some time prior to 1900. Through this study a number of new questions have emerged regarding specific details of the WDS beyond those involved with the role of wampum. We do not know if the sex of the dog was significant, but it may not have been a concern to people focused on coat color. Alan Mounier (personal communication, 2007) notes that only selective breeding could have insured that there were white dogs available for this rite. This was unlikely, and there is no evidence to determine whether these were albino dogs or if the coat color was simply white or tan, or if both might have been used. Genetic limitations may not have been a reason for the apparently restricted distribution of the WDS.

The sacrificial burning of white baskets, adorned with ribbons that also may have been white, generally replaced the sacrifice of white dogs at least among the Onondaga. Since many native communities had developed market economies that included traditional crafts, we can infer that these baskets were native made. The specifics of the modern form of the ritual as practiced among the Seneca and the Onondaga, the only two groups for which this has been documented, provide an interesting question for students of culture history and cultural change among others of the Six Nations or their many descendant groups.

Were there further uses for the ashes remaining once the sacrificial dog had been cremated? The pyre that consumed the body of the sacrificial dog, along with the wampum and other gifts, are not mentioned in any of these narrations. We do not know if the burned remains were simply abandoned or if the outside reporters simply lost interest once the burning had been completed (see Becker, manuscript C). What would remain from this rude cremation process is more than the simple gray wood ash and a few crumbling bones from the dog and any surviving bits of wampum. Experience with human cremations (e.g., Becker 2005a, 2005b) reveals that a great deal of the skeleton can survive when the burning takes place on a large pyre. Of interest is the finding that smaller pyres, with lower temperatures, in the long term may be more destructive to bones. Beauchamp (1888: 195) notes that there were other rituals during which "sprinkling with ashes" was still common among the Onondaga. For example, ashes were used in treating the sick (Beauchamp 1888: 197), but the origins of these ashes are not known. We should inquire as to the possibility that "sacred" ashes from the WDS were retrieved for medicinal purposes (Ober-holtzer 2003)

Midwinter rituals of some type are known from among all sedentary peoples in the temperate zone, particularly in the Core Area of diplomatic wampum use. The presence of midwinter rites among the Mohawk and Cayuga may lead some readers to infer that they had variant forms of the WDS, but we would disagree. The strong correlation between the use of white dog rituals and the heart of the Core Area of wampum use and the complete absence of the WDS among the foraging peoples living on the periphery of diplomatic wampum use also is notable (Becker 2007b, 2010).

The significance of white or albino animals as divine signs appears widespread among Native American peoples. Personal names such as White Dog (Schultz 1962: chapter 1) or White Buffalo appear often in the literature, perhaps reflecting special interests. What we do not know is how significant these appearances were prior to European contact and whether the "mystical" aspects of these beasts only became linked as divine signs as elements of revitalization in the post-contact period (cf. Applebome 2012).

Sacred Uses for Wampum?

The research for this volume began with a simple quest to identify a sacred use for wampum among aboriginal peoples of the Northeast. The association of strings of wampum and the sacrificed white dogs was well documented. The variations in the use of strings of wampum associated with the WDS all appear purely ornamental. In examples of the WDS where strings were seen, they may have been decorative as well as used as verifications of the legitimacy or honesty of the prayers and confessions (messages) borne by the sacrificed white dogs.

A parallel use for wampum is seen in condolence messages. Usually strings of wampum were presented to condole for the loss of a kinsperson, but in some cases wampum bands were employed. Often the more important the deceased was ranked (higher status in these egalitarian cultures), the larger were the quantities of wampum sent and the greater the distances. But did condolence wampum serve a ritual purpose, or what could be called a "sacred use"? There are innumerable accounts of condolence messages associated with wampum presentation, but no specific details on what became of these gifts. The ritual of presenting wampum certainly has sacred overtones, but is the wampum itself sacred or simply an important cultural symbol of the sincerity (validity) of the sentiment conveyed? While not quantified, we suggest that prior to the 1800s any wampum presented after a death had strongly financial functions. As such, the wampum became the personal property of the survivors. During the nineteenth century, when wampum seems to become less available, perhaps because of its trade value on the western frontier, the presentation of condolence wampum became more formal. In many cases these strings of wampum, the usual gift during that later period of the 1800s, were conserved. That is, the rarity of this ritual commodity led the community to create formal processes whereby the recipient was obliged to hold the wampum as if in a sacred trust, but to forward it to the heirs of the next person in the community to die. Thus the handing on of the condolence wampum was a trust shared within the community.

11

Discussion

We are not the first observers to recognize that the WDS emerged as part of the Midwinter Feast at some point around 1800. Beauchamp (1885: 235; 1888: 198; 1895: 198; cf. Tooker 1970: 102–103) recognized the WDS as a recent addition to midwinter rituals. Perhaps Beauchamp's 1892 summary says it best:

> "In its essential feature of sacrifice the white dog feast seems quite modern, but in point of time [season of the year] it corresponds with the old Dream Feast, taking its place and retaining some of its features."
>
> Beauchamp 1892: 85

Boyle (1898), Waugh (1916: 133), and Lloyd (1922: 261–263) all agreed with Beauchamp. Waugh had spent time from 1912 to 1915 among the Iroquois of Ontario, Quebec and New York, when the WDS was ending, but he, as those before him, must have read enough of the literature to reach a similar conclusion. Waugh believed the sacrifice to be a survival of earlier dog feasts, whereas we might call it an evolutionary transformation.

Lloyd (1922) listed the only eight references in which he could find any form of dog sacrifice anywhere in the Northeast that predated the period of Handsome Lake. Lloyd's listing includes a number of errors, but the overall pattern is the same. Dog sacrifice existed in forms that may be ancestral to what emerged after 1800. Several of these accounts also are mentioned in the Whipple Report (1889: 419, 425, 448; see under New York [State] Assembly). All of them have been summarized or detailed in this volume.

Reconstructing Origins: Why Two Dogs?

The very first known or prototypic WDS was reported by Kirkland in 1800. He noted the killing or sacrifice by strangulation of pure white dogs. Cord strangulation, often specified, does not mar or damage the pelt or skin, nor stain it with blood. Kirkland indicates that three dogs were killed, only two of which were cremated. Reports of the sacrifice of two dogs are common in early accounts. Fenton's recognition (1944: 161) that the offering of two dogs reflected the gifts of the moieties to the Creator, reflecting the roles of moiety divisions in these feasts, has been noted only by Tooker (1970: 41) but not pursued by other scholars. We've pointed out that Kirkland's account in 1800 clearly specifies that two wampum bands worn by the sacrificed dog, hung up to rot, represented the moieties of the Oneida. The decline in traditional Iroquoian kinship, and a shift to patrilineal descent, appears correlated with a loss of functional duality in each of these cultures. The sacrifice of a single dog may be one of the most evident indications of the decline in the kinship system with which Lewis Morgan, fortunately, became so concerned. The evidence for moiety participation in the early WDS is strongest in Kirkland's account, where we are not placing undue emphasis on the significance of cooking of two dogs. The number sacrificed may be another element of the rite that was improvised by the elders or reflects peculiarities of the situation of any specific year.

Two observations on native Iroquoian culture by outside observers (Sir William Johnson and later C. A. Hirschfelder) reveal aspects of overall stability in various implicit designs for living that should be considered here. Some basic elements of culture may have remained unchanged despite hundreds of years of European contacts. The earlier of these two observation dates from 1771, while the other is more recent; yet each reveals why small changes (or perhaps variations) within the culture can be irrelevant to the overall trajectory of change. In 1771 a letter written by Sir William Johnson and pointed out by William Starna (2008: 300) contains observations that reveal Sir William as a brilliant ethnographer. Sir William's observations of the differences in the customs and manners of the distinct tribes of the Five Nations are as follow:

> In all inquiries of this sort we should Distinguish between the more remote Tribes & those Ind[ns] who from having been next to our settlem[ts] for sev[l] years, & relying solely on oral Tradition for the support of their Ancient usages, have lost [a] great part of them, & have blended some with Customs [from] amongst ourselves, so as to render it Extremely

difficult, if not impossible to Trace their Customs to their origin or to discover their Explication.

Sir William, speaking of the Mohawk as the tribe nearest to the colonial settlements, emphasized that like the Onondaga, Cayuga, and others occupying lands farther from colonial settlements,

> "tho' they still retain many Ancient Customs, they are much at a Loss to account for them . . .".
>
> Sir William Johnson 1771

Sir William recognized not only influences from among the Dutch and English colonist but how much French Jesuits had come to influence the Mohawk. He was aware of differences in various cultural elements as they appeared among the Five Nations tribes and the relative effects of distance on culture change. In this compendium, we reveal that such differences are evident within the many reports of the WDS, both within a single tribe and also through the space occupied by several, but not all, of the Five Nations. The synthetic accounts produced by several twentieth-century scholars have, in effect, homogenized the differences and obscured the origins of each. A century ago, J. N. B. Hewitt (1917) reviewed three volumes relating to the Indians of New York State that had appeared over the previous decade. His critique and his ample corrections were directed mostly to Arthur Parker's work, the product of a native-descent scholar.

> Too much credence is placed in the authenticity of the so-called past wampum traditions, which are of course concerned with the activities of the 'Iroquois' settled at Caughnawaga and elsewhere on the St. Lawrence, Canada, and so have little bearing on the early history of the Five Nations of New York.
>
> Hewitt 1917: 432

Hewitt, echoing Sir William's remarks of more than a century earlier, was concerned with a number of inauthentic (post-1800) developments in native culture that were being promulgated as ancient traditions. Hewitt dispatched the idea that the founders of the League

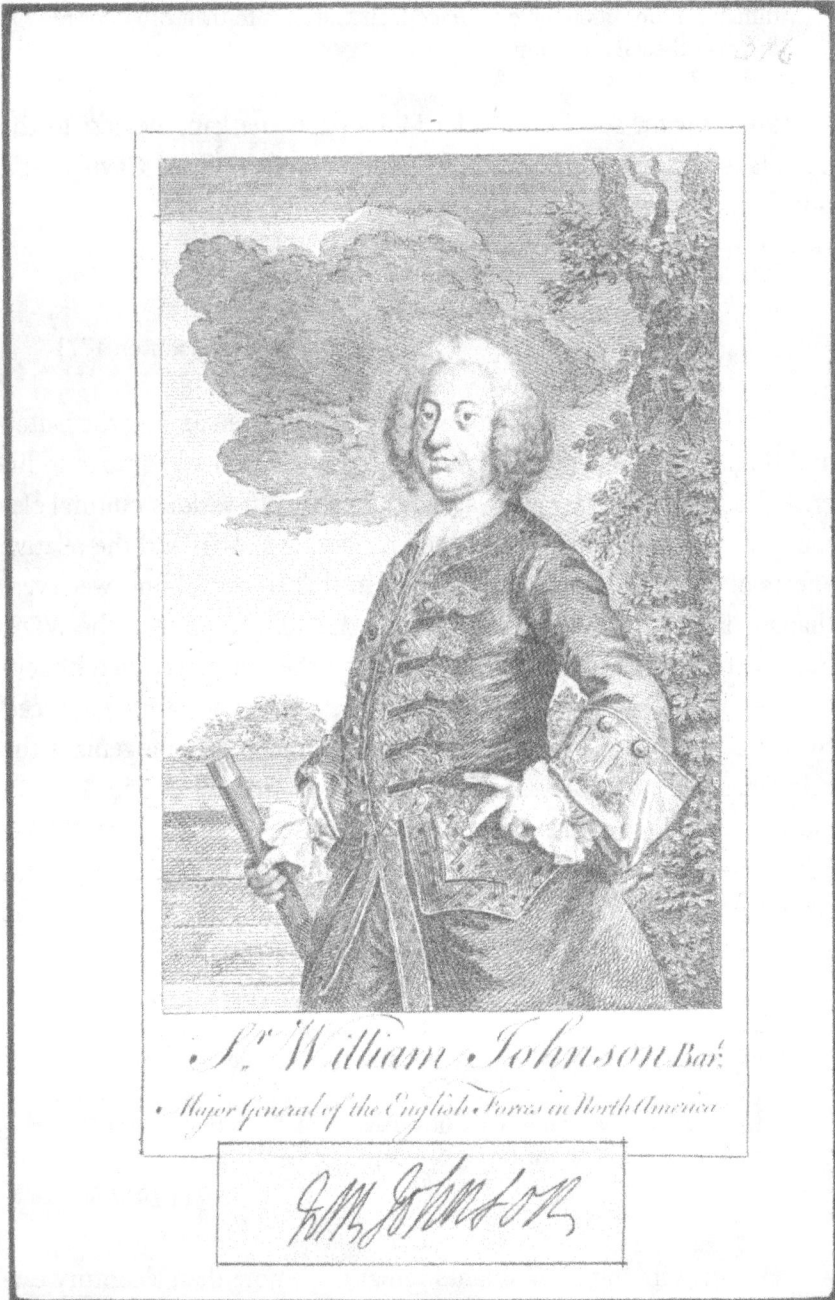

FIGURE 12: Sir William Johnson, superintendent of Indian Affairs in North America (c1715–1774)
Reference: Library and Archives Canada, Mikan no. 4313142.

knew anything at all about wampum (see Merriam 2010a, 2010b). Hewitt (1917: 433) recognized that "the great religious festivals all antedating the time of Handsome Lake are today still in vogue" in various locations. We may suppose that he was referring to the midwinter rites and other seasonal festivals in their general form but without accepting the WDS as an ancient ritual.

We believe that many fundamental cultural rules of hospitality and terminology were shared among the Five Nations and perhaps other traditional cultures in the Northeast. The basic cultural rules of hospitality have remained unchanged among descendants of traditionalists even if the modes of expression have become vastly different. More than 30 years ago, M. J. Becker passed some days living with a family of Oklahoma Delaware in Nowata, a village in the area of Bartlesville. During that period, MJB stayed with Henry and Belva Secondine. They simply opened their home, and together with many of their kin they graciously banqueted MJB during the entire visit. For these meals we returned thanks, but to whom remained unknown to MJB. By listening to the Secondines and others, MJB realized that the English term "feast" had specific ritual connotations. Secular dining was always a banquet, regardless of the quantity of food being shared—and it was always shared. They provided MJB with an excellent banquet three times each day, but probably no meal included dog. In fact, I do not recall anyone having a dog in the house. Since that visit, MJB noted that other cultures make similar distinctions when using terms from the English language. Of relevance here is C. A. Hirschfelder's description (1886b) of how the "Crees banqueted" him in Canada, nearly a century before Becker's trip to Oklahoma. Hirschfelder briefly described the Cree dog feast and how it differed from secular banqueting.

Hirschfelder's observation about eating dog meat during ritual meals is important and may relate to a dog sacrifice reported by John Cooper. Cooper vaguely reports hearing of a dog sacrifice at Albany, but never at Moose. Cooper (1933: 66, 90, 93) says that at times of stress "a type of dog sacrifice" is made to Vitico and "sometimes a dog is painted and killed" as a sacrifice. If the meat was not consumed, the sacrificial nature certainly sounds similar to the WDS. Rogers (1978:

764) reports a dog sacrifice among the southeastern Chippewa where the dog was bound and thrown into a stream.

Archaeological and ethnographic evidence for the ritual use of dogs and wolves in the entire Midwestern region is brilliantly surveyed by Robert Cook (2012). In his efforts to decode the meanings of archaeological data from Fort Ancient and other sites, he has assembled evidence remarkably parallel, but not demonstrably overlapping, with the information for the Iroquoian peoples presented here.

Because dogs were common if not ubiquitous among the many tribes of the Northeast, dog sacrifice might be expected to have developed among many native tribes through parallel and independent cultural processes. The ritual sacrifice of dogs, however, is very different from killing and eating them. True sacrifice involves the burning or abandonment of the carcass, and thus the loss of this significant protein source. Many of the tribes encountered by explorers Lewis and Clark hosted them with meals of dog, but these same people were reluctant to sell these valuable animals to them.

Traditional banqueting, with dog meat as a special treat, was common among various native peoples in North America. What is crucial to recognizing innovative aspects of the WDS is the use of the dog, or dogs, as ritual objects whose flesh is, in effect, sacrificed rather than being consumed. The ability to use such a large quantity of choice meat in a purely ritual manner speaks to an increase in the resource base of the participants. This would be particularly true in the winter or spring when most food resources traditionally were at their lowest. However, JL points out that winter hunting trips could produce significant amounts of meat. The Midwinter Feast also was reported as timed to a winter hunt.

Never discussed in any accounts of the WDS is the actual size of the dog or dogs that were sacrificed. In general, we presume that dogs eaten or used in the WDS were larger than a fox and smaller than a wolf. However, April Beisaw (personal communication, 27 March 2012) suggests "that Native Americans in the northeast had two 'breeds' of dogs" of which one was large and wolf-like and the other was much smaller" (see also Morey 2006). Artistic depictions of the WDS generally suggest that the dogs were of small to medium size, perhaps 50 cm (19 to 20 inches) tall and weighing about 10 to 15 kg (22–30 pounds). These drawings for illustrations, however, are not optimal sources of information for this subject. Dogs of smaller size would be more easily cremated and would cause less loss of meat. The sizes of dogs consumed at feasts are similarly unreported. Larger dogs yield more meat, but this may not have been a relevant factor in either feasting or sacrifice.

Dogs used for hunting often are valued for skill in tracking rather than ability to challenge the game. A good hunting dog would not be a candidate for a feast, regardless of size. Beisaw (2007) offers some data on the sizes of dogs found in archaeological contexts in New York based on tooth measurements. Her taphonomic studies reflect the common use of dogs for food, but Beisaw also includes possible ceremonial contexts (Beisaw 2006; see also Handley 2000). We suggest that feasting people may have selected larger animals, whereas the WDS may have utilized smaller canines. Bones of four wolves (Canis lupus) have been found at a Susquehannock archaeological site in Pennsylvania dating to 1600–1625 (Guilday et al. 1962: 61), and wolf mandibles are part of surviving Susquehannock artifacts of that same period (Becker 2011a, 2012a).

Despite finds of wolf bones at Susquehannock sites and the use of wolf mandibles in the construction of some artifacts, there has never been a missionary or other account of dog sacrifice among these people. Although Susquehannock villages were destroyed and the peoples scattered by the Five Nations by 1675, we have no evidence for anything approaching dog sacrifice. This is another piece of evidence, negative as it may be, that none of the Iroquoians were conducting a WDS prior to the end of the eighteenth century.

William Beauchamp made numerous brilliant observations that have contributed enormously to our understanding of various Iroquoian cultures. Beauchamp (1888: 203, n1) listed and reviewed more than a dozen accounts of the WDS, including that which was written by Samuel Kirkland during his work among the Oneida.[18] Despite the inclusion of Kirkland's account in his inventory, Beauchamp concluded that "[t]he Onondagas and Senecas only seem to have observed this feast" (Beauchamp 1888: 203, n1). We have now gathered all of the known firsthand accounts of the WDS and have confirmed the limited distribution of this ritual.[19] Beauchamp's careful review should have been better known to anthropologists of the twentieth century. The present review also points out specific details commonly lost in the many synthetic accounts that fill the post-1900 literature (e.g., Wallace 1970, see above).

We cannot yet confirm that Handsome Lake introduced to the Seneca various rituals involving the sacrifice of a white dog connected with ideas regarding forgiveness of sins, but his message facilitated the acceptance of rituals relating to sin and forgiveness. These Christian-influenced ideas developed simultaneously or spread to the Onondaga, but no further to the east. The innovations that entered the rites of the Midwinter Feast are derived from Catholic concepts of sin and redemption. The concept of sin and the sacrifice of a white dog appeared during the period when efforts were being made to revitalize some of the Five Nations Iroquois cultures in the aftermath of the Revolutionary War. This was an interval that Susan Johnston (personal communication, 3 October. 2011) identifies as a period of accelerated change, during which external events trigger episodes of rapid cultural change. The many variations on the theme of the WDS, as demonstrated, were recognized long ago, as was the limited distribution of these changes.

The late Cath Oberholtzer (personal communication, June 2008), and many others, pointed out that the concept of sin and rituals to remove sin are Christian concepts. Sacrifice to carry away sins of believers is an introduced idea, distinct from any religious form relating to any of the Five Nations or other known horticultural peoples. Horticulturalists are strongly propitiatory in their rituals. As indicated by the Jesuit commentary, traditional Iroquoian "prayers" involved supplication or propitiation, not a request for absolution from sins committed. The Christian elements in Handsome Lake's "Good Word" entered into the beliefs system of some Seneca at a time when they were deliberately trying to shift away from traditional subsistence systems and toward European style agriculture. But for a single word we agree with Tooker that

> "the reforms introduced by Handsome Lake merely adapted Iroquois religion to changed conditions. They did not change the basic structure of the Iroquois religion and belief systems."
>
> Tooker 1970: 3

We find that Tooker's use of the word "merely" underestimates the significant cognitive shift involved in the acceptance of sin and how this view influenced other aspects of the culture of those who became followers of this new native view of the world. Tooker (1970: 139–140) expends considerable effort to deny that the sacrificed dogs carried sins away. Tooker was familiar with the Newtown Long House at Tonawanda. The Sand Hill Long House at Tonawanda was defunct by the 1870s. She may have decided that Morgan reported on the Sand Hill customs because they differed from what she was told in the 1950s at Newtown.[20] She uses the differences between Morgan's reporting and her findings from a second Long House to explain differences in behaviors, in effect denying that there had been "changes in the Midwinter ceremonial" itself (Tooker 1970: 143). This denial of culture change from the 1850s to the 1950s reflects Tooker's belief that the WDS is an ancient rite.

The impact of Iroquoian culture change around 1800 on the shifts of gender roles and other aspects of society were considerable. In this process of change, we propose that there developed a syncretism between the confessions of sin to the Maker and the validating properties of wampum sent with the white dog. The act of confession plus the attachment to the sacrificial dog of confessional strings of white wampum would be appropriate aspects of the rituals that related to the WDS in the period after 1800.

In most of the accounts of the WDS, the activities involving the rituals occur from late in January or in February, long after the actual winter solstice but during the period identified by Iroquoians as midwinter. Speck and General (1995: 49) report on the timing of the midwinter rites of the Cayuga, among whom there has never been any mention of a WDS. The timing of these events provides an interesting demonstration that these midwinter activities were the products of peoples practicing a very low level of horticulture rather than an agricultural subsistence system. Agrarian economies tend to generate complex calendar mechanisms, recognizing and often celebrating solstices and equinoxes. The very timing of the WDS reflects the degree to which these tribes utilized maize production as a supplement to an extensive foraging strategy. Lewis Henry Morgan, of course, recognized aspects of these economic systems in his prototypic classification of what might be called "societal evolution."

Notable to this research is the recognition of various elements that were *not* associated with the WDS in any of the reports. Alcohol use is entirely absent from all of the many ceremonies of the WDS described here, as would be expected in rituals derived from the teachings of Handsome Lake. In one case, sugar and tobacco are brought as gifts by outsiders, but alcohol is nowhere involved. While those hostile to native traditions often note "senseless drumming and dancing" (Titley 1986: 162), drumming is not specifically noted in these reports, although music and dancing is often mentioned. The absence of alcohol from the WDS could suggest that these rituals reflect new directions in traditional cultural behaviors; changes that began around 1800 CE and were parts of an acculturative process still developing by the end of that century. In the 1890s there remained a great range of vibrant native cultures throughout Canada, despite some significant attempts to repress them. Section 114 of the Indian Act adopted universally in Canada in 1895 proscribed a number of traditional behaviors known among several of the tribal populations. These included "arm-biting" and "also applied to the dog feast and [to] rites of some coastal Tribes" (Titley 1986: 166, also 207, n19). This may relate to Shimony's (1994: 185) unreferenced mention of efforts by the Canadian government to put "considerable pressure on the Longhouse to outlaw the burnings." The WDS may also have been targeted by laws prohibiting "the wounding or mutilation of the dead or living body of any human being or animal" (Titley 1986: 166), "crimes" punishable by two to six months in prison.

How significant were external pressures to the abandonment of dog sacrifice? The midwinter rites of the village-dwelling Iroquoians and other peoples appear to have attracted interest only among anthropologists, whereas the two tribes among whom dogs were sacrificed gained a great deal of attention. In addition, popular as well as anthropological interest in the WDS was sufficient to lead many serious scholars to believe that the Seneca and Onondaga examples were representative of all the Five Nations. From the earliest records the practitioners of the WDS graciously hosted outsiders who came to witness, if not to join the rituals. These visitors probably provided tacit support for the WDS rather than a source of pressure to abandon this sacrifice. The sacrifice itself seems to have replaced the eating of dogs, a cultural change that has attracted no interest at all. The ultimate cessation of the dog sacrifice, like the dropping of dog from the diet among native people in general, may have been as much a result of internal changes in attitudes toward pet dogs as external pressures by governments or neighbors. Increased wealth and available beef throughout North America may have ended demand for dog as human food. As dogs became pets among native peoples, attitudes toward their sacrifice seem to have changed.

As dog sacrifice exited from the rituals of two Iroquoian peoples, the wampum commonly used as ornament has taken on an increasing role in Indian identity. Since the 1950s, wampum has attained considerable status among many of the native peoples of the northeast, even among claimant groups for which there is no history of wampum use in diplomacy. Our research into the WDS began as an effort to define and clarify how, and if, wampum was used in rituals within the region where it once was a significant commodity (Becker 2013). Modern claims to the sacredness of all forms of wampum are no more than that—modern claims.

Conclusions

The nineteenth-century White Dog Sacrifice (WDS), a ritual documented from among only two of the Iroquoian Five Nations, represents a Christian-influenced addition to their midwinter feasting. The sacrifice of white dogs as well as the use of wampum as an optional ornament reflect innovations that emerged in parallel with the new Code of Handsome Lake (ca. 1735–1815), who was a major figure in Seneca history. At the end of the 1700s, the traditional consumption of dog meat as part of healing rites merged with the ritual sacrifice of dogs in bargaining with the spirits or forces (or gods) as part of a more specific ritual behavior. By 1800, the feasting on dog at various rituals and festive occasions had become, among some Iroquoian groups, transformed into a sacrifice of dogs in which the flesh of the victims was not consumed. Allowing all of a highly desirable meat to go uneaten represents a considerable transformation in cultural behavior. This new ritual reflected an improved economy in which the members could sustain a significant sacrifice of resources.

This review of all of the evidence relating to the WDS suggests that ritual consumption of dog meat during the midwinter festivities of the Seneca and Oneida, and to a lesser extent the Onondaga, were shifting after 1800 to become the more elaborate WDS. By 1830 a variety of elements in the sacrificial aspect of the Midwinter Feast had coalesced into a ritual that had become known as the WDS. Wampum was not always a part of this sacrifice, suggesting that when used, it served as an ornament rather than as a presentation to the Creator.

A critical element of this ritual is the cremation of the sacrificed dog, or dogs, with no intention to consume its flesh. This shift appears to have paralleled changes taking place in Iroquoian subsistence systems, from traditional foraging supplemented by low-level horticulture to a semi-agrarian pattern based on European agriculture. Perhaps the most significant aspect of the newly emerging WDS was the introduction of Christian concepts of sin and sacrifice to a religious system that did not incorporate such beliefs.

A possible Oneida origin for the WDS has been noted, but the classic WDS as associated with Handsome Lake was strongly noted among the Seneca at the far western margins of the Five Nations' range.

From there it spread only to other groups resident in the east of Seneca territory. The rite soon after was reported among the Onondaga.

The earliest indication of the use of wampum in the WDS began at the end of the decades when the exchange of diplomatic wampum was coming to an end, about 1830. This also was about the time that the last native "religious" or "ecclesiastical" wampum band was made and presented, in 1831. Of particular note is our discovery that wampum played no significant part in these midwinter rites before the 1850s, after which time it was more regularly incorporated as a part of the WDS

The sacrifice and cremation of one or more dogs, representing a loss of a significant quantity of very desirable meat, seems to have attracted disproportional outside attention to this aspect of the Midwinter Feast. Over the years the addition of ribbons, tobacco, wampum, and other notions to the sacrificed dogs increased the value of the goods that were communal offerings at midwinter. These items, representing the sins of the donors, appear to have masked the importance of the baskets into which they were placed. The baskets literally became the containers used to carry away the sins that were burned while the dogs served as messengers. Hewitt revealed how strings of wampum were used to validate the messages, each message being a confession of sins. The means of collecting small items from the participants, as representations of their sins from the past year, was often overlooked by observers and has not been presented in detail in this collection. Some reports indicate that items were given as food (bread, vegetables, etc.) to be consumed as part of the feast, while other items were presented to be ritually burned. These details, and any cultural variations, have not been reported here. Our focus on wampum and the limited space available to reproduce these many direct observations in their entirety provide yet another avenue for research into the acculturative process. How these two tribes incorporated the concept of sin and the sacrifice of white dogs into their traditional feast cycle remains to be documented. The role of baskets, a traditional product that had become of economic importance among these peoples in the nineteenth century, appears significant in this process.

Did the value of the sacrificial goods donated by individuals increase? If donations revealed sins, participants would be hesitant to confess to significant quantities of contributions. Yet one might see the allocation of wealth to these activities as a form of ritual destruction that replaced the extensive burial offerings so well known from graves. Burial of a person's goods plus gifts presented by survivors formerly had been a significant means by which wealth was withdrawn from the Iroquoian villages. The increased use of resources needed for house construction and for sacrifice after the period around 1800 may be compared with archaeological evidence from earlier periods. We suggest that the nineteenth century saw a decline in burial offerings, reflecting a trend toward Christianization of belief. This process could be studied as a quantifiable process through archaeological research.

By the early 1900s the use of wampum in the WDS had ended, but not because these shell beads had become scarce. The end of wampum use in the WDS, and in general, reflects important changes in native material culture. The uses for wampum, which had been so important in diplomacy among the Five Nations Iroquois and many other people from around 1600 to 1800, shifted to new aspects of cultural behavior. Along with Christian religious elements, wampum entered into rituals where it had not previously existed. External interpretations of the WDS, with concerns for the sacrificed dogs and the destruction of valuables (cf. potlatches in the Canadian west), masked the cognitive significance of the baskets acting as vehicles for transporting sins. These innovations were among the many aspects of culture change among these native-descent peoples that marked accommodations to the complex society that was surrounding these traditional peoples.

Afterward

After this volume had gone into production, J. L. was notified that the canadiana.org database had recently added a number of obscure Canadian journals. Lainey's review of these provided some additional obscure newspaper accounts in which the White Dog Sacrifice (WDS) is mentioned. Being informed of this project, our colleague George Hamell also identified a series of references from American sources. Given the need to maintain a production schedule we are limiting our use of these recently discovered records to a brief comment rather than attempting to insert the individual notes into the text. Only one of these texts (Webster 1870) includes extensive details relating to the WDS, but it has limitations similar to those that we had previously associated with second-hand narrations, or what we have termed synthetic accounts.

The earliest of these newly discovered items (Anon. 1850a, 1850b) both report on a WDS that had first appeared in an 1850 issue of the Syracuse Journal; an issue that has yet to be located. The celebrants of that apparent Midwinter Feast were Onondaga, presumably resident in the area near Syracuse, New York. They were noted as "convoking the tribes of the several cantons." The WDS (burning of the dog) took place "Friday last" with the ninth and closing day being "Tuesday last" on which a "war dance" was held. The Midwinter aspects of this gathering are not detailed. The longer of these two versions (Anon. 1850a) emphasizes the installation of officers and adoption of individuals of "other nations, and occasionally white people, into the Onondaga nation." This particular Feast may have come to public attention only because it included the adoption of J. V. H. Clark, Esq. into the Wolf "tribe" (clan). He was given the name Go-yah-da Kae-nah-has. Only the year before Joshua Clark had published (1849) his detailed ethnographic account of the Onondaga in which he described a WDS that he had witnessed in 1841.

The longest and most complete account of a WDS among these newly found texts was published by Thomas Webster (1870). This Thomas Webster (1809–1901) was a Methodist clergyman born in Ireland, and not related to Oh-yah-do-ja-neh (Thomas Webster) of the Snipe Clan (Converse 1888: 84–85) or any of his native kin. Rev.

Webster had immigrated to Canada, married, and ultimately settled in Newbury, Ontario. The last two chapters of his long, serialized work in 1870 offer a brief ethnography of "[t]he pagans on the Grand River." Although he specifically mentions the Cayuga in his two opening paragraphs, the remaining five pages include no reference to any specific one of the Six Nations who had then been resident near Brantford, nor any of the other four or five native tribes living in that location. We suggest that he witnessed a Seneca WDS. Webster's 1870 publication states that he had "visited a modern pagan temple on the Grand River" some years earlier with the intent of witnessing a WDS but that he had arrived too late. His published account, though far from first hand, refers to events that we place around 1860, a period for which we have little evidence for any WDS. Thus this narration serves to suggest that the WDS continued to be held during this period, but that interest on the part of non-Native Canadians was low. The period of active suppression of Native rituals by the Canadian government had not yet begun.

The Rev. Webster had missed the ritual sacrifice but had, after the fact, met "the priest who had officiated at the recent festival" and through an interpreter heard an account of the events. Webster's valuable account of the "temple" and its forest location are presented as if they were first hand. Webster's account (1870: 26) reports that the dog was killed on the first day of the Feast and hung from a beam extending side to side at the middle of the house, along with a string of deer hoofs worn by "the officiating priest" during the dance. A turtle shell rattle is described in detail as are "a few dried pelts . . . made to assist in supplying music, they being pounded with sticks—by way of drums, probably" (Webster 1870: 27). The only other example of folded-hide drums known are attributed to the "Delaware." These details pertaining to the ritual objects that Webster actually saw are separated in his text from the account of the dog sacrifice that he states had been relayed to him by a translator.

Webster was told that on the last day of the feast, the actual length of which is not specified, at a time just before or at the rising of the sun, the dog is burned "at a convenient distance from" the "temple." The dog, adorned with ribbons and other small items, was said to convey the message from the people to the Great Spirit. While the dog is burning the attendees were permitted to "supplement their previous offerings" by throwing additional items into the fire (Webster 1870: 28). After the burning of the dog, "the fire and ashes are scattered about" (Webster 1870: 29). No mention was made of the scattering of household ashes that was so central to the renewal aspects of the Midwinter Feast. Webster's extensive account makes no mention of baskets or non-dog related aspects of this important event that we believe was part of the Seneca ritual calendar.

Two other brief published reports of the Midwinter Festival, both from the 1890s, reveal the transition away from the burning of dogs and the "substitution" of baskets as a center of the ritual. We believe that the significance of baskets had always been a central part of the Native ritual, but long overshadowed by the strangulation and burning of dogs. The use of baskets for the gathering of objects to be burned, or what we had concluded was the gathering of sins for a ritual offering, became the foremost aspect of the Midwinter Feast. An 1895 account of the New Year rituals from the Tonawanda Reservation makes no mention of the Seneca by name, but we infer that they were the principles in this event. The 1895 publication indicates that the Feast began on 30 January. One the first day "The Pagan Indians... William Poodry and George Hotbread were appointed to go through the town with corn husks braided around them ... each carrying a basket in which to receive whatever might be bestowed" (Anon. 1895). The items they collected were mostly offerings of tobacco. The scattering of household ashes began on the second day and continued for two or three days.

> "Early in the morning of the fifth day they burn Indian tobacco, using this instead of burning the white dog for a sacrifice. After this they dance what is called the peace dance. The sixth and seventh days they have games of chance and dances at night."
>
> Anonymous 1895

Apparently the festivities at this Feast lasted only seven days. This brief anonymous recounting provides a good summary of what seems to have been a very traditional Midwinter Feast.

A brief mention of the replacement of the Dream Feast by the White Dog Feast appears in another published account from the following year. The 1896 article is only a short pastiche, and it treats the Six Nations as if they formed a single entity. The length of the Feast ritual is given as "fourteen days; on the ninth day two white dogs were burned" (W. H. D. 1896). Aside from mentioning that the "False Faces . . . always opened the ceremonies" nothing of note is offered. The numbers 14 and nine do not correlate with any other reports we have collected and we believe that their use here derived from earlier publications, perhaps from one of the two anonymous accounts of 1850 recorded from among the Onondaga in which the ninth day is cited as the closing day.

The construction date of the log Onondaga longhouse (Council House) at Ohsweken on the Grand River Reserve is not known, but it must have been the location of the last WDS as well as the first Winter Feast at which only white baskets were burned. Hale (1885: 314) describes it as "about thirty-five feet long by twenty wide . . .". By 1898 a large longhouse had been erected nearby and the old log structure became a cookhouse (Spittal 1989: 362). Both buildings are seen in a photograph from 1898 (Boyle 1898: Pl. VI, Spittal 1989: Pl. 20). A listing of the various publications by Boyle and others that are related to the First Nations in Canada has been compiled by Charles Garrad (1987).

The newly located references to the WDS noted here provide readers with additional sources referring to this ritual. They confirm our original conclusion that the sacrifice of dogs appears to have ended by 1890, with the burning of baskets becoming the aspect of the ritual that continues to be used to atone for sins. These data led us to review the photograph added to Hale's 1885 publication by William Guy Spittal, the editor of the 1989 reprint (Spittal 1989). The photograph added as Plate 19, captioned "THE LAST BURNING OF THE WHITE DOG. Onondaga Longhouse, Ohsweken, c. 1931–33" is believed by Spittal to represent the last occasion on which a dog was actually sacrificed. While the warmly dressed onlookers seen in the photograph reveal a winter event, there is no clear evidence of a pyre or of a dog upon it. MJB perceives a large, steaming kettle tended by a man with a cup or mug in his hand. This may be a vat of food for the Midwinter Feast, or perhaps depicts a boiling down of maple syrup. It is not evidence of an actual dog sacrifice. It is, however, evidence of altered perceptions between the 59 years between 1931 and the publication of this photograph in 1989. In 1989 many of the elder adults, who may or may not have been present when this picture had been taken, may have recalled events of those earlier days. The caption indicates that some of the Onondaga people chose to remember having strong continuities with their ritual past; continuities that made linkages to events that they had not witnessed. Recall of events, recent or distant, as all public narrative is subject more to volition than to evidence.

The various dates of these recently identified accounts of the WDS indicate that the ceremonies had been conducted in some of the years for which we have no other records of the Feast. However, the addition of these reports to our coverage does not answer the question of how regularly the WDS was incorporated into the Midwinter Feast, or even how regularly each of the several Iroquoian peoples convened these rites. While the Webster account (1870) is silent regarding a specific nation, his mention of Cayuga in conjunction with what we believe to be a Seneca WDS brings up the possibility of conjoined rituals at which both Seneca and Onondaga, and perhaps individuals from other tribes, joined together to celebrate the Midwinter Feast. The evidence collected here reveals the importance of examining the complete record, and for specifying details of each event in order to understand process as well as culture in general. The writing of ethnography cannot generalize from one culture to another no matter how closely related they may be. Understanding the operating rules of any specific culture is a significant task when the participants are operating with only an outline of the ritual, and not a set script. Learning the grammar of their language and the many other rules of their culture is a task confronting every person born into the group. Entering from another cultural milieu, as does every anthropologist, presents a difficult challenge to understanding the rule system. While the task may be difficult, it is not impossible to master.

Appendix I

Beauchamp's Newspaper Clippings and the WDS

Within this text we have included several newspaper accounts in which the WDS is described. These are among the more extensive ethnographic reports available for these cultural events. William Beauchamp's massive data base (Beauchamp 1840) includes nine boxes filled with scrapbooks into which Beauchamp inserted cuttings from various newspapers. We have identified in these scrapbooks a total of six newspaper reports about the WDS, most if not all from among the Onondaga, published between the years 1878 and 1902. We list these six accounts here for scholars interested in Beauchamp's diligent amassing of information regarding the native peoples of New York.

Box	Volume	Years	Page	Title
31	2	1878–84	67	Burning the White Dog (see Anonymous 1884a)
3		1885–88	72	Curious Indian Customs (The Sacrifice of the White Dog at The Onondaga Reservation) (Possibly Converse 1888)
33	5	1893–94	29	Red Skins Reform (Burning of the White Dog and Other Barbarous Customs, Now Historic)
33	5	1893–94	30	Annual Feast of the White Dog
34	7	1897–1902	30	Onondaga White Dog Feast
			92	White Dogs Wait in Heaven for Masters. Such the Teaching to Which Pagan Indians at Reservation Listen When Blind Zealot Preaches Doctrines of Handsome Lake.

Appendix II

First Nations Aggregates in Canada

The Seven Nations of Canada, a post-Contact confederacy of First Nation peoples established along the St. Lawrence valley, enables us to consider how the classic study of within-village diversity conducted by Fredrik Barth (1993) in northern Bali applies to the interactions among the distinct peoples who were resident within the same immediate area, often identified as a single "village."

Villages of the Seven Nations of Canada included three occupied by Iroquois (Kahnawake, Kanesatake, Akwesasne), one occupied by Wendat-Huron (Lorette-Wendake), one by Algonquin (Pointe-du-Lac, Three-Rivers) and two where the residents came from among the Abenaki (Wolinak and Odanak), which is a collective term applied to those several Eastern peoples, such as the Penobscot and Pasamaquoddy, who had moved west. The village of Odanak also included Sokoki from inland New England, a people today commonly identified as Western Abenaki. The mission station at Kanesatake also included separate villages for the Algonquin and Nepissing, who maintained separate residential areas and dispersed into their respective hunting territories for half the year. (cf. Becker 2006).

The classic study of within-village diversity was conducted by Barth (1993) based on his research in northern Bali many years earlier. In that area, Bali-Hindu villages are interspersed with Islamic villages. All those economies are strongly agricultural, yet hierarchical structures are strong in some of these villages while others are egalitarian. The range of variation within the same general ecological situation is impressive and offers multiple models for how members from several cultures in residential proximity may interact.

Barth's observations of an egalitarian agricultural society also apply to the Tuscarora, who joined the confederacy of the Five Nations Iroquois about 1722. Uncertain at this time is whether these people were foragers or a low level horticultural people before this relocation. Becker suspects they were horticulturalists but there's no archaeological evidence to support this commonly accepted belief. Wallace (2009: 252) sees the "factionalism" or diversity within the Tuscarora as "a form of adaptation." This view provides better definition to Snyderman's

(1961) earlier observations that Iroquoian flexibility had similar implications for adaptation.

Also important to this study of the WDS is Wallace's observation (2009: 253) that "ignoring diversity is also a phenomenon worthy of attention in itself." In our quest to understand a specific culture we may work diligently to reconcile what seem to be contradictory themes and sets of conflicting information when these apparently opposite views may reveal the reality of differing perceptions within the group.

As among the villages of the Five Nations Iroquois in New York, each of the Canadian villages of First Nation peoples in the St. Lawrence valley may have held a considerable collection of wampum relating specifically to the political history of its own residents. The history and village composition of the Seven Nations of Canada, called by several different names, is equally complex. Today there is in Canada intensive ethnohistoric and archaeological research directed toward decoding the specific areas of residence of the specific tribes gathered in such multicultural villages. There are several good studies of the villages of the Seven Nations of Canada, and ethnographic studies as well (cf. Becker 2006a for the Lake of the Two Mountains). Less well-documented, the village of the Algonquin of Pointe du Lac at Three-Rivers also is the subject of considerable interest at this time. Since these villages have been continually occupied for several hundred years, archaeological investigations within each require careful planning. The results of recent work include an archaeological report for the old part of Wendake, and ongoing research at Odanak. Archaeological research within each of these communities provides clues that enable us to understand cultural dynamics within such residential aggregates as reported in the historical documents.

Endnotes

1. The arrival of the WDS reflects the post 1800 shifting of the locations of various groups of Seneca, Oneida, and Onondaga. The diplomatic wampum received by the Seven Nations of Canada (*Federation des Sept-Feux*; see Lainey 2004: 46–47) may have been held at Caughnawaga (Kahnawake) at Sault-St-Louis. The area called Kahnawake has moved at least three times before reaching its current location. This was the principal group within the complex assemblage of Canadian Haudenosaunee and other cultures.

   Kanesatake may have included three or four distinct villages or residential areas, together identified collectively as Iroquois. Akwesasne is the Mohawk village. Traditionally, these peoples all had been extensive users of diplomatic wampum. The use of wampum in diplomacy among the other peoples of the Seven Nations of Canada varied considerably.

2. Snyderman (1961: 576) confuses the sacrifice of the dogs, the offering of wampum, and other details found in a Jesuit Relation of 1655–1656 (Thwaits 1890, 42: 195–199) with rituals then connected to the New Year celebration. Snyderman's effort to link the post-1800 WDS to earlier events is unconvincing. He even confused the dates, claiming that the events as he described them took place in 1636. This is one of the more obvious examples of Snyderman's attempts to project the WDS back to a period long predating 1799.

3. The transformation of a ritual meal of dog flesh into the "blood" sacrifice of the WDS reflects a constellation of changes in these communities. As regards culture change, note should be made of the 2007 controversy regarding dog fighting as a sport in the United States. When this activity was widely reported in the press, most academics perceived this "sport" as cruel, while aficionados decried the pressure put on their traditional sporting activities. A long history of lethal competitions between animals or human and animal, as in bull fighting in Western Europe and elsewhere, can be documented as part of the history of "sport." We ought to consider that only recently have these blood sports become separated from a parallel religious activity—that of sacrificing living animals.

4. Wallace (1970) synthesized his account of the WDS from the two Jackson volumes (1830a,b) and his own field notes taken at Cold Spring (Allegheny Seneca group) in January and February of 1952. Wampum was not a part of the WDS or any other rituals described by Wallace, nor is wampum mentioned elsewhere in his study. Conversely, metallic ornaments are not associated with any of the accounts of the WDS that we have read.

When discussing an earlier account of the WDS (Anonymous 1872a) Beauchamp (1908: 326) reported that "Clark's circumstantial account (1841) differs widely from this, two dogs being burned at that time." Clark (1849) had made his observations in 1841, but some of his commentary appears to include information provided to him, possibly by Abraham La Fort using information from other examples. I suspect that Beauchamp's use of circumstantial events applies to what we here have defined as synthetic.

The late Cath Oberholtzer (personal communication, 9 June 2008) believed that it is possible that a WDS did take place at the green corn season (late in August) and possibly at Pentecost or other times during the year besides the Midwinter Feast. We believe that feasting on dog meat may have been part of rituals at any season but find no support for the idea that a WDS took place other than at the midwinter ceremonies. Not a single record of a WDS other than at midwinter has been documented (see Fenton 1936, 1941). Speck and General (1995: 20–29) specifically distinguish, among the Cayuga, between winter rituals considered part of male activities and summer harvesting ceremonies that were in the realm of women. Women did not sacrifice dogs.

5. The changes taking place among the Seneca and other Iroquoians around 1800 indirectly led to a changed perception of the lifestyles and cultures of the Aboriginal Lenape in southeastern Pennsylvania. Halliday Jackson was a Quaker missionary to the Seneca around 1800. His role in creating an erroneous view of the foraging Lenape of southeastern Pennsylvania is a narrative only recently revealed. Many bands of the foraging Lenape, the aboriginal native people of the Philadelphia region (Becker 2006b), had

left the Delaware Valley by the 1660s to become involved in the pelt trade (Becker 2011b). Between 1681 and 1701 (Kent 1979), they returned home for short stays only to join other bands in selling all of their traditional lands. The traditionalist bands remaining in Penn's colony had their locations of residence exempted from these sales of the period 1682–1701. Regardless, all the traditionalist bands had left by 1740. Other individual Lenape simply merged into the colonial population.

By the early 1800s those individuals or small groups of Lenape who had remained behind were aging and dying (Becker 1990), as were those elder colonists who had actually seen the warm weather fishing encampments and lifeways of these native people. By 1810, no one living in the Delaware Valley had a firsthand view of life as it actually was lived by the Lenape of the Delaware Valley. Halliday Jackson's books (1830a, 1830b) described "contemporary" Indian lifestyle, but not that of the *Lenape*. Jackson's "Indians" were the acculturating Seneca living near Lake Erie at that time. The erroneous belief created by Jackson's works included the idea that the Lenape lived in large palisaded villages and practiced maize horticulture. This view persisted among scholars as well as a naïve public for more than 150 years, despite the documentary record and the failure of archaeologists to locate any supposed Lenape "villages" (cf. Becker 2006c). MJB was surprised to learn at a conference in October 2012 that Jackson's portrayal persists not only in the public mind but also among many historians and a surprising number of anthropologists. Prior to the development of the popular myth that all Indians rode horses and hunted bison, which emerged after the 1870s, popular mythology perceived all Indians as living like the Five Nations Iroquois.

6. Tooker (1970: 134) inserts a line into the Osgood account, but her source for this is unknown, or may be an error. Tooker says that corn [maize] is placed "in a basket carried by an aged female" (see also her page 138). Earlier (1970: 116), Tooker had distorted the 1800 Kirkland account and placed it in the latter part of the

eighteenth century in order to give greater age to the WDS than the evidence supports.

7. Reports that the body of the dog had been suspended from a pole for some days before being cremated are in contrast to those reports stating that the killing and burning took place on the same day. These variations in timing may reflect aspects of the evolution of this ritual as well as variations among the several practicing communities. More significant in our review of the WDS is that most reports of this ritual indicate that the bodies of the dogs were suspended from poles. Oberholtzer notes that poles were important in both Iroquoian and Algonquian rituals. Individual trees, such as the Iroquois Great Pine, and prepared poles were considered to be cosmic axes (Oberholtzer 1986). Sun disk wands as well as scalps often were suspended from naturally colored (debarked?) poles, or from poles that had been painted red. Oberholtzer believes that a sun disk wand with a white dog depicted on the reverse was reported around 1915 on the Six Nations Reserve in Canada. This may relate to a ceremonial cane from the Six Nations Reserve, Brantford. That account has a string of black and white wampum attached and a dog figure carved on it (cf. Beauchamp 1895: 316). The cane, dated 1800s–1915, is curated in the Canadian Museum of Civilization, Gatineau (Object III-I-1068a-b).

A possible relationship with the pole used to suspend the dog or dogs in some versions of the WDS can be seen in Hale's (1883: 127) list of activities following a death. Number 27 on Hale's list directs mourners to "suspend a pouch upon a pole, and will place in it some mourning wampum—some short strings—to be taken to the place where the loss was suffered."

Oberholtzer (1986) described an Iroquoian sun disk wand with an anthropomorphic face, specific tribe not known, on the back of which a white dog is incised (Canadian Museum of Civilization CMC-III-I-401). No mention of such wands appears in any of the account of the WDS, and the decoration on this wand may be incidental to its use and to the WDS.

8. Seneca pronouns do distinguish gender. Professor Wallace Chafe (personal communication, 16 July 2008) notes that Seneca pronouns appear as pronominal prefixes attached to verbs. The sex of the white dog is seldom specified in the English language accounts and may not have been relevant. Jackson's 1799 account specifically notes a male dog. Oberholtzer suggests that paintings on dogs may have been intended to achieve equality between male and female dogs.

9. Tooker's studies in the 1950s reached conclusions remarkably similar to those published by Fenton in 1936. She agrees with Fenton that no Seneca then alive had ever seen a WDS, but that the Cold Spring Seneca agreed that the burning took place on the fifth to seventh day (Tooker 1970: 73). According to Tooker (1970: 76–78), the Sour Springs Seneca "Anciently" burned the dogs on the fourth day. We believe that her reports reflect both flexibility and the irrelevancy of specifying a specific day in the midwinter rituals for the killing and/or burning of the sacrificial dog.

10. Tooker (1970: 161–169) presents Clark's entire account as an appendix to her review, but she neglected to refer to it in her index.

11. Snyderman (1961: 590) incorrectly reports that Beauchamp had observed the WDS ceremony at Onondaga in 1894, and that wampum was no longer being used as part of this ceremony. Beauchamp's statement, however, may reflect a hiatus in the use of wampum or simply a single case in which no wampum was seen or used. We also suspect that Beauchamp was annoyed to learn that Converse had seen a WDS in 1888, perhaps the last one held.

12. Kirkland's long residence at a major Oneida village is generally credited with influencing many of the Oneida people, as well as some of the newcomer Tuscarora in their villages, to support the American rebels in their War for Independence. Most of the entire career of the Reverend Kirkland was focused among the Oneida in the area of central New York. He eventually founded Hamilton-Oneida Academy, now Hamilton College, where his important

records of Oneida life and culture change are among his papers. Dr. Christine Sternberg Patrick's research (e.g., 2009) reveals the extent of Kirkland's records and the many copies of his journals made for various sponsoring organizations. Her research also suggests that during this period of Kirkland's residence there were no Mohawk residents among the Oneida (personal communication, April 2012). This leads us to believe that "one of the professed Pagans" noted by Kirkland on 22 August was a traditionalist Oneida and not a Mohawk as MJB had thought.

13. Also of interest is Samuel Kirkland's use of the Oneida term that Pilkington offers as "gyanse." The following, with limitations on our use of the characters to represent Oneida language, provides an excellent explanation of this term. We had previously inferred that matrilineal cousins were suggested or more generally, "close kinsmen," but Chafe provides excellent clarification.

> "This verb base is used to refer to matrilineal cousins, but also (and frequently in ceremonial usage) to members of the opposite moiety. Thus *agá:'se:'* 'we (exclusive dual) are cousins', *já:'se:* 'we (inclusive plural) are cousins', *yá:'se:'* 'they (dual) are cousins . . .'"
>
> Wallace Chafe (personal communication, 16 June 2013)

Karin Michelson (personal communicatino, 26 February 2013) identifies the contemporary Oneida word for "gyanse" as "kya:se, which means Cousin! (see Michelson and Doxtater 2002). Clifford Abbott (personal communication, 26 February 2013) identifies "gyanse" as the "direct address term for cousin." Michael Foster compares Pilkington's transcription of "gyanse" to Cayuga "oⁿkya'se:'," translated as "we two are cousins" (also see the Seneca term, in Chafe 1967: 37, #12). Woodbury (2003) provides related Onondaga terms.

14. Sciulli and Purcell (2011) discuss dog burials from central Ohio that date from 4,000–5,000 BP (Early Archaic) and provide references to many others. No cultural continuity between these Archaic period behaviors and those of the Late Prehistoric Monongahela peoples is implied.

15. Today it remains unclear exactly how many wampum strings, bands, and other artifacts incorporating wampum are held within the ancient center of their diplomatic use; the region we identify as the Core Area (Becker 2013). The wampum now held by the Oneida Indian Nation, Inc. (OIN) consists almost entirely of examples purchased recently (Becker 2007a, 2007b). Study of the wampum now owned by the OIN has raised several questions regarding the once extensive holdings of bands and strings by natives and colonials alike within the area of present New York State. These studies explore how wampum bands and strings were used prior to 1800 and reveal significant changes that took place around that date.

16. The late Cath Oberholtzer (personal communication, 9 June 2008) had made the interesting suggestion that the wampum might have had meaning greater than simple ritual ornamentation or for the dog's use in delivering a message. The adornment of a dog might be interpreted as the dog being "given" a string of wampum in condolence for its death, and not as an offering as part of an effort to remove sins. The late date during which wampum was first associated with these rituals and the late introduction of wampum strings to the rituals associated with confession support her idea.

17. Snyderman (1961: 607) suggested that the wampum objects associated with post-Handsome Lake rituals were "old" belts and strings that "are now associated with the religion" and kept at Tonawanda in the 1950s. His belief in the supposed presence of wampum belts and wampum strings, deemed "sacred" and not to be viewed by outsiders, is another of Snyderman's personal and biased ideas that is contradicted by his own data sets. Had any collection of belts and strings been held at Tonawanda, the loss of a small string of wampum used in confession rituals would not have become such an issue. Its replacement required a major effort that extended beyond the community.

    Snyderman made the unlikely suggestion (1961: 590) that the ceremony faded away because wampum became rare. Loose wampum beads continued to be plentiful at least into the 1950s

(Einhorn 1974). In the post-1950 revitalization period, loose beads became valuable for various purposes, including the construction of replica wampum bands. Most of the replica "wampum" bands of late date are fashioned from glass beads or from a wide range of other materials. Reports of bands recently (post-1995) fashioned from real wampum cannot be verified.

18. Of note is Beauchamp's listing of only one supposed report of the custom from New England, as an occasional sacrifice, said to be in Mather's *Magnalia*. Since this would be the only account of the WDS in New England, the exception to the rule would be of interest. Becker scanned this volume (Mather 1702) for the reference that Beauchamp claimed to have seen, but without success. There is, in Mather's recounting of the captivity narrative of Hannah Swarton, captured near Casco Bay in May of 1690 and taken to Canada, note of eating "*Dogs flesh*" (Mather 1702, Book VI, Chapter II, p. 10). Mather's section on scapegoats, however (1702, Bk. VI, Chapter VII: 66), makes no reference to native parallels, a category into which the WDS would fall. Thus we believe that Beauchamp made an error in this aspect of his narration, and like the use of diplomatic wampum, the WDS never took place in New England (see Becker 2010).

19. Snyderman (1961: 589, n14) claimed that an undated report on the white dog "ceremony as witnessed by J. C. Starr 'some time ago'" appeared in *The Indian Moccasin* for February 1895. This publication, edited by Jeremiah Hubbard, began in Afton, Indian Territory (later Oklahoma) in 1893, but ceased publication in 1894. We have been unable to identify this report or to secure copies of this publication, but Lainey has tracked a microfilm source. We also have been unable to locate *The Barrie Examiner* for the month and year in which a relevant article is said to have appeared, although copies of this newspaper are held in several locations. A copy may be in Snyderman's papers at the APS (Series II: Newspaper Clippings).

Snyderman (1961: 589, n13) also cites a report by the Presbytery of Buffalo for 1889 as stating "that there 'had been no sacrifice of White Dogs . . . for the last 13 years [since ca 1876] and the superstitions are fast disappearing. . . .'" Whether this refers to a specific Onondaga group or the Onondaga in general is not certain.

20. Tooker's account of the midwinter festival at the Newtown Long House, nearest Tonawanda on the Cattaraugus Reservation, is based on reports by Parker (1913: 81–85) and Brush (1901: 67–69), both of which are synthetic accounts. Presumably she projects her belief that "anciently" the white dog was strangled on the first day and burned on the sixth (Tooker 1970: 52, 67–68).

Acknowledgments

Our sincere thanks are due to the late Cath Oberholtzer for her gracious sharing of information and for her many important suggestions regarding this work. Thanks also are due to Christine Sternberg Patrick and Kathryn L. Merriam for providing data from their research and for careful readings of earlier versions of this text. Thanks also are due Wallace Chafe for his input into various linguistic matters. The extremely insightful evaluations of two anonymous reviewers and Bernard Powell also are deeply appreciated.

Thanks also are due to Clifford Abbott, Leon Arredondo, H. Blau, Joy Bedo Chapman, Gary A. Chapman, Robert A. Cook, Angela Cookson, Arthur Einhorn, William Engelbrecht, Jennifer Fitzgerald, Michael Foster, Professor Kurt Jordan, Neal Kenney, Kevin McBride, Martha McCartney, Karin Michelson, Martin H. Murphy, Mary Lynn Rainey, Ruben E. Reina, Martha Sempowski, Fabien Tremblay, Dianne Wayman, Jane Weiss, Hanni Woodbury, and Daniel Yeh for their various useful contributions. Special thanks are due to Alan Mounier, Stephen Marvin, Gregory Lattanzi, and Kathleen Geesey for their important editorial efforts with earlier drafts of this manuscript, and to Richard Swain, Traci Meloy, and the entire library staff at the West Chester University. Thanks also are due to Vincent Lafond (Canadian Museum of Civilization) for his help in getting the picture of the longhouses.

The support of Dr. Lori Vermeulen (Dean of Arts and Science, West Chester University) and F. P. and M. E. Gillon enabled much information to be processed for this publication. Thanks also are due the U.S. Congress for the encouragement provided by the federal tax rules supporting research. The ideas expressed here and any errors of interpretation or presentation are, of course, solely the responsibility of the authors.

References

Aborigines' Committee. (1844). *Some Account of the Conduct of the Religious Society of Friends Towards the Indian Tribes . . . with a Brief Narrative of . . . the Civilization and Christian Instruction of the Indians.* London: Edward Marsh [for] The Aborigines' Committee of the Meeting for Sufferings.

Abrams, George. (1967). "Moving of the Fire: A Case of Iroquois Ritual Innovation." In *Iroquois Culture, History, and Prehistory: Proceedings of the 1965 Conference on Iroquois Research, Glens Falls, NY,* Elisabeth Tooker, ed., pp. 23–24. Albany: New York State Museum and Science Service.

Anonymous. (1850a). "Indian Council Extraordinary." The Spectator [New York City], 4 February: p. 3 (From the *Syracuse Journal*).

———. (1850b). "Indian Councils." *New Hampshire Sentinel* [Keene, NH], 7 February. Vol. LII (6): 2 (From the *Syracuse Journal*).

———. (1872a). "The Onondaga Indians" [From Photographs by Ranger and Austin]. *Harper's Weekly* XVI (No. 790, for 17 Feb.): 141–142.

———. (1872b). "Sacrifice of a White Dog by the Onondaga Indians." *New York Times,* From the *Syracuse Journal,* Jan. 18. Jan. 21, p. 4.

———. (1884a). "Burning the White Dog: A Sacrificial Ceremony by the Onondago Indians." *The New York Times,* Jan. 22, p. 3.

———. (1884b). GI-YE-WA-NO-US-QUA-GO-WA. Solemn and Impressive Ceremony of the Iroquois Indians. Sacrifice of the White Dog. THE MAIL (Toronto). Clipping on file, Library and Archives of Canada (LAC), Elliott Moses fonds [collections], MG30–C169, Vol. 2, file 1, "Scrapbook, 1858–1888" (assembled by Jonas Moses).

———. (1886). "Burning the White Dog." [Dateline: "Jamestown, [NY] Feb. 21"]. *New York Times,* Feb. 22 [Seneca at Cattaraugus; No page].

———. (1895). "Celebrating the Indian New Year. Curious Customs of the Pagan Indians on the Tonawanda Reservation." *New York Times,* 10 February, p. 24.

Applebome, Peter. (2012). "Farm Oddity Turns Out to Be Sacred. A White Bison Is Born in Rural Connecticut." *The New York Times.* July 16: A16–A17.

Barth, Fredrik. (1993). *Balinese Worlds.* Chicago: University of Chicago Press.

Beauchamp, William M. (1840–1944). William M. Beauchamp, Papers. Index to Scrapbooks of Newspaper Clipping. Boxes 31–39, New York State Library, Albany.

———. (1879). "Wampum belts of the Six Nations." *The American Antiquarian* 2 (3): 228–230.

———. (1885). "The Iroquois White Dog Feast" [Onondaga]. *American Antiquarian and Oriental Journal* 7: 235–239.

———. (1888a). "Onondaga Customs" [in New York]. *Journal of American Folk-Lore* 1 (3): 195–203.

———. (1888b). "Onondaga White-Dog Feast." Letters to the Editor. *Science* 12 (No. 285, 20 July): 36.

———. (1889). White Dog Feast. *Journal of American Folk-Lore* 2 (5): 160.

———. (1892). *The Iroquois Trail, or, Foot-Prints of the Six Nations in Customs, Traditions, and History, in which are included David Cusick's Sketches of Ancient History of the Six Nations.* Fayetteville, New York: H. C. Beauchamp, Recorder Office.

———. (1895a). "Onondaga Notes" [White Dog Feast]. *Journal of American Folk-Lore* 8 (30): 209–216.

———. (1895b). "An Iroquois Condolence." *Journal of American Folk-Lore* 8 (30): 313–316.

———. (1901). "Wampum and Shell Articles Used by the New York State Indians." *Bulletin of the New York State Museum*, Number 41, Vol. 8. Albany: University of the State of New York.

———. (1908). *Past and Present of Syracuse and Onondaga County New York from Prehistoric Times to the Beginning of 1908.* New York and Chicago: The S. J. Clarke Publishing Company.

——— (Arranger and Editor). (1916). *Moravian Journals Relating to Central New York 1745–1766.* Syracuse: Dehler Press. [Reprinted 1976 by AMS Press, New York].

Becker, Marshall Joseph. (1975). "Moieties in Ancient Mesoamerica: Inferences on Teotihuacan Social Structure. Parts I and II." *American Indian Quarterly* 2: 217–236, 315–330.

———. (1980). "Wampum: The Development of an Early American Currency." *Bulletin of the Archaeological Society of New Jersey* 36: 1–11.

———. (1990). "Hannah Freeman: An Eighteenth-Century Lenape Living and Working Among Colonial Farmers." *Pennsylvania Magazine of History and Biography* 114: 249–269.

———. (2001). "The Vatican Wampum Belt: An 1831 Example of an 'Ecclesiatical-Convert' Belt and a Typology and Chronology of Wampum Belt Use." *Bollettino—Monumenti, Musei e Gallerie Pontificie* XXI: 363–411.

———. (2002). "A Wampum Belt Chronology: Origins to Modern Times." *Northeastern Anthropology* 63: 49–70.

———. (2004). "A Penobscot Wampum Belt in the Vatican Museums: A Possible Nineteenth Century Example of Native American Diplomacy." *Bollettino—Monumenti, Musei e Gallerie Pontificie* XXIV: 225–270.

———. (2005a). "Cremations in Five Hut Urns in the Museo Gregoriano Etrusco: Implications for Iron Age Cultural Diversity. In Mandolesi, Alessandro, *Materiale protostorico: Etruria et Latium Vetus.* Cataloghi/ Museo gregoriano etrusco, 9, pp. 485–495. Rome: "L'ERMA" di Bretschneider.

———. (2005b). "Penobscot Wampum Belt Use during the 1722–1727 Conflict in Maine." In *Papers of the Thirty-Sixth Algonquian Conference*, H. C. Wolfart, ed., pp. 23–51. Winnipeg: University of Manitoba.

———. (2005c). The Human Skeletal Remains. Appendix A. In Sweetman, Rebecca, *Knossos Medical Faculty Site* [KMF '78]: *Late e Antique Graves and Other Remains, pp. 370–383. The Annual of the British School at Athens* 100: 331–386.

———. (2006a). "The Vatican 1831 Wampum Belt: Cultural Origins of An Important American Indian Artifact and Its Meaning as the Last 'Ecclesiastical Convert' Belt." *Bulletin of the Archaeological Society of New Jersey* 61: 79–134.

———. (2006b). "Anadromous Fish and the Lenape." *Pennsylvania Archaeologist* 76 (2): 28–40.

———. (2006c). "Foragers in Southern New England: Correlating Social Systems, Maize Production and Wampum Use." *Bulletin of the Archaeological Society of Connecticut* 68: 75–107.

———. (2007a). "Studying Wampum: A Visit to the Oneida Indian Nation." *Susquehanna River Archaeological Center* newsletter 3 (3): 1–3, 6.

———. (2007b). "Wampum Held by the Oneida Indian Nation, Inc. of New York: Research Relating to Wampum Cuffs and Belts." *The Bulletin: Journal of the New York State Archaeological Association* 123: 1–18.

———. (2007c). "Unique Huron Ornamental Bands: Wampum Cuffs." *Material Culture Review* 66: 59–67.

———. (2008a). "Small Wampum Bands Used by Native Americans in the Northeast: Functions and Recycling." *Material Culture* 40 (1): 1–17.

———. (2008b). "Wampum on the Fringe: Explaining the Absence of a post-1600 CE Native-Produced Commodity in Delaware." *Bulletin of the Archaeological Society of Delaware* 45 (2012, New Series); 23–36.

———. (2010). "Wampum Use in Southern New England: The Paradox of Bead Production without the Use of Political Belts." In *Nantucket and Other Native Places: The Legacy of Elizabeth Alden Little*, E. S. Chilton and M. L. Rainey, eds., pp. 137–158. Albany, New York: SUNY Press with the Massachusetts Archaeological Society.

———. (2011a). "Important Illustrations of Susquehannock Material Culture: A Review of 'A Glimpse of the World Non-European in Skokloster Castle,' edited by E. Westin Berg (2006)." Norrköping, Sweden: Pressgrannar AB. Skokloster-studier Nr. 37 (Skokloster Studies 37). *The SRAC Journal (Susquehanna River Archaeological Center)* 7 (1): 1–3.

———. (2011b). "Lenape Culture History: The Transition of 1660 and its Implications for the Archaeology of the Final Phase of the Late Woodland Period."
Journal of Middle Atlantic Archaeology 27: 53–72.

———. (2012a) "Susquehannock Material Culture Revisited: Eight Pennsylvania
Ethnographic Artifacts in the Skokloster Castle Collection in Sweden and
a Possible Connection to Capt. John Smith." *Pennsylvania Archaeologist* 82
(1): 66–73.

———. (2012b). "Two Penobscot Wampum Bands in Florence, Italy: Origins
and Functions of One Subset of Bias Woven Artifacts." *International Journal
of Anthropology* 27 (4): 233–274.

———. (2012c). "Wampum Chronology: An Update on the Origins and Varied
Uses of a Native American Commodity." *Bulletin of the Archaeological Society
of Connecticut* 74: 47–66.

———. (2013). "Wampum Bags and Containers from the Native Northeast."
Material Culture 45 (1): 21–48.

———. (In review, A). Wampum Keepers. *American Indian Culture and Research
Journal*.

———. Manuscript A, "A wampum basket from New England." In circulation.

———. Manuscript B, "Wampum Crowns and Cuffs: Two Rare Categories of
Woven Wampum Bands." Manuscript on file, West Chester University of
Pennsylvania.

———. Manuscript C, "Ashes to Caches: Is 'Dust' Dust among the Ancient Maya?"
Manuscript on file, West Chester University of Pennsylvania.

———. Manuscript D, "Who Held the Wampum in the 17th Century Native
Communities!" Manuscript in circulation.

Becker, Marshall J. and Jonathan Lainey. (2004). "Wampum Belts with Initials
and/or Dates." *American Indian Culture and Research Journal* 28 (2): 25–45.

———. (2008). "Wampum and the White Dog Ceremony: Preliminary Notes on
a Ritual Use for This Specific Type of Shell Beads." *Newsletter of the Archaeological Society of New Jersey* 219 (January): 3–6.

Bieder, Robert E. (1980). "The Grand Order of the Iroquois: Influences on Lewis
Henry Morgan's Ethnology." *Ethnohistory* 27 (4): 349–361.

Biesaw, April M. (2006). "Deer, Toads, Dogs, and Frogs: A New Interpretation
of the Faunal Remains from the Englebert Site, Tioga County, New York."
Northeast Anthropology 72 (Fall): 1–23.

———. (2007). Osteoarchaeology of the Englebert Site: Evaluating Occupational
Continuity through the Taphonomy of Human and Animal Remains. Ph.D.
thesis, State University of New York at Binghamton.

Blau, Harold. (1964). "The Iroquois White Dog Sacrifice: Its Evolution and Symbolism." *Ethnohistory* 11 (2): 97–119. [Article noted in *Anthropos* 59 (5/6): 945].

———. (1969). *Calendric Ceremonies of the New York Onondaga.* Doctoral dissertation in Anthropology, The New School for Social Research, New York City [c. 1970]. University Microfilms International, Ann Arbor, Michigan.

———. (1972). *Harold Blau Collection of Onondaga Songs and Spoken Word* (1956). Nine tape reels, American Folklife Center. Library of Congress, Washington, DC.

Boyle, David. (1898). "Pagan Iroquois." *Annual Archæological Report, being part of APPENDIX to the Report of the Ministry of Education Ontario.* Vol. 13: 54–196. Toronto: Warwick Brothers and Rutter for the Legislative Assembly. [Available online].

———. (1900a). "Ontario: Religion. The Paganism of the Civilised Iroquois of Ontario." *The Journal of the Anthropological Institute of Great Britain and Ireland* 30: 46–47.

———. (1900b). "Music of the Pagan Iroquois" [Seneca]. *Annual Archæological Report for 1899, being part of APPENDIX to the Report of the Ministry of Education Ontario.* Vol. 15. Toronto.

———. (1902). "On the Paganism of the Civilized Iroquois of Ontario." *Annual Archæological Report [for] 1901, being part of APPENDIX to the Report of the Ministry of Education Ontario.* Vol. 16, pp. 115–125. Toronto: L. K. Cameron.

Brébeuf, Jean de. (1896). "Relation of what Occurred among the Hurons in the Year 1635." *Jesuit Relations and Allied Documents.* Vol. VIII, Reuben Gold Thwaites, ed. Cleveland: Burrows Brothers.

Brinton, Daniel G. (ed.). (1885). *The Lenâpé and their Legends.* Philadelphia: D. G. Brinton.

Browne, William H. (ed.) (1890). "Proceedings of the Council of Maryland, 1687/8–1693." *Archives of Maryland,* Vol. VIII. Baltimore: Maryland Historical Society.

Bruce, Dwight Hall. (ed.) (1896). *Onondaga's Centennial: Gleanings of a Century.* Vol. II. Boston: Boston History Company.

Brush, Edward Hale. (1901). *Iroquois, Past and Present.* Buffalo, New York: Baker, Jones and Company.

Buckingham, James Silk. (1841). *America, Historical, Statistic, and Descriptive.* Three volumes. London: Fisher.

Butler, Eva L. and Wendell S. Hadlock. (1949). Dogs of the Northeastern Woodland Indians. Bulletin, *Massachusetts Archaeological Society* 10 (2): 17–35.

C., A. F. and I. C. C. (1900). Record of American Folk-Lore. *Journal of American Folk-Lore* 13 (49): 135–145.

Campbell, William W. (1831). *Annals of Tryon County, or, The Border Warfare of New York during the Revolution*. New York: J. and J. Harper.

Campisi, Jack and William A. Starna. (1995). On the Road to Canandaigua: The Treaty of 1794. *American Indian Quarterly* 19 (4): 467–490.

Caswell, Harriet S. (1834–?) (1892). *Our Life Among the Iroquois Indians* [Seneca]. Boston: Congregational Sunday-School and Publishing Company.

———. (2007). *Our Life Among the Iroquois Indians* [Seneca]. Lincoln: University of Nebraska Press. Reissued with a new Introduction by Joy A. Bilharz.

Ceci, Lynn. (1978). "Watchers of the Pleiades: Ethnoastronomy among the Native Cultivators in Northeastern North America." *Ethnohistory* 24 (4): 301–317.

———. (1982). "The Value of Wampum Among the New York Iroquois: A Case Study in Artifact Analysis." *Journal of Anthropological Research* 38 (1): 97–107.

———. (1985). Shell Bead Evidence from Archaeological Sites in the Seneca Region of New York State. Paper presented at the Annual Conference on Iroquois Research (11–13 October), Rensselaerville, New York.

———. (1989). [1988] Tracing Wampum's Origins: Shell Bead Evidence from Archaeological Sites in Western and Coastal New York. In Proceedings of the 1986 Shell Bead Conference: Selected Papers, pp. 63–80. Charles F. Hayes III, General Editor. Research Records No. 20, Research Division, Rochester Museum and Science Center. Rochester, New York.

Chafe, Wallace L. (1961). "Seneca Thanksgiving Rituals." Smithsonian Institution, Bureau of American Ethnology, *Bulletin* 183. Washington, DC: U.S. Government Printing Office.

———. (1967). *Seneca Morphology and Dictionary*. Washington, DC: Smithsonian Press.

Clark, Joshua V. H. (1849). *Onondaga, or Reminiscences of Earlier and Later Times; Being a Series* . . . . Vol. I. Syracuse, New York: Stoddard and Babcock.

Clayton, W. Woodford. (1878). *History of Onondaga County, New York*. Syracuse, New York: D. Mason and Company.

Conklin, Harold C., and William C. Sturtevant. (1953). "Seneca Indian Singing Tools at Coldspring Longhouse: Musical Instruments of the Modern Iroquois." *Proceedings of the American Philosophical Society* 97: 262–290.

Converse, Harriet Maxwell. (1888). "The Festival of the Sacrifice of the White Dog as Now Practised [sic] at the Onondaga Reservation." *Journal of American Folklore* 1 (1): 83–85. From the *Elmira Telegram* (Elmira, New York) 29 January 1888.

———. (1930). "The Seneca New Year Ceremony." *Indian Notes and Monographs* 7: 68–89. Museum of the American Indian–Heye Foundation, New York.

Cook, Robert A. (2012). "Dogs of War: Potential Social Institutions of Conflict, Healing, and Death in a Fort Ancient Village." *American Antiquity* 77 (3): 498–523.

Cooper, John M. (1933). "The Northern Algonquian Supreme Being." *Primitive Man* 6 (3–4): 41–111. Reprinted (1934) in *Catholic University of America Anthropological Series* 2. Washington, DC: Catholic University of America.

———. (1936) "Notes on the Ethnology of the Otchipewe of Lake of the Woods and of Rainy Lake." *The Catholic University of America Anthropological Series* 3: 1–29.

Coventry, T. L. (1889). Religious Customs of the Iroquois. *Hamilton Literary Monthly* XXIV (June): 11–18.

Crouse, Florence. (1944a) "The New Years [sic] Dance at the Indian Long House." In *Seneca Indians: Home Life and Culture*, pp. 81–85. Conservation Society of York County [PA], Inc. York, Pennsylvania: Maple Press for the Society.

———. (1944b) "Tribal Dances and ceremonials; Bread Feast; The Ten Day Feast." In *Seneca Indians: Home Life and Culture*, pp. 57–60. Conservation Society of York County [PA], Inc. York, Pennsylvania: Maple Press for the Society.

Crowell, Samuel. (1877). "The Dog Sacrifice of the Senecas." In *Indian Miscellany: Containing Papers on the History, Antiquities, Arts, Languages, Religions, &c of the American Aborigines*, William Wallace Beach, ed., pp. 323–332. Albany, New York: J. Munsell. Library of American Civilization 14493.

———. (1944) "Rites of the Aborigines." *Northwest Ohio Quarterly* 16 (3–4, July–Oct.): 147–157.

Cuoq, Jean André. (1882). *Lexique de la langue Iroquoise avec Notes et Appendices*. Montreal: J. Chapleau & Fils.

Curtin, Jeremiah, and J. N. B. Hewitt (1918). *Seneca Fiction, Legends, and Myths: Thirty-Second Annual Report of the Bureau of American Ethnology for 1910–1911*. Washington, DC: U.S. Government Printing Office.

Cusick, David. (1848). *David Cusick's Sketches of Ancient History of the Six Nations—Comprising–First–A Tale of the Foundation of the Great Island (etc.)* [from the 1827 edition]. Lockport, New York: Turner & McCollum. Library of American Civilization 40089; American Culture Series, Microfilm Reel 85.4. [Reissued in 2004].

D., W. H. (1896). "Six Nation Indian Traditions." *The Lamp* [Toronto, Theosophical Society] Number 29, 15 December. Volume III (5): 76–77.

Deardorff, Merle H. (1951). "The Religion of Handsome Lake: Its Origin and Development." In *Symposium on Local Diversity in Iroquois Culture*, William N. Fenton, ed., pp. 77–108. Smithsonian Institution, Bureau of American Ethnology, *Bulletin* 149. Washington, DC: U.S. Government Printing Office.

Deardorff, Merle H. and George S. Snyderman. (1956). "A Nineteenth-Century Journal of a Visit to the Indians of New York." *Proceedings of the American Philosophical Society* 100 (6): 582–612.

Delâge, Denys. (2005). "Vos chiens ont plus d'esprit que les nôtres: histoire des chiens dans la rencontre des Français et des Amérindiens." *Les Cahiers des dix* 59: 179–215.

Dennis, Matthew. (2010). *Seneca Possessed: Indians, Witchcraft, and Power in the Early American Republic.* Philadelphia: The University of Pennsylvania Press.

Dorsey, J. O. (1894). A Study of Siouan Cults. In *Eleventh Annual Report of the Bureau of Ethnology, for 1889–90,* pp. 361–544. Washington, DC: U.S. Government Printing Office.

Doty, Lockwood L. (1876). *A History of Livingston County, New York, from its Earliest Traditions to the Present.* Geneseo, New York: Edward L. Doty [reissued in 1905].

Duis, E. (1874). *The Good Old Times in McLean County, Illinois. Old Settlers of McLean County.* Bloomington, Illinois: Leader Publishing.

Dunnell, Robert C. (1980). "A Monongahela Settlement in Central Ohio County, West Virginia." *West Virginia Archeologist* 29: 1–37.

Dwight, Timothy. (1823). *Travels, in New England and New-York.* Vol. 4. London: For William Bynes and Son.

Einhorn, Arthur. (1974). "Iroquois-Algonquin Wampum Exchange and Preservation in the Twentieth Century." *Man in the Northeast* 7: 71–86.

Fenton, William N. (1936). "An Outline of Seneca Ceremonies at Coldspring Longhouse." *Yale University Publications in Anthropology* 9. New Haven, Connecticut: Yale University Press.

———. (1942). Editor (and recorder) of *Songs from the Iroquois Longhouse.* Program Notes for an Album of American Indian Music from the Eastern Woodlands. [34 pages; the five sound discs were issued from the Recording Lab, 1947] From recordings in the Archive of American Folk culture (AFS L6). The Library of Congress, City of Washington, The Smithsonian Institution. *Bureau of American Ethnology,* Publication 3691. Recording laboratory 1947.

———. (1944). "Samuel Crowell's Account of a Seneca Dog Sacrifice near Lower Sandusky, Ohio in [the] 1830s: A Commentary." *Northwest Ohio Quarterly* 16 (3–4, July–Oct.): 158–163.

———. (1950). "Review of Midwinter Rites of the Cayuga Longhouse, by Frank Speck, with Alexander General (1949)." *American Anthropologist* 52 (4): 521–523.

———. (1956). "Toward the Gradual Civilization of the Indian Natives: The Missionary and Linguistic Work of Asher Wright (1803–1875) among the

Senecas of Western New York." *Proceedings of the American Philosophical Society*, Vol. 100 (6): 567–581.

———. (1957). (Ed.), "Seneca Indians by Asher Wright (1859)." *Ethnohistory* 4 (3): 302–321.

———. (1987). *False Faces of the Iroquois*. Norman: University of Oklahoma Press.

———. (1991). *The Iroquois Eagle Dance: An Offshoot of the Calumet Dance*. Syracuse, New York: Syracuse University Press, reprint of the 1953 *Report of the Bureau of American Ethnology*.

———. (1998). *The Great Law and the Longhouse: A Political History of the Iroquois Confederacy*. Norman: University of Oklahoma Press.

Fitzgerald, Jennifer. (2009). "Native Dog Burials and Associated Ritual in Coastal Virginia and Beyond." Thesis for B.A. in Anthropology, College of William and Mary, Williamsburg, VA.

Folts, James D. (1999). "Before the Dispersal: Records of New York's Official Relations with the Oneidas and Other Indian Nations." In *The Oneida Indian Journey: From New York to Wisconsin*, L. M. Hauptman and L. G. McLester III, eds., pp. 151–170. Madison: University of Wisconsin Press.

G., B. D. (1860). "Sacrifice of the Senecas." *The Historical Magazine and Notes and Queries* 4 (March): 87–88.

Garrad, Charles (compiler). (1987). *The Annual Archaeological Reports of Ontario 1887–1928: A Research Guide*. Toronto: A Special Publication by The Ontario Archaeological Society.

George, Richard. (2011). "The Wylie #3 Site (36WH283): Part II." *Pennsylvania Archaeologist* 81 (2): 1–43.

Gomme, George Laurence. (1883). *Folk-lore Relics of Early Village Life*. London: Elliot Stock.

Grant, George Monro. (1882). *Picturesque Canada: The Country as It Was and Is*. Vol. 14. Toronto: Belden Brothers.

Gregory, Leverette B. (1980). "Hatch Site–Preliminary Report." *Quarterly Bulletin, Archaeological Society of Virginia* 34 (4): 239–248.

Hale, Horatio. (1883). *The Iroquois Book of Rites*. D. G. Brinton, ed., no. 2. Philadelphia: Library of Aboriginal American Literature.

———. (1885). "The Iroquois Sacrifice of the White Dog." *American Antiquarian and Oriental Journal* 7: 7–14.

———. (1886). "The Origin of Primitive Money." *Popular Science Monthley* 28: 296–307.

———. (1897). "Four Huron Wampum Records: A Study of Aboriginal American History and Mnemonic Symbols." *Journal of the Anthropological Institute of Great Britain and Ireland* 26: 221–247.

————. (1989). "The Iroquois Sacrifice of the White Dog." Reprint of Hale 1885 plus a recent photograph. In *The Iroquois Book of Rites and Hale on the Iroquois*, pp. 314–322. Ohsweken [Ontario]: Iroqrafts (Iroquois Reprints).

Handley, B. M. (2000). "Preliminary Results in Determining Dog Types from Prehistoric Sites in the Northeastern United States." In, *Dogs Through Time: An Archaeological Perspective*, edited by S. J. Crockford, ed., pp. 205–215. BAR International Series 889. Oxford, England.

Harmon, Daniel Williams. (1820). *A Journal of Voyages and Travels in the Interior of North America . . . Montreal to the Pacific (1800–1819)*. Andover, Massachusetts: Flagg and Gould.

Harris, Mr. (1829). "Indians in New York: Extracts from a Communication of Mr. Harris." *The Missionary Herald, The Proceedings . . . American Board of Commissioners of Foreign Missions . . . 1829*. Vol. XXV, pp. 90–92. Boston: Crocker & Brewster.

Hauptman, Laurence M. (1999). The Oneida Nation: A Composite Portrait, 1784–1816. In *The Oneida Indian Journey: From New York to Wisconsin*, edited by L. M. Hauptman and L. G. McLester III, eds., pp. 19–37. Madison: University of Wisconsin Press.

————. (2008). "Designing Woman: Minnie Kellogg." In *Seven Generations of Iroquois Leadership: The Six Nations since 1800*. Syracuse, New York: Syracuse University Press.

Hewitt, John N. B. (1910). "White Dog Sacrifice." In *Bureau of American Ethnology, Bulletin 30*, Vol. 2, pp. 939–944. Washington, DC: U.S. Government Printing.

————. (1917). Review of *The Constitution of The Five Nations*, by Arthur C. Parker (1916), *Traditional History of The Confederacy of the Six Nations*, by Duncan Campbell Scott (1911), and *Civil, Religious and Mourning Councils and Ceremonies of Adoption of the New York Indians*, by William M. Beauchamp (1907). *American Anthropologist* 19 (3): 429–438.

Hirschfelder, C. A. (1886a). "GI-YE-WA-NO-US-QUA-GO-WA. Sacrifice of the White Dog." *The Indian*, Vol. I (7): 73–74, (8): 86–87, (9): 98–99.

———(1886b). "How the Crees Banqueted Me." *The Indian*, Vol. I (No. 10), 26 May: 110–111.

Hobsbawn, Eric J. (1992). "Introduction: Inventing Traditions." In *The Invention of Tradition*, edited by E. J. Hobsbawm and T. Ranger, eds., pp. 1–14. Cambridge, Massachusetts: Cambridge University Press.

Holmes, William H. (1883). "Art in Shell of the Ancient Americans." In *The Second Annual Report of the Bureau of Ethnology, Smithsonian Institution*, pp. 179–305. Washington, DC.

Houghton, Frederick. (1920). "History of the Buffalo Creek Reservation." *Buffalo Historical Society Publications* 24: 1–181.

Hurd, Isaac. (Manuscript A). "The Onondaga Nation: Their new year's feast, the sacrifice of the white dog, their dances, their present condition, the school lately established among them with a few reflections [ca. 1846]." On file in the Lewis Henry Morgan Papers, Box 21: 15, New York: University of Rochester.

Hyde, Jabez Backus. (1903). "A Teacher among the Senecas: Historical and Personal Narrative of Jabez Bachus Hyde, Who Came to the Buffalo Creek Mission in 1811, Written in 1820." *Buffalo Historical Society Publications* 6: 239–274.

Jackson, Halliday. (See under Wallace 1952)

———. (1806). (See under Snyderman 1957)

———. (1830a). *Civilization of the Indian Natives; or, a brief view of the friendly conduct of William Penn towards them in the early settlement of Pennsylvania; the subsequent care of the Society of Friends in endeavouring to promote peace and friendship with them by pacific measures; and a concise narrative of the proceedings of the yearly meeting of Friends, of Pennsylvania, New Jersey, and parts adjacent, since the year 1795, in promoting their improvement and gradual civilization.* Philadelphia: Marcus T. C. Gould; New York: Isaac T. Hopper.

———. (1830b). *Sketch of the Manners, Customs, Religion and Government of the Seneca Indians in 1800.* Philadelphia: Marcus T. C. Gould.

Jemison, Mary. (1824). *A Narrative of the Life of Mrs. Mary Jemison, who was taken by the Indians in the year 1755 . . . . As told to, and with an Appendix by James E. Seaver in 1823.* Canandaigua New York: J. D. Bemis and Company.

Jenness, Diamond. (1935). "The Ojibwa Indians of Parry Island, Their Social and Religious Life." Canada Department of Mines, *Bulletin* 78. *Anthropological Series* 17. J. O. Patenaude, Printer.

Johnson, Sir William. (1771). Letter to Anthony Lee, Esq., from Johnson Hall, 28 February. In *Documentary History of the State of New York, 1851* E. B. O'Callaghan, ed. Albany, New York: Charles Van Benthuysen. Vol. 4: 270.

Kent, Donald H. (editor). (1979). Pennsylvania and Delaware Treaties, 1629–1737. In *Early American Indian Documents: Treaties and Laws, 1607–1789*, Vol. 1, A. T. Vaughan, ed. Washington, D.C.: University Publications of America.

Kirkland, Rev. Mr. Samuel. (1800). *Samuel Kirkland Papers for 1800.* Hamilton College, New York: Archives. (26 Feb. 1800; 30 May 1800). [See under Pilkington 1980.]

Knapp, Samuel L. (1837). "The Sacrifice of the White Dog." *The New-York Mirror: A Weekly Gazette of Literature and the Fine Arts.* Vol. 15 (1) (July 1): 3.

Kuhn, Robert and Martha L. Sempowski (2001). "A New Approach to Dating the League of the Iroquois." *American Antiquity* 66 (2): 301–314.

Lainey, Jonathan. (2004). *La «Monnaie des Sauvages»: Les colliers de wampum d'hier à aujourd'hui*. Quebec: Septentrion.

Lang, William. (1880). *History of Seneca County, from the Close of the Revolutionary War to July 1880*. Springfield, Ohio: Transcript Printing Company.

Lismer, Marjorie. (1941). *Seneca Splint Basketry*. Bureau of Indian Affairs, Washington, D.C.

Lloyd, Herbert M. (1922). "Appendix B." In *League of the Ho-de-no-sau-nee or Iroquois*. From the 1851 edition, H. M. Lloyd, ed., pp. 145–312. New York: Dodd, Mead [reissue of the 1901 edition].

Lyford, Carrie A. (1945). *Iroquois Crafts*, W. W. Beatty, ed. Publications of the Education Division, United States Office of Indian Affairs. Phoenix: Printing Department of the United States Indian School. *Indian Handicraft* 5. (Reprinted 1982 by Irocrafts in Ohsweken, Ontario.)

Mather, Cotton. (1702). *Magnalia Christi americana: or, The ecclesiastical history of New-England, from its first planting in the year 1620 unto the year of our Lord, 1698*. In seven books. London: Thomas Parkhurst (Microfilm: American Culture Series, Reel 9.99).

———. (1855). *Magnalia Christi americana: or, The ecclesiastical history of New-England, from its first planting etc.* Two volumes, with an Introduction and Notes by Thomas Robbins. Hartford, Connecticut: S. Andrus and Son.

McBride, Kevin A. (1993). "'Ancient and Crazie': Pequot Lifeways during the Historic Period." In *Algonkians of New England: Past and Present*, P. Barnes, ed., pp. 63–75. Boston: Boston University Press.

Merriam, Kathryn Lavely. (2005). "Mr. Hewitt and Mrs. Kellogg." Paper presented at the Conference on Iroquois Research, Rensselaerville, New York (October 1). Copy on file, Becker Archives, West Chester University.

———. (2010a). "The Preservation of Iroquois Thought: J. N. B. Hewitt's Legacy of Scholarship for His People," Doctoral dissertation in History, University of Massachusetts Amherst. Copy on file, Becker Archives, West Chester University of Pennsylvania.

———. (2010b). "The Wampum Chase: Smithsonian Ethnographer J. N. B. Hewitt's Years in Pursuit of the Preservation and Meaning of Wampum." *American Society for Ethnohistory*, Ottawa, Ontario (5 October).

Michelson, Karin and Mercy Doxtater. (2002). *Oneida-English/English-Oneida Dictionary*. Toronto: University of Toronto Press.

Michelson, Truman. (1925). The Mythical Origin of the White Buffalo Dance of the Fox Indians. In *Bureau of American Ethnology, 40th Annual Report, 1918–1919*, pp. 23–290. Washington, D.C.: Government Printing Office.

Morey, Darcey F. (2006). "Burying Key Evidence: The Social Bond between Dogs and People." *Journal of Archaeological Science* 33: 158–175.

Morgan, Lewis Henry. (1851). *League of the Iroquois*. Two volumes. Rochester, New York: Sage & brother.

———. (1852). *Fifth Annual Report of the Regents of the University of New York on the Condition of the New York State Cabinet of Natural History*. Albany, New York.

———. (1901). League of the Ho-de-no-sau-nee or Iroquois. Two volumes. From the 1851 edition, H. M. Lloyd, ed. New York: Dodd, Mead [reissued in 1922].

———. (1962). *League of the Iroquois*. With an Introduction by William N. Fenton. Secaucus, New Jersey: Citadel Press.

———. (N.d.) "Journals" [of L. H. Morgan]. Vol. 1, Number 1. Manuscript, in the Collections of the University of Rochester Library. Rochester, New York.

Morrison, Alvin H. (1990). Dawnland Dog-Feast: Wabanaki Warfare, c. 1600–1760. In *Papers of the Twenty-First Algonquian Conference*, W. Cowan, ed., pp. 258–278. Ottawa: Carleton University.

N., C. D. (1861). "The [Seneca] Sacrifice of the White Dog." *The Historical Magazine and Notes and Queries* 5 (January): 28–29.

New York [State] Assembly ["the Whipple Report"]. (1889). "Report of [the] Special Committee Appointed by the Assembly of 1888 to Investigate the Indian Problem of the State." Assembly Document 51. Albany. New York State Library Cat. No. E78 N7 N77 1977; copy on file in Becker Archives, West Chester University of Pennsylvania.

Oberholtzer, Cath Ann. (1986). "Iroquoian Sun Disc Wands. A Condensed Symbol." Trent University thesis for the Master of Arts in Anthropology.

———. (2003). "Fleshing Out the Evidence: From Archaic Dog Burials to Historic Dog Feasts." *Ontario Archaeology* 73: 3–14.

O'Callaghan, Edmund Bailey (transcriber). (1849). *Manuscripts of Sir William Johnson. In The Documentary History of the State of New York*. Vol. II. Albany, New York: Weed, Parsons, & Company.

———. (1851). *The Documentary History of the State of New York*. (Vol. IV). Albany, New York: Weed, Parsons, & Company.

Oneida Elders. (1999). "Stories of the Oneida Language and Folklore Project, 1938–1941." In *The Oneida Indian Journey: from New York to Wisconsin*, L. M.

Hauptman and L. G. McLester III, eds., pp. 110–125. Madison: University of Wisconsin Press.

O'Reilly, Henry (Arranger). (1838). *Settlement in the West: Sketches of Rochester; with Incidental Notices of Western New York.* Rochester, New York: William Alling.

Osgood, Thaddeus. (See Dwight 1823)

Osgood, Thaddeus. (1829 [?]). *The Canadian Visitor: Communicating Important Facts and Interesting Anecdotes Respecting the Indians and Destitute Settlers in Canada and the United States of America.* London: Hamilton and Adams (also Westley and Davis; J. Nisbet; and J. Miller).

————. (1851). *The Seamens and Strangers' Friends Society has Strong Claims upon Christianity.* Boston: n.p.

Parker, Arthur C. (1912). "Code of Handsome Lake, the Seneca Prophet." *New York State Museum Bulletin* 163. Albany: University of the State of New York.

Patrick, Christine Sternberg. (2009). "The Samuel Kirkland Journals." Paper presented at the Annual Meeting of the Iroquois Conference, Rensalaersville, New York. October.

Pierard, J., M. Cote, and L. Pinel. (1987). Le chien de l'occupation archaïque du site Cadieux in La Période archaïque. *Recherces amérindiennes au Québec* 17 (1–2): 47–61.

Pilkington, Walter (ed.). (1980). *The Journals of Samuel Kirkland; 18th-century Missionary to the Iroquois, Government Agent, Father of Hamilton College.* Clinton, New York: Hamilton College.

Potts, William John. (1889). "Indian Tobacco among the Modern Iroquois." *Journal of American Folk-Lore* 2 (7): 307–308.

Red Eye, Clara. (1944). "The Great Snake Ritual." In *Seneca Indians: Home Life and Culture. Conservation Society of York County* [PA], Inc., pp. 61–62. York, Pennsylvania: Maple Press for the Society.

Rogers, E. S. (1978). "Southeastern Chippewa." In *Handbook of North American Indians*, Vol. 15: *Northeast*, B. G. Trigger, ed., pp. 760–771. Washington, D.C.: Smithsonian Institution.

Sagard Théodat, Gabriel. (1865). *Le grande voyage du pays des Hurons. situé en l'Amérique vers la mer douce, ès derniers confins de la Nouvelle France dite Canada, avec un dictionnaire de la langue huronne.* New edition by M. Émile Chevalier. Paris: Tross.

Sanfaçon, André. (Manuscript A.). *Wampums "paroles" chrétiennes (1654–1831). Offrandes de "colliers de porcelaine" par les Amérindiens des missions et réductions de la Nouvelle-France et du Canada à des sanctuaires européens et canadiens,* J. Lainey, ed. In review, Septentrion.

Schultz, James Willard. (1962). *Blackfeet and Buffalo: Memories of Life among the Indians*, K. C. Seele, ed. Norman: University of Oklahoma Press [Reissued 1980].

Schwartz, Marion, with Susan Hochgraf. (1997). *A History of Dogs in the Early Americas*. New Haven, Connecticut: Yale University Press.

Sciulli, Paul W., and Joseph Purcell. (2011). "Two Archaic Dogs from Central Ohio." *Pennsylvania Archaeologist* 81 (2): 54–64.

Seaver, James Everett (See Jemison)

Setzler, F. M. (1944). "Samuel Crowell's Account of a Seneca Dog Sacrifice: An Introduction." *Northwest Ohio Quarterly* 16 (3–4, July–Oct.): 144–146.

Severance, Frank H. (1903). "Narratives of Early Mission Work on the Niagara frontier and Buffalo Creek." *Buffalo Historical Society* 6.

Shatttuck, George C. (1991). *The Oneida Land Claims: A Legal History*. Syracuse, New York: Syracuse University Press.

Shimony, Annemarie Anrod. (1961). "Conservatism among the Iroquois at the Six Nations Reserve." *Yale University publications in Anthropology* 65. New Haven, Connecticut: Department of Anthropology, Yale University [reissued 1994 by Syracuse University Press: Syracuse, NY].

———. (1978). "Alexander General, 'Deskahe,' Cayuga-Oneida, 1889–1965." In *American Indian Intellectuals of the Nineteenth and Twentieth Centuries (1976 Proceedings of the American Ethnological Society)*, Liberty, ed., pp. 177–198. St. Paul, Minnesota: West Publishing Company.

Smith, Harlan I. (1897). "The Monster in the Tree: An Ojibwa Myth." *Journal of American Folk-Lore* 10 (No. 39): 324–325.

Smith, James Haddon. (1881). *History of Livingston County, New York*, with illustrations and biographical sketches. Syracuse, New York: D. Mason and Company.

Snyderman, George S. (1954). "The Function of Wampum." *Proceedings of the American Philosophical Society* 98 (6): 469–494.

———. (1957). "Halliday Jackson's Journal of a Visit Paid the [Seneca] Indians of New York (1806)," Describer and ed. *Proceedings of the American Philosophical Society* 101 (6): 565–588.

———. (1961). "The Function of Wampum in Iroquois Religion." *Proceedings of the American Philosophical Society* 105: 571–608.

———. (1982). "An Ethnological Discussion of Allegheny Seneca Wampum Folklore." *Proceedings of the American Philosophical Society* 126 (4): 316.

Speck, Frank G., with Alexander General (Deskáheh). (1949). *Midwinter Rites of the Cayuga Longhouse*. Philadelphia: University of Pennsylvania Press.

———. (1995). *Midwinter Rites of the Cayuga Longhouse* (Bison Book Edition). Lincoln: University of Nebraska Press.

Spittal, William Guy. (1989). "Preface." Pages 5–6 and figure captions in, *The Iroquois Book of Rites and Hale on the Iroquois*, by Horatio Hale (Reprint of the 1883 edition). Ohsweken, Ontario, Canada: Iroqrafts Ltd.

Starna, William A. (2008). "Retrospecting the Origins of the League of the Iroquois." *Proceedings of the American Philosophical Society* 152 (3): 279–321.

Starr, J. C. (1895?) "White Dog Ceremony." *The Indian Moccasin*, Jeremiah Hubbard, ed. Afton, Indian Territory [Oklahoma]) February.

Stevens, Edward T. (1870). *Flint Chips: A Guide to Pre-Historic Archaeology*. London: Bell and Daldy.

Stiles, Ezra. (1901). *The Literary Diary of Ezra Stiles*, F. Bowditch Dexter. ed. Vol. III: Jan. 1, 1782–May 6, 1795. New York: Charles Scribner's Sons.

Strong, John A. (1985). "Late Woodland Dog Ceremonialism on Long Island in Comparative and Temporal Perspective." *Bulletin: Journal of the New York State Archaeological Association* 91: 32–38.

Sullivan, John. (1887). *Journals of the Military Expedition of Major General John Sullivan*. Auburn, New York: Knapp, Peck and Thomson.

Swanton, John R. (1938). "John Napoleon Brinton Hewitt [1859–1937]." *American Anthropologist* 40 (2): 286–290

Swatzler, David. (2000). *A Friend among the Seneca*. Mechanicsburg, Pennsylvania: Stackpole Books.

Thomas, Stephen Cox. (1966). "The House 7 Multiple Dog Cremation Burial. Pages 171–179 in, The Archaeology of the Dunsmore Site: A Late Iroquoian Community in Southern Simcoe County [Ontario]." Site Report. Archaeological Services, Inc. report (Ms.) filed with The Ministry of Citizenship, Culture and Recreation, Toronto (as cited by Oberholtzer 2003).

Thwaites, Reuben Gold (ed.). (1890–1901). *Jesuit Relations and Allied Documents: Explorations of the Jesuit Missionaries in New France, 1610–1791* (in 73 volumes). Cleveland: Burrows Brothers. Reissued 1959 by Pageant Book Company, New York. (Also, Library of American Civilization 21463–21490; 1970). Vol. VIII: 1634–1636, XLII: 1655–1656.

Titley, E. Brian. (1986). *A Narrow Vision: Duncan Campbell Scott and the Administration of Indian Affairs in Canada*. Vancouver: University of British Columbia Press.

Tooker, Elisabeth. (1964). "An Ethnography of the Huron Indians, 1615–1649." *Bureau of American Ethnology Bulletin* 190. Washington, DC.

———. (1965). "The Iroquois White Dog Sacrifice in the Latter Part of the Eighteenth Century." *Ethnohistory* 12 (2): 129–140. Summarized in *Anthropos* (1967) 62: 949–950.

————. (1970) *The Iroquois Ceremonial of Midwinter*. Syracuse, New York: Syracuse University Press.

————. (1994) *Lewis H. Morgan on Iroquois Material Culture*. Tucson: University of Arizona Press.

Underhill, Ruth (1965). *Red Man's Religion*. Chicago: University of Chicago Press.

Vanesse, Joseph L. (1907). "The White Dog Feast." *The Canadian Magazine* 30 (1): 62–64.

Wallace, Anthony F. C. (ed.) (1952). "Halliday Jackson's Journal to the Seneca Indians, 1798–1800." *Pennsylvania History* 19 (2 & 3): 117–147, 325–349.

————. (1956). "Revitalization Movements: Some Theoretical Considerations for their Comparative Study." *American Anthropologist* 58: 264–281.

————. (1958). "The Dekanawideh Myth Analyzed as the Record of a Revitalization Movement." *Ethnohistory* 5 (2): 118–130.

————. (1961). *Culture and Personality*. New York: Random House.

————. (1970). *The Death and Rebirth of the Seneca*. New York: Alfred A. Knopf.

————. (2009). "Epilogue: On the Organization of Diversity." *Ethos [Society for Psychological Anthropology]* 37 (2): 251–255.

Waugh, F. W. (1916). "Iroquis [sic] Foods and Food Preparation." Canada Department of Mines, *Geological Survey Memoir* 86. Government Printing Bureau.

Webster, Thomas. (1870). "Early Scenes in Canadian Life." Chapters XXXV–XXXVII. *New Dominion Monthly* Volume III (September); 23–30.

Whipple Report. (1889). (See under New York [State] Assembly)

Wonderley, Anthony W. (2004). *Oneida Iroquois Folklore, Myth, and History: New York Oral Narrative from the Notes of H. E. Allen and Others*. Syracuse, New York: Syracuse University Press.

Woodbury, Hanni. (2003). *Onondaga-English, English-Onondaga Dictionary*. Toronto: University of Toronto Press.

Woodward, Asbell. (1880). "Wampum; A paper presented to the Numismatic and Antiquarian Society of Philadelphia." 2nd ed. (56 pages). Albany, New York: J. Munsell (reprint of the 62-page edition of 1878).

Tables

TABLE I: Eyewitness Accounts; Seneca White Dog Sacrifice

Date of Observation (published)	Day of Fest. Killed/Burned	Time of the Day*	No. of Dogs	Wampum Used	Who Saw	Hang Dog(s) On Pole(s) Or on Image
After 23 March 1799 (1952)	7/?: 7/?	Midday to PM	1?	"String of beads"	H. Jackson	On an Image
1812 (Dwight 1823)	1?/?:7/?	?	2	?	Th. Osgood	Suspended (on pole?)
1813 (O'Reilly 1838)				—	Edwin Scranton	—
7 Feb. 1816	1/7: 6/7	Morning	1	5 strings of purple beads	J. Horsford	"to a post"
Genesee Seneca at Buffalo Creek Before 1823	1/9: 8 or 9/9	?	2	None?	Mary Jemison	20-foot post
1829	5/?	?	1	—	Mr. Harris	Post
1 Feb. 1830 (1877)	2/?/?	Noon	2	None	S. Crowell	"cross"

1832? (1860) ·	5?/7?	Twilight	2	"strings of wampum" [1 each?]	Unknown; Told to BDG	Horiz. pole
1846** (Morgan N.d.)	1?/7: 5/7	Soon after dawn	1	"string"	Morgan	On a pole
Cattaraugus 1886	?/?	?	1	—	Anon.	—
31 Jan. 1898	10/10***	Sunrise****	1	Small string	Boyle	—
1901	No burning	?	—	—	Brush	
Cattaraugus Newtown Feb. 1906	?4/ Basket	?	Bask	—	Parker	

*If strangled and burned on the same day, times may vary.

** These data are a combination of what Morgan saw and what was reported to him (see text).

***Unclear when this Midwinter Feast began, and even the number of days may be a synthetic inference. Tooker (1970: 175) says that the ceremony described by Boyle "probably lasted 10 days."

****Set for sunrise (killing and burning?), but delayed. The delay suggests variations in scheduling were common, as the killing had been scheduled for "sunrise on Monday morning."

TABLE II: Eyewitness Accounts; Onondaga White Dog Sacrifice

Date of Observation (published)	Day of Fest. Killed/Burned	Time of the Day*	No. of Dogs	Wampum Used	Who Saw	Hang Dog(s) On Pole(s) Or on Image
1841 (J. Clark 1849)	6?/7? : 6?/7?	9 in the Morning	2	"small belts of wampum"	Joshua Clark	Ladder against the House
1846	—	-	—	—	Isaac Hurd (from Tooker 1970)	—
1872	?**	2pm	1			
1878	?	—	1	String—white	Woodward 1880	A pole
1884 A	Early in Feast	Late in day?	1	—	Anon. 1884a	Not hung
1884 B—Canada (Onondaga sect.)	5/7*** : 5/7	Possibly sunrise	1	String of wampum	Hirschfelder 1886 (& Anon. 1884b)	Not hung
1885 Canada	—	—	1?	String of wampum	H. Hale 1885	—
1888	—	—	1	Beads of wampum	Harriet Converse	—
– 1969+	/ 9/9	Morning	"2"*	—	Blau (synthesized)	—

**Strangled in the early forenoon and burned at 2 p.m. on the same day.

***Hirschfelder (Anon. 1884b) states that in "ancient days the killing of the white dog took place on the first day ...." The strangulation of 1884 is not described by Hirschfelder, but we presume it took place early in the day. Fenton's synthetic account (1941:17) posits that the "dog must be strangled before sunrise."

*Four baskets were burned, with two of them representing dogs.

TABLE III: Kirkland's Eyewitness Account of an Oneida Ritual Similar to the White Dog Sacrifice.

Date of Observation (published)	Day of Fest. Killed/Burned	Time of the Day*	No. of Dogs	Wampum Used	Who Saw	Hang Dog(s) On Pole(s) Or on Image
1800 (fall, harvest)		—	3 (Eat 2)	The hung dog has 1 white & 1 black belt	S. Kirkland	12 foot pole (for 1 dog)

TABLE IV: Synthetic Accounts

Author	Tribe
Hyde 1903 (1820)	"Rochester area" (Seneca?)
Knapp 1837: 3	Seneca near Buffalo
Cusick 1848: 31	Seneca?
Morgan 1851, I: 175–179 (also 1922: 207–213; 1962: 215–217; 1901, I: 208).	Tonawanda Seneca*
Stevens 1870: 462	Seneca (via Morgan)
Gomme 1883: 89	Seneca
Caswell 1892: 214–219.	Seneca
Bruce (editor) 1896, II:1063	"Seneca"
Fenton 1936: 11 (see also Fenton 1942: 17; 1991: 8, 15, 146).	Oneida "context" but probably Onondaga.
Shimony 1961; 1994: 186	Onondaga at Six Nations, Ohsweken, "Iroquois"
Tooker 1970: 110**	At the "time of the American Revolution" (Iroquois?)
Wallace 1970: 50–58, 344 n1	Seneca?

* Tooker (1970: 138) believed that Morgan's description derived from the Sand Hill Long House; one of two at Towanda. Some data may come from Sand Hill, but the entire published account is synthetic. Some additional data were taken by Tooker from his notes.

** "This basket with all its contents, was first cast into the fire…" [before the dog] (Tooker 1970: 110). Tooker is the only scholar to include mention of a basket in her synthetic "account."

List of Figures

Page

Index